PHOTO

The International Annual of Advertising,
Editorial and Television Photography

Edited by Walter Herdeg

A document that records all changes in objectives, techniques and taste, but also reveals—behind the professional aspects of advertising—how a changing economic situation affects the photographer.

The wide range of creative styles and the many different trends visible in modern photography are displayed in the 10 sections of the book:

Advertisements — Booklets — Calendars — Packaging — Record Covers — Film/TV — Editorial Photography — Magazine Covers — Book Covers — Annual Reports.

"The definitive recap of what's been going on in the wonderful world of photography vis-à-vis design and vice versa."—*Publishers Weekly*. "An accurate mirror of our times ... ad people are employing the best photography has to offer."—*Photo Weekly*.

THE TWO COMPANION ANNUALS:

Edited by Walter Herdeg

GRAPHIS POSTERS 76

This 4th edition of GRAPHIS POSTERS presents the foremost selection of poster art available today. "The contemporary poster in its diverse usage for art, the stage, trade and industry and political propaganda fills the need for many purposes", reports *Creative Signs & Displays*. "An outstanding state-of-the-art commentary", *CA Magazine* observed. This edition offers visual evidence arranged in four major categories: *Advertising* Posters, *Cultural* Posters, *Social* Posters, *Decorative* Posters.
Published annually in March/April.

GRAPHIS ANNUAL 1975/76

The International Annual of Advertising
and Editorial Graphics
This is the 24th annual edition of the original cornerstone of the *"Graphis* trilogy". It continues its survey of graphics in advertisements, annual reports, booklets, book jackets and magazine covers, trademarks, letterheads, packaging, record covers, film, television and editorial design. It is an endless source of ideas and a perfect "swipe file" for art directors, illustrators and designers.
Published annually in October/November.

Other Graphis Books, Edited by Walter Herdeg:

A NEW SERIES IN 'SQUARE BOOKS' FORMAT (9-¼" × 9-⅜"):

FILM AND TV GRAPHICS 2

GRAPHIS/RECORD COVERS

GRAPHIS/DIAGRAMS

The Graphic Visualization of Abstract Data

IN 9-½" × 12" FORMAT:

GRAPHIS/ANNUAL REPORTS

Text by Richard A. Lewis

GRAPHIS/PACKAGING 2

Write for a complete catalogue:

VISUAL COMMUNICATION BOOKS

Hastings House, Publishers
10 East 40th Street, New York, N.Y. 10016

PHOTOGRAPHIS76

PHOTOGRAPHIS 76

The International Annual of Advertising, Editorial
and Television Photography

Das internationale Jahrbuch der Werbephotographie
und der redaktionellen Photographie

Le répertoire international de la photographie
publicitaire et rédactionnelle

Edited by: / Herausgegeben von: / Réalisé par:

Walter Herdeg

Walter Herdeg, The Graphis Press, Zurich (Switzerland)

Distributed in the United States by

Hastings House

Publishers
10 East 40th Street, New York, N.Y. 10016

PUBLICATION No. 143   [ISBN   0–8038–5816–7]

Contents   Inhalt   Sommaire

Abbreviations Abkürzungen Abréviations

Australia	AUL	Australien	AUL	Afrique du Sud	SAF
Austria	AUS	Belgien	BEL	Allemagne	GER
Belgium	BEL	Dänemark	DEN	Australie	AUL
Canada	CAN	Deutschland	GER	Autriche	AUS
Czechoslovakia	CSR	Finnland	FIN	Belgique	BEL
Denmark	DEN	Frankreich	FRA	Canada	CAN
Finland	FIN	Griechenland	GRE	Danemark	DEN
France	FRA	Grossbritannien	GBR	Espagne	SPA
Germany	GER	Hongkong	HGK	Etats-Unis	USA
Great Britain	GBR	Iran	IRN	Finlande	FIN
Greece	GRE	Italien	ITA	France	FRA
Hong Kong	HGK	Japan	JPN	Grande-Bretagne	GBR
Iran	IRN	Jugoslavien	YUG	Grèce	GRE
Italy	ITA	Kanada	CAN	Hongkong	HGK
Japan	JPN	Marokko	MOR	Iran	IRN
Mexico	MEX	Mexico	MEX	Italie	ITA
Morocco	MOR	Niederlande	NLD	Japon	JPN
Netherlands	NLD	Norwegen	NOR	Maroc	MOR
Norway	NOR	Österreich	AUS	Mexique	MEX
Singapore	SIN	Schweden	SWE	Norvège	NOR
South Africa	SAF	Schweiz	SWI	Pays-Bas	NLD
Spain	SPA	Singapore	SIN	Singapour	SIN
Sweden	SWE	Spanien	SPA	Suède	SWE
Switzerland	SWI	Süd-Afrika	SAF	Suisse	SWI
USA	USA	Tschechoslowakei	CSR	Tchécoslovaquie	CSR
Yugoslavia	YUG	USA	USA	Yougoslavie	YUG

Cover/Umschlag/Couverture: Henry Wolf

Editor's Note

Photography is becoming an ever more versatile medium. As it enters new fields of imaginative picture-making, the standards become more exacting, the peak achievements more immaculate in their perfection. We are grateful to all those who, by regularly sending us their best work, help us to record the new criteria and the new break-throughs and thus to set up guidelines for all who are involved in the advancement of applied photography.

Anmerkung des Herausgebers

Die Photographie entwickelt sich mehr und mehr zu einem äusserst vielseitigen Medium. Je mehr die technischen Möglichkeiten ausgedehnt und je phantasiereicher die Aufnahmen werden, umso anspruchsvoller werden die Normen, umso stärker die Forderung nach Perfektion, die von Spitzenphotographen verlangt wird. – Wir danken all jenen, die es uns durch regelmässiges Einsenden ihrer besten Arbeiten ermöglichen, die neuen Trends auf diesem Gebiet nachzuzeichnen und damit auch neue Richtlinien festzulegen für die-jenigen, die sich für die Weiterentwicklung der angewandten Photographie einsetzen.

Note de l'Editeur

La photographie est un medium d'une diversité toujours croissante. Plus elle s'empare des domai-nes techniques et imaginatifs jusqu'ici inaccessi-bles, plus on réclame des photographes éminents un niveau plus élevé et une exécution qui frise la perfection. Nous adressons nos remerciements à tous ceux qui nous permettent par leurs envois réguliers de mettre en évidence les récentes tendances et les nouveaux critères et de jeter des jalons pour ceux qui s'intéressent à l'avancement de la photographie appliquée.

Henry Wolf

Preface

HENRY WOLF wrote the introduction to PHOTOGRAPHIS 67 and supplied the cover photograph for PHOTO-GRAPHIS 70. This time he combines the two functions. His career as an editorial art director took him from *Esquire* to *Harper's Bazaar* and *Show* and in 1973 to *Sesame Street*. He has worked widely in advertising, for instance in Trahey/Wolf Advertising, Inc., and runs a design studio of his own. But he will probably be best known to most of our readers as a photographer in his own right, and one with an unusually alert eye, lively wit and professional polish. His alert eye serves him in equally good stead as an observer of the human (and photographic) scene, whose comments are as apt and unaffected as they are refreshing.

Twenty years ago or so, on my first visit to Rome, I stood in front of St. Peter's, taking in the enormity of it, when a girl art student walked up to me and started a conversation. "Did you know there is a brass star sunk into this pavement and if you put your heels exactly on this star you can see only the front row of columns of the Bernini colonnade which is really four columns deep? But if you move even a centimetre in any direction, all the columns pop out in perspective and there are suddenly four times as many." We found the star and I tried it; to her delight — as if she were the only one to know this secret — it worked. Standing in the exact centre of this great stone circle blocked its own depth from one's vision. I was reminded of this interlude when I reread the foreword I wrote for the 1967 edition of this book.

I am still here and Photography is still essentially the same, but a slight shift in position gives me a very different perspective.

Eight years ago I made much of the fact that "before the photograph there was no really believable image", and that it was this built-in credibility that made photography so valuable, particularly as used by advertising as a means of persuading the public to buy the more or less useful products of industry. Some weeks after the book appeared, Konrad Halle, the bookseller who sold it to me and who is also an erudite booklover, sent me a clipping from the London *Times* of 29 June 1967 which carried a review of *Photographis* and commented mostly on my introduction. After quoting a phrase of mine on "photography's inability to lie", the reviewer asked: "Cannot photography lie with greater conviction than any other medium?" The question bothered me. Maybe I had been too insistent on one aspect of photography, too absolute in trying to isolate just what it was that made this relatively new imagery so all-pervasive in our daily lives that most of us cannot spend an hour without seeing a photograph.

What I had overlooked is the fact that a photograph is not the truth but an abstraction. A convention which gets re-translated in the observer's mind. Let's take an example: A photographer is assigned to do a reportage on a new nightclub. He shoots 20 rolls of Tri-X film and, that night, he goes back to his darkroom and processes the film. The next day he looks at some prints and feels disappointed. The photographs fail to capture what the nightclub was like, even though they are "true"; the people in the photos are the people who were there, the mirrored columns are the same shape as in reality and the singer wears a low-cut sequin dress — just as she did.

What's missing? Colour for one thing. The photograph is black and white. No one has ever seen anything in black and white. Sound for another. The blaring music, voices, the clinking of glasses — all missing. Also, the prints fall short in evoking the smell of the place. It was tightly packed, sweaty, hot. The photographer felt people pushing him. Elbows. A sense of claustrophobia. People stepping on his feet. Movement is also missing. The photograph is still, motionless, frozen. No one has ever seen another person not breathing, not blinking their eyes. A photograph shows them breathless, blinkless. Also depth is lacking. The photograph is two-dimensional, and no human eye has ever seen a two-dimensional scene. The eye scans and doesn't always stop within the boundaries of the 24×36-mm cut-off in the camera.

The disappointed photographer, on reflection, feels better: it's amazing how much the photograph *does* retain. After all, it is an arbitrary fragment without sound, smell, motion, colour, depth or a sense of touch. It is really more of a reminder which helps to reconstruct a memory.

This is where I am reconsidering my stand of years ago: the important ingredient in a photograph worth considering at all is the ingenuity with which the artist uses this abstraction to evoke in the observer the same feeling that he himself was enveloped by at the moment of picture-taking.

To achieve this, it isn't enough to repeat with the proper technical knowledge what the photographer saw through the viewfinder and print it on sensitized paper: it's also necessary to use other conventions which help to reconstruct the feeling.

Another example: A racing car travelling at 180 miles per hour passes in front of a press camera; the photographer snaps the picture at $1/2000$ of a second. This shutter speed "stops" the car and in the resulting Kodachrome the car looks like it is parked in front of the grandstand. There are many photographic conventions possible to give the car its speed back. The important thing is the re-interpretation that has to be built into the picture as it is taken. Which brings me to another change of opinion. Years ago, as an occasional photographer, when I was also an Art Director and mostly my own client, I had a healthy disregard, even disdain, for technique. Now, as a photographer who has to solve other people's visual problems, I have learned to respect the necessity of the technical expertise I used to sneer at: it is needed for the building of the illusion. The noises and feeling of the party, the speed of the car have to be "re-invented" in photographic terms. It is essential to be familiar with them all to pick the most effective ones.

Photography can never be "pure" fantasy like music or painting. The subject has to be there in front of the lens. It cannot be imagined or conjured up. You can always touch it.

The genius which is possible in photography is only concerned with the means of giving the earthbound subject wings. To make it seem unique, beautiful or ugly, thoughtful or desirable beyond its mere depicted physical existence.

Henry Wolf

Vorwort

HENRY WOLF, der für PHOTOGRAPHIS 67 das Vorwort verfasste und für PHOTOGRAPHIS 70 den Umschlag gestaltete, zeichnet dieses Jahr sowohl als Autor des Einführungstextes wie auch als Umschlaggestalter. Als künstlerischer Leiter war er für die Präsentation verschiedener Zeitschriften verantwortlich, so für *Esquire, Harper's Bazaar, Show* und seit 1973 für *Sesame Street.* Ebenso bedeutend ist aber auch seine ausgedehnte Tätigkeit auf dem Gebiet der Werbung – z. B. bei Trahey/Wolf Advertising, Inc. Heute führt er ein eigenes Design Studio. Unsere Leser werden ihn jedoch am besten als Photographen kennen – als Photographen mit einem ungewöhnlich wachen Auge, mit spritzigem Geist und beruflichem Schliff. Sein waches Auge macht ihn auch zum glänzenden Beobachter der menschlichen (und photographischen) Szene, dessen Kommentare durch ihre Brillanz, ihre Klarheit und ihre Frische überzeugen.

Bei meinem ersten Besuch in Rom vor rund zwanzig Jahren stand ich vor dem Petersdom und liess dessen Enormität auf mich einwirken, als eine Kunststudentin auf mich zukam und mich in ein Gespräch verwickelte. «Wussten Sie, dass hier im Pflaster ein Messingstern eingelassen ist, von dem aus man, wenn man genau mit den Fersen daraufsteht, nur die vorderste Säulenreihe der Bernini-Kolonnade sehen kann, die in Wirklichkeit vier Säulenreihen hat? Weicht man auch nur einen Zentimeter davon ab, treten alle Säulen perspektivisch hervor und es sind plötzlich viermal so viele.» Wir fanden den Stern und probierten es aus. Zu ihrem Entzücken – als wäre sie die einzige, die von diesem Geheimnis wüsste – traf das Vorhergesagte zu. Stand man genau in der Mitte des grossen Steinkreises, verbarg sich dessen räumliche Tiefe vor den eigenen Blicken. An diesen Vorfall wurde ich erinnert, als ich wieder das Vorwort las, das ich für die Ausgabe dieses Buches von 1967 schrieb.

Ich bin noch immer hier und die Photographie ist im wesentlichen noch dieselbe – und doch eine kleine Positionsveränderung bewirkt für mich schon eine sehr veränderte Perspektive.

Vor acht Jahren strich ich gross heraus, dass es vor der Photographie kein wirklich glaubhaftes Bild gegeben habe, und dass diese ihr eigene Glaubwürdigkeit die Photographie so wertvoll mache, insbesondere auch als Mittel in der Werbung, um zum Kauf mehr oder weniger nützlicher Industrieprodukte zu verlocken. Einige Wochen nach Erscheinen des Buches schickte mir der Buchhändler und belesene Buchliebhaber Konrad Halle einen Ausschnitt aus der Londoner *Times* vom 29. Juni 1967 mit einer Besprechung von *Photographis,* die sich eingehend mit meiner Einleitung auseinandersetzte. Nach dem Zitat einer meiner Sätze über die Unfähigkeit der Photographie zu lügen fragte der Rezensent: «Kann Photographie nicht mit grösserer Überzeugung lügen als irgendein anderes Medium?» Die Frage liess mich nicht los. Vielleicht hatte ich mich zu sehr auf einen Aspekt der Photographie versteift, um dingfest zu machen, was eigentlich diese relativ neue Bilderflut unsere Alltagswelt so durchdringen lässt, dass die meisten Menschen kaum eine Stunde verbringen können, ohne ein Photo zu sehen.

Ich hatte übersehen, dass Photographie nicht Wahrheit, sondern eine Abstraktion ist. Eine Konvention, die im Geist des Betrachters zurückübersetzt wird. Ein Beispiel: Ein Photograph soll eine Reportage über einen neuen Nachtclub machen. Er verbraucht 20 Tri-X Filme, die er noch in derselben Nacht in seiner Dunkelkammer entwickelt. Am nächsten Tag sieht er einige Abzüge an und ist enttäuscht. Obwohl die Photos «stimmen», fangen sie den Nachtclub nicht ein, wie er war. Wohl sind die Menschen auf den Photos diejenigen, die anwesend waren, die abgebildeten Säulen haben dieselbe Form wie in Realität und die Sängerin trägt ein tiefausgeschnittenes Paillettenkleid – wie in Wirklichkeit.

Was fehlt? Zum einen die Farbe. Die Photographie ist Schwarzweiss. Niemand hat je etwas in Schwarzweiss gesehen. Zum anderen der Ton. Die laute Musik, das Stimmengewirr, das Gläserklingen, all das fehlt. Ausserdem evozieren die Abzüge nicht den Geruch der Lokalität. Es war dort proppenvoll, schweisstreibend heiss. Der Photograph spürte wie ihn die Leute stiessen. Ellbogen. Ein Gefühl der Platzangst. Leute traten ihm auf die Füsse. Auch die Bewegung fehlt. Das Photo ist still, reglos, eingefroren. Noch nie hat jemand andere Menschen nicht atmend und nicht blinzelnd gesehen. Eine Photographie zeigt sie ohne Atem und ohne Blinzeln. Auch die Raumtiefe geht ab. Das Photo ist zweidimensional, und kein Mensch hat je eine zweidimensionale Szene gesehen. Das Auge schweift umher und bleibt nicht innerhalb der Grenzen des 24×36mm-Ausschnitts der Kamera stehen.

Dem enttäuschten Photographen wird wieder wohler, wenn er bedenkt, wie erstaunlich es eigentlich ist, wie *vieles* doch in dem Photo festgehalten ist. Es ist zwar ein willkürliches Fragment ohne Ton, Geruch, Bewegung, Farbe, Tiefe oder körperliche Nähe, aber es hilft, die Erinnerung heraufzubeschwören.

In dieser Beziehung überdenke ich meinen früheren Standpunkt: Wichtig an einem beachtenswerten Photo ist die Erfindungsgabe, mit der der Künstler diese Abstraktion benützt, um beim Betrachter dasselbe Gefühl auszulösen, das er im Augenblick des Photographierens hatte.

Um das zu bewirken, genügt es nicht, mit dem nötigen technischen Wissen zu wiederholen, was der Photograph durch den Sucher sah, und es auf lichtempfindlichem Papier abzuziehen: Es bedarf noch des Einsatzes anderer Konventionen, um Eindrücke und Atmosphäre zu rekonstruieren.

Noch ein Beispiel: Ein Rennauto rast mit 270 km/h vor einem Pressephotographen vorbei, der das Bild mit $1/2000$ Sekunde Belichtungszeit aufnimmt. Die Verschlussgeschwindigkeit «hält» das Auto an und es sieht auf dem entstehenden Kodachrome-Bild aus, als wäre es vor der Zuschauertribüne geparkt. Es gibt viele photographische Konventionen, wie man dem Auto seine Geschwindigkeit wiedergeben kann. Wichtig ist dabei die Wiederausdeutung, die bei der Aufnahme ins Bild eingebaut werden muss. Das bringt mich zu einem anderen Meinungswandel. Vor Jahren, als Gelegenheitsphotograph, als ich Art Director und meist mein eigener Kunde war, hatte ich Aufnahmetechniken gegenüber eine gesunde Missachtung, ja sogar Verachtung. Jetzt, als Photograph, der die visuellen Probleme anderer Leute lösen muss, habe ich die Notwendigkeit technischer Sachkenntnis schätzen gelernt, die ich einst so geringschätzte: Sie ist vonnöten, um die Illusion aufzubauen. Lärm und Atmosphäre der Party, die Geschwindigkeit des Autos müssen auf photographischem Wege «neu erfunden» werden. Es ist wesentlich, mit allen Techniken vertraut zu sein, um die effektvollsten auszuwählen.

Photographie kann nie «reine» Phantasie sein wie Musik oder Malerei. Der Gegenstand muss vor dem Objektiv sein. Er kann nicht erdacht oder heraufbeschworen werden. Man kann ihn immer anfassen.

Das in der Photographie mögliche Geniale befasst sich nur mit den Mitteln, die dem erdgebundenen Gegenstand Flügel verleihen. Es will ihn über seine rein abgebildete physische Existenz hinaus einzigartig scheinen lassen, schön oder hässlich, nachdenklich oder begehrenswert.

Henry Wolf

Préface

HENRY WOLF – auteur de la préface de PHOTO-GRAPHIS 67 et auteur de la photo de couverture de PHOTOGRAPHIS 70 – a combiné cette année-ci ces deux fonctions. – Henry Wolf a été chargé successivement de la direction artistique des magazines *Esquire, Harper's Bazaar* et *Show*, et dès 1973 de *Sesame Street*. A part son travail rédactionnel, il s'est fait un nom par ses activités étendues dans le domaine de la publicité – p.ex. auprès de Trahey/Wolf Advertising, Inc. Depuis quelques temps il travaille aussi à son propre compte. Pourtant, nos lecteurs l'estiment sans doute en premier lieu comme photographe de profession – photographe accompli à l'œil vif et à l'esprit pétillant. Ces facultés le permettent également d'observer la scène humaine (et photographique) et de la commenter d'une façon aussi perspicace que rafraîchissante.

Il y a une vingtaine d'années, lors de mon premier séjour à Rome, je me trouvais devant St-Pierre, me laissant pénétrer de la splendeur de l'édifice, quand une étudiante des beaux-arts s'approcha de moi et engagea la conversation: «Vous savez qu'il y a une étoile de cuivre scellée dans le sol et que, si vous mettez les talons exactement sur cette plaque, vous ne voyez que la rangée avant de la colonnade de Bernini? Mais si vous vous déplacez ne serait-ce que d'un centimètre dans n'importe quelle direction, toutes les autres rangées de colonnes apparaissent, et la colonnade est multipliée par quatre.» Nous nous sommes mis en quête de l'étoile, l'avons trouvée et essayée. La jeune fille exultait, comme si elle avait été la seule à connaître le grand secret. Et cela marchait: en se plaçant au centre du grand cercle de pierre, la perspective disparaissait. C'est à quoi je pensais en relisant la préface que j'ai écrite pour l'édition 1967 du présent ouvrage.

Je suis toujours là, et la photographie n'a guère changé pour l'essentiel; pourtant, un léger déplacement suffit déjà pour faire apparaître une perspective très différente.

Il y a huit ans, j'ai beaucoup insisté sur le fait qu'avant l'avènement de la photographie, il n'y avait pas d'images vraiment dignes de foi et que c'est cette crédibilité attachée au processus même qui a fait de la photo une acquisition aussi précieuse, particulièrement dans le domaine publicitaire où il s'agit de convaincre le public d'acheter les produits plus ou moins utiles de l'industrie. Quelques semaines après la parution du volume, Konrad Halle, mon libraire, qui est un expert en livres, me fit parvenir un compte-rendu paru dans le *Times* de Londres du 29 juin 1967. Le critique relevait l'une de mes phrases sur «l'impossibilité, pour la photo, de mentir» et la mettait en question en écrivant ceci: «Est-ce que la photo ne peut pas mentir avec bien plus de conviction que tout autre média?» Cette question ne me lâcha plus. Peut-être avais-je trop insisté sur un seul aspect de la photo en tentant de déterminer de manière trop absolue ce qui rendait cette imagerie relativement récente si omniprésente et influente dans notre vie quotidienne qu'il ne se passe guère une heure sans que la plupart d'entre nous soient confrontés à une photo.

Ce que j'avais négligé, c'est le fait qu'une photo n'est pas la vérité toute nue, mais une abstraction, une convention qui est retransposée dans l'esprit de l'observateur. Prenons un exemple: Un photographe se voit confier un reportage sur une nouvelle boîte de nuit. Il noircit une vingtaine de pellicules Tri-X et les développe le soir même dans son labo. Le lendemain, certaines de ces images lui semblent décevantes, sans attrait. C'est qu'elles n'arrivent pas à reproduire l'ambiance du night-club, tout en reproduisant fidèlement tous les détails enregistrés par l'appareil: les gens visibles sur ces photos étaient vraiment là, les piliers à miroirs sont les mêmes que dans la réalité, et la chanteuse porte exactement la robe décolletée en paillettes d'or qu'elle arborait au club – et pourtant, quelque chose ne joue pas.

Qu'est-ce qui manque? La couleur, d'abord, puisque la photo est noire et blanche. Personne n'a jamais rien vu de ses yeux en noir et blanc. Puis, le son. La musique envoûtante, les voix, le tintement des verres – tout cela est absent. Les photos ne réussissent pas non plus à enregistrer les odeurs de cette salle comble où l'on nageait dans la transpiration et la chaleur. Le photographe a senti des gens le bousculer, il a reçu des coups de coude dans les côtés. Sa vieille angoisse de claustrophobe s'est réveillée. Les gens lui marchaient sur les pieds. Rien de tout cela sur la photo. Le mouvement manque, lui aussi. La photo est figée, immobile. Personne n'a jamais vu hors de la morgue une personne qui ne respirait pas, qui ne bougeait pas les yeux. Sur la photo, ils oublient de respirer, de cligner des yeux. La profondeur manque. La photo n'a que deux dimensions, et aucun œil humain n'a jamais perçu de scène bidimensionnelle. Puis, la vision naturelle n'est pas fixe, l'œil scrute sans cesse tout le champ visuel et n'est pas accoutumé à se mouvoir uniquement dans la découpe de 24×36 mm de l'appareil photo.

A la réflexion, le reporter déçu reprend courage: après tout, c'est quand même étonnant ce qu'une simple photo arrive à reproduire, alors qu'elle n'est au fond rien d'autre qu'un fragment arbitraire sans mouvement, sans odeur, sans son, sans couleur, sans profondeur, sans impression tactile. Son rôle essentiel est de servir de support pour la reconstruction qu'opère la mémoire.

C'est là que je reviens sur ma constatation d'il y a quelques années: l'élément essentiel d'une photo qui vaut la peine d'être retenue, c'est l'ingéniosité avec laquelle l'artiste utilise cette abstraction pour évoquer dans l'esprit de l'observateur les sensations et sentiments qui l'animaient, lui, quand il a appuyé sur le déclencheur.

Pour ce faire, il ne suffit pas de reproduire avec tout le savoir technique nécessaire ce que le photographe a vu à travers son viseur, puis de l'imprimer sur du papier sensibilisé; il faut encore mettre en œuvre d'autres conventions permettant de reconstruire les sensations et sentiments qui agitaient le photographe au moment de la prise de vue.

Prenons un autre exemple: Un bolide passe à 270 km à l'heure devant l'appareil d'un photographe de presse, qui réalise une superbe photo à $1/2000^e$ de seconde. Seulement, à ce temps de pose-là, la voiture paraît immobile, et la photo Kodachrome la montre comme parquée devant les tribunes. Il y a de nombreuses conventions photographiques susceptibles de restituer l'impression de vitesse. L'essentiel, c'est le support de réinterprétation qui doit être inclus dans la photo au moment où elle est prise. Ce qui me fait adopter une autre position nouvelle. Il y a des années, je fonctionnais de temps à autre comme photographe, j'étais directeur artistique et la plupart du temps mon propre client, et — je tenais en peu d'estime l'aspect purement technique. Maintenant que je travaille surtout comme photographe au service d'autres gens dont j'aide à résoudre les problèmes visuels, j'ai appris à respecter la nécessité de la spécialisation technique que j'écartais jadis avec un certain dédain. C'est que cette technicité est essentielle pour créer l'illusion. Les bruits et l'ambiance de la soirée, la vitesse du bolide doivent être réinventés en quelque sorte sur le plan photographique. Il est donc important de maîtriser toutes les possibilités de la technique pour mettre en œuvre celles qui s'avèrent le plus efficaces.

La photo ne peut jamais être œuvre d'imagination pure comme le sont la musique ou la peinture. Le sujet doit être là, devant l'objectif. Il ne peut être ni imaginé ni évoqué. Il est là, matériel, palpable.

Le génie qui peut s'affirmer dans une photo concerne exclusivement la manière dont le sujet peut échapper à la pesanteur de la terre, dont il peut être paré d'unicité, de beauté, de laideur, d'intellectualité ou d'attrait par-delà sa seule existence physique mise en image.

Index to Photographers
Verzeichnis der Photographen
Index des photographes

Index to Designers
Verzeichnis der Gestalter
Index des maquettistes

Index to Art Directors
Verzeichnis der künstlerischen Leiter
Index des directeurs artistiques

Index to Agencies, Studios and Producers
Verzeichnis der Agenturen, Studios und Produzenten
Index des agences, studios et producteurs

Index to Publishers
Verzeichnis der Verleger
Index des éditeurs

Index to Advertisers
Verzeichnis der Auftraggeber
Index des clients

■ Entry instructions may be requested by anyone interested in submitting samples of exceptional photography or graphics for possible inclusion in our annuals. No fees involved. Closing dates for entries:
PHOTOGRAPHIS (advertising and editorial photography): 30 May
GRAPHIS ANNUAL (advertising and editorial art and design): 15 December
GRAPHIS POSTERS (an annual of poster art): 30 March
Write to: The Graphis Press, Dufourstrasse 107, 8008 Zurich, Switzerland

■ Einsendebedingungen können von jedermann angefordert werden, der uns Beispiele hervorragender Photographie oder Graphik zur Auswahl für unsere Jahrbücher unterbreiten möchte. Es werden keine Gebühren erhoben. Einsendetermine:
PHOTOGRAPHIS (Werbe- und redaktionelle Photographie): 30. Mai
GRAPHIS ANNUAL (Werbe- und redaktionelle Graphik): 15. Dezember
GRAPHIS POSTERS (ein Jahrbuch der Plakatkunst): 30. März
Adresse: Graphis Verlag, Dufourstrasse 107, 8008 Zürich, Schweiz

■ Tout intéressé à la soumission de travaux photographiques et graphiques recevra les informations nécessaires sur demande. Sans charge de participation. Dates limites:
PHOTOGRAPHIS (photographie publicitaire et rédactionnelle): 30 mai
GRAPHIS ANNUAL (art graphique publicitaire et rédactionnel): 15 décembre
GRAPHIS POSTERS (annuaire sur l'art de l'affiche): 30 mars
S'adresser à: Editions Graphis, Dufourstrasse 107, 8008 Zurich, Suisse

Editor, Art Director: Walter Herdeg
Assistant Editor: Stanley Mason
Project Manager: Vreni Monnier
Art Assistants: René Sahli, Klaus Schröder, Otmar Staubli, Peter Wittwer

1

Magazine Advertisements

Newspaper Advertisements

Zeitschriften-Inserate

Zeitungs-Inserate

1

2

3

4

PHOTOGRAPHER / PHOTOGRAPH / PHOTOGRAPHE:

1, 2, 4 Klaus P. Ohlenforst
3 George de Gennaro
5, 6 Mario Zappala
7, 8 Marco Emili

ART DIRECTOR / DIRECTEUR ARTISTIQUE:

1, 2 Horst Schug
3 Brian Mc Carthy
4 Klaus Hergert
5–8 Piero Mora

AGENCY / AGENTUR / AGENCE – STUDIO:

1, 2 Gramm & Grey GmbH + Co. KG
3 Tracy-Locke Advertising
4 Heumann, Ogilvy & Mather GmbH
5–8 Young & Rubicam Italia S.p.A.

5

6

1, 2 Full-colour magazine advertisements from a series for *Knorr* soups, "Germany's most popular tinned soups", here mushroom and tomato. (GER)
3 Magazine advertisement for the *Dole* banana as a low-calorie snack for those who need to slim. Banana in full colour. (USA)
4 Full-colour magazine advertisement for a *Wasa* wheat crispbread with sesame seeds. (GER)
5, 6 From a series of full-colour magazine ads for *Barilla* pasta, each explaining differences in quality of spaghetti, macaroni, etc. (ITA)
7, 8 "Our Board of Directors has decided that only yellow peaches will be used for our fruit juices this year." Full-page magazine advertisement and detail of the colour photograph for *Valfrutta* fruit juices. (ITA)

1, 2 Ganzseitige Zeitschrifteninserate für preiswerte *Knorr*-Dosensuppen. Mehrfarbig. (GER)
3 Mehrfarbiges Zeitschrifteninserat für kalorienarme *Dole*-Bananen. (USA)
4 Ganzseitiges Inserat für *Wasa*-Knäckebrot mit Sesam-Körnern. Mehrfarbig. (GER)
5, 6 Zwei Beispiele aus einer ganzseitigen Zeitschriften-Inseratenserie für *Barilla*-Teigwaren, die im Gegensatz zu Konkurrenzprodukten nicht zusammenkleben. Mehrfarbig. (ITA)
7, 8 Zeitschrifteninserat und Ausschnitt für *Valfrutta*-Fruchtsäfte, die von einer aus Bauern und Fachleuten bestehenden Genossenschaft hergestellt werden und besonders naturrein sind. (ITA)

1, 2 D'une série d'annonces de magazine pour les potages *Knorr*, les plus vendus en Allemagne. Les reproductions en couleur se réfèrent à la crème de champignons et à la crème de tomates. (GER)
3 Annonce de magazine pour les bananes *Dole* pauvres en calories – pour ceux qui désirent amaigrir. (USA)
4 Annonce de magazine en couleur pour un pain croustillant aux graines de sésame. (GER)
5, 6 D'une série d'annonces de magazine pour les pâtes alimentaires *Barilla*; chaque annonce donne des détails concernant la différence en qualité des spaghettis, des macaroni etc. Polychrome. (ITA)
7, 8 «Le conseil des directeurs a décidé de ne prendre que les pêches jaunes pour les jus de fruit cette année.» Annonce de revue et détail de la photo couleur pour les jus de fruits *Valfrutta*. (ITA)

7

8

Lahden Vaalea

Lahden Vaalean alkoholipitoisuus on enintään
3,7 painoprosenttia ja sitä saa sekä pulloissa että tölkeissä

9

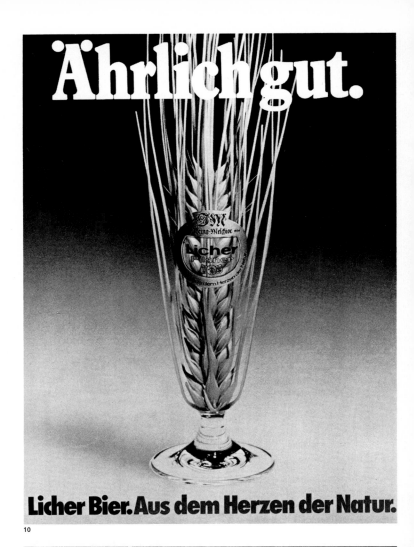

Ährlichgut.

Licher Bier. Aus dem Herzen der Natur.

10

Täglich Brot.

Licher Bier. Aus dem Herzen der Natur.

11

9 Full-colour magazine advertisement for *Lahden Vaalea*, a pale ale made by Oy Mallasjuoma. (FIN)
10, 11 "Honestly good."—"Daily bread". Full-colour magazine advertisements on a green ground for *Licher* beer, "from the heart of nature". Fig. 10 puns on *ehrlich* (= honest) and *Ähre* (= a spike of wheat). (GER)
12 Magazine advertisement as part of a campaign to popularize *Guinness* beer with the feminine sex, for whom beer-drinking was formerly not considered "ladylike". (GBR)
13 Magazine advertisement showing a glass of beer among antiquities from a museum in Leyden—a reference to its long tradition. (NLD)
14 Magazine advertisement for a *Pilsner* beer "born in Pilsen, at home in the whole world". (GER)
15 Full-colour magazine advertisement from a campaign for *Guinness* beer. See Fig. 12. (GBR)

9 Ganzseitiges Zeitschrifteninserat einer finnischen Brauerei für *Lahden Vaalea*, ein helles Bier. Mehrfarbig. (GER)
10, 11 Mehrfarbige Zeitschrifteninserate für *Licher*-Biere aus reinen Naturprodukten. Grüner Grund. (GER)
12 Aus einer Serie Zeitschrifteninserate für *Guinness*-Bier, das auch für Damen geeignet, d.h. «ladylike», sein soll. (GBR)
13 Zeitschrifteninserat für Bier der Grolschen Brauerei in Enschede. Die ägyptischen Grabbeigaben aus einem Museum in Leiden versinnbildlichen den Begriff der Tradition. (NLD)
14 Ganzseitiges Zeitschrifteninserat für das echte, in Pilsen gebraute und in viele Länder exportierte *Pilsner-Urquell*-Bier. (GER)
15 Ganzseitiges Zeitschrifteninserat für *Guinness*-Bier. Vorwiegend zarte Braun- und Blautöne. (GBR)

9 Annonce de magazine en couleur pour une marque de bière blonde. (FIN)
10, 11 «Honnêtement, elle est bonne.» «Le pain quotidien.» Annonces de magazine sur fond vert pour la bière *Licher*. La fig. 10 présente un jeux de mots – *ehrlich* = honnête, et *Ähre* = un épi. (GER)
12 Annonce de magazine figurant dans une campagne publicitaire qui vise à une plus grande popularité de la bière *Guinness* parmi les femmes – car auparavant une femme qui buvait un verre de bière n'était pas considérée comme étant «lady-like». (GBR)
13 Annonce de magazine présentant un verre de bière parmi des antiquités provenant d'un musée de Leyde – photo qui fait allusion à sa longue tradition. (NLD)
14 Annonce de magazine pour un pils qui «est né dans la région de Plzen», mais qui est très populaire dans le monde entier. (GER)
15 Annonce de magazine pour la bière *Guinness*. Voir la fig. 12. (GBR)

PHOTOGRAPHER:

9 Kaj G. Lindholm
10, 11 S.S.M.
12 Harry Peccinotti
13 Paul Huf
14 Dieter Bork
15 Richard Dunkley

DESIGNER / GESTALTER:

9 Kari Torkler
10, 11 S.S.M.
12 Anne Carlton
14 Coordt von Mannstein
15 Mike Trumble

ART DIRECTOR / DIRECTEUR ARTISTIQUE:

9 Kari Torkler
10, 11 S.S.M.
12 Anne Carlton
14 Coordt von Mannstein
15 Mike Trumble

AGENCY / AGENTUR / AGENCE – STUDIO:

9 SEK Advertising Ltd.
10, 11 S.S.M.
12 J. Walter Thompson Co. Ltd.
13 Grolsche Bierbrouwerij B.V.
14 von Mannstein' Werbeagentur
15 J. Walter Thompson Co. Ltd.

LADYLIKE

GUINNESS

12

RIJKSMUSEUM VAN OUDHEDEN
LEIDEN

13

Geboren in Pilsen.
Zuhause in aller Welt.

Pilsner Urquell

14

ANYONE FOR GUINNESS?

Summer. When a girl can play it cool
and still get what she wants.
There's one drink that keeps its head

and its refreshingly dry, clean taste,
even when it's been left on the cold shelf.
Cold Guinness. The perfect serve.

15

29

16

Proef de naam.

Importeur Johnnie Walker: Mähler-Besse B.V. Amsterdam.

17

18

King Gordon and the longdrinks.

Is er echt niet alleen voor de perfekte gin tonic. Maakt cola, up en sinaasappelsap tot wis en waarachtige longdrinks. Doet bitter lemon, lime juice en tomatensap zich hooggerheven voelen in het glas. Is onmisbaar ingrediënt van de enige echte Dry Martini cocktail.

Staat vaker dan welke drank ook in cocktailrecepten. Schudt mee in shakers over de hele wereld. Dat is Gordon's Gin, de koning van het mixen en het shaken. Want niet voor niets is Gordon's de meest verkochte gin ter wereld. Gordon's Gin. King Gordon.

19

Reserve a box for the interval.

20

16 Magazine advertisement for *Schultheiss* beer "with the honest taste". (GER)
17 "Taste the name." Magazine advertisement for *Johnnie Walker* whisky. (NLD)
18 Double-spread magazine advertisement for *Famous Grouse* Scotch whisky, with full-colour illustration and a text on the effects of ice on scotch. (USA)
19 Magazine advertisement for *Gordon's* gin, showing bottle-tops of some of the drinks with which it can be mixed. (NLD)
20 Magazine advertisement for *Benson and Hedges* cigarettes. Red-brown fur, beige gloves, gold box on red cloth. (GBR)
21 Magazine advertisement (inside back cover) for *Benson and Hedges* cigarettes. Full colour, gold box. (GBR)
22 "Call me *Peroni*. I shall be your beer." Full-colour magazine advertisement for *Peroni* beer. (ITA)

16 Ganzseitiges Zeitschrifteninserat für Pilsner-Bier der Brauerei *Schultheiss*. (GER)
17 Zeitschrifteninserat für *Johnnie-Walker*-Whisky, mit der Aufforderung, auf die Marke zu achten. (NLD)
18 Doppelseitiges Zeitschrifteninserat für *Famous Grouse*, mit einer Erklärung, welchen Einfluss die Eiszugabe auf den Geschmack dieses schottischen Whiskys hat. (USA)
19 Ganzseitiges Zeitschrifteninserat für den aus England eingeführten *Gordon's* Gin; Verschlusskapseln und Früchte weisen darauf hin, dass er sich gut mixen lässt. (NLD)
20, 21 Ganzseitige, mehrfarbige Zeitschrifteninserate für *Benson and Hedges* Zigaretten bei festlichen Gelegenheiten, z. B. Theaterbesuch oder Festessen. (GBR)
22 Ganzseitiges, mehrfarbiges Zeitschrifteninserat für Bier. «Nenne mich *Peroni*, ich werde dein Bier sein.» (ITA)

16 Annonce de magazine pour la bière *Schultheiss,* «la bière au goût honnête». (GER)
17 «Goûtez le nom!» Annonce de magazine pour une marque de whisky. (NLD)
18 Annonce de magazine sur page double pour un whisky écossais. Illustration en couleur avec texte se référant à l'effet que produit la glace dans le scotch. (USA)
19 Annonce de magazine pour une marque de gin; les capuchons représentent les boissons qui se prêtent le mieux à être mélangées au gin. (NLD)
20 Annonce de magazine pour les cigarettes *Benson & Hedges*. Fourrure en rouge brun, gants beiges, boîte dorée sur fond rouge. (GBR)
21 Annonce de revue – parue sur la 3e page de couverture – pour les cigarettes *Benson & Hedges*. Polychrome, boîte dorée. (GBR)
22 «Appelez-moi *Peroni*. Je serais votre bière.» Annonce de magazine en couleur pour la bière *Peroni*. (ITA)

Some occasions call for the golden touch.

21

chiamami Peroni
sarò la tua birra

sono la birra più bevuta in Italia
Lo sapevi?

BIRRA PERONI

22

PHOTOGRAPHER/ PHOTOGRAPH/ PHOTOGRAPHE:

23 Jurriaan Eindhoven
24 Ilimari Kostiainen
25 Klaus P. Ohlenforst
26 Gillean Proctor
27 Henry Wolf
28 Julian Cottrell
29, 30 Ben Oyne

23 "I do what I like. I drink what I like." Full-colour magazine advertisement selling *Coebergh* fruit cordials to emancipated women. (NLD)
24 Magazine advertisement for a mocca coffee made by *Paulig*. Cup and saucer in golden yellow and brown shades. (FIN)
25 "How long should a good Pilsen beer mature?" Full-colour magazine advertisement for a brewery in Herrenhausen. (GER)
26 Magazine ad in black, gold and white for *Black Velvet*, a *Gilbey's* Canadian whisky. (CAN)
27 Magazine ad for imported *Hennessy* cognacs. Bottles and initial in colour. (USA)
28 Magazine advertisement for *Schweppes*, from a series underlining the high degree of aeration of their table waters. Full colour. (GBR)
29, 30 Complete colour magazine advertisement and detail of the photography for *Granini* fruit juices ("Drink something for your figure"). (GER)

23 Ganzseitiges Zeitschrifteninserat für *Coebergh*-Fruchtschnaps. «Ich tue, was mir passt; ich trinke, was mir passt.» Mehrfarbig. (NLD)
24 Inserat für *Paulig*-Kaffee und -Mokka. (FIN)
25 Ganzseitiges Zeitschrifteninserat für *Herrenhäuser* Pilsener Bier. Mehrfarbig. (GER)
26 Zeitschriftenanzeige für den kanadischen Whisky *Black Velvet*. Schwarz, Gold, Weiss. (CAN)
27 Ganzseitiges, mehrfarbiges Zeitschrifteninserat mit Preisangaben für vier verschiedene Sorten von *Hennessy*-Cognac. (USA)
28 Mehrfarbiges Zeitschrifteninserat für *Schweppes*-Tafelgetränke. Die Finger messen die Höhe der aufsteigenden Bläschen. (GBR)
29, 30 Ganzseitiges Zeitschrifteninserat und Ausschnitt für das kalorienarme *Granini*-Fruchtgetränk, das sich zur Erhaltung und Wiedergewinnung der schlanken Linie empfiehlt. Mehrfarbig. (GER)

23 «Je fais ce que je veux. Je bois ce que je veux.» Annonce de magazine en couleur pour une eau-de-vie fruitée qui est destinée particulièrement aux femmes qui désirent s'émanciper. (NLD)
24 Annonce de magazine pour la promotion du mocca *Paulig*. Tasse et soucoupe en teintes jaune doré et brunes. (FIN)
25 «Combien de temps faut-il pour que la bonne pils soit affinée?» Annonce de magazine pour une brasserie à Herrenhausen. (GER)
26 Annonce de magazine en noir, or et blanc pour le whisky *Black Velvet*. (CAN)
27 Annonce de magazine pour un cognac importé. Bouteilles et initiale en couleur. (USA)
28 Annonce de magazine pour *Schweppes*, tirée d'une série qui souligne la haute gazéification de leurs eaux minérales. Polychrome. (GBR)
29, 30 Annonce de magazine complète et détail de la photo pour les jus de fruits *Granini*. (GER)

ART DIRECTOR / DIRECTEUR ARTISTIQUE:

23 Bob Bernard
24 Pertti Vaajakallio/Riitta Markkanen
25 Werner Würdinger
26 Robert Glynn
27 Gene Federico
28 Mel Wright
29, 30 Peter Warfelmann

AGENCY / AGENTUR / AGENCE – STUDIO:

23 KVH/CDP
24 SEK Advertising Ltd.
25 Gottschling & Würdinger GmbH & Co.
26 Cockfield, Brown & Co. Ltd.
27 Lord, Geller, Federico, Inc.
28 J. Walter Thompson Co. Ltd.
29, 30 Masius

Advertisements / Inserate
Annonces

DESIGNER / GESTALTER / MAQUETTISTE:

24 Pertti Vaajakallio
25 Werner Würdinger
26 Gillean Proctor
27 Gene Federico/Helen Federico
28 Mel Wright
29, 30 Peter Warfelmann

29

Advertisements
Inserate
Annonces

PHOTOGRAPHER / PHOTOGRAPH:

31 Tony Blake
32 David Montgomery
33 Mane Weigand
34 Richard Noble

DESIGNER / GESTALTER / MAQUETTISTE:

31 Raimund Lunz
32 Ton Vergouw
33 John Buchner
34 Clive Challis

ART DIRECTOR / DIRECTEUR ARTISTIQUE:

31 Gerd Ziegler/Rainer Diekerhoff
33 John Buchner
34 Clive Challis

AGENCY / AGENTUR / AGENCE – STUDIO:

31 J. Walter Thompson GmbH
32 J. Walter Thompson Co. B.V.
33 Young & Rubicam GmbH
34 Lord, Geller, Federico, Inc.

31 "Everything goes with *Bacardi* rum." Double-spread magazine advertisement in full colour using the simple life to promote *Bacardi* rum. (GER)
32 "I am pure." Full-colour magazine advertisement for *Agio* Havanna cigars, which claim to be natural and unadulterated. (NLD)
33 "How good that tomorrow is Christmas again." Magazine advertisement in colour showing an almost empty bottle of *Dimple* Scotch whisky. (GER)
34 Magazine advertisement using some Eastern European local colour to sell the Polish *Wyborowa* vodka. Roughly actual size. (USA)

31 Doppelseitiges Zeitschrifteninserat für *Bacardi*, einen weissen Rum von den Karibischen Inseln, mit Vorschlägen zum Mischen mit Coke, Tonic und Bitter Lemon. Farbig. (GER)
32 «Ich bin rein.» Farbiges Zeitschrifteninserat für *Agio*-Zigarren aus kubanischem Tabak. (NLD)
33 Mehrfarbiges, ganzseitiges Zeitschrifteninserat für den 12 Jahre alten schottischen Whisky *Dimple*. Das Inserat erschien kurz vor Weihnachten. (GER)
34 Originalgrosser Ausschnitt aus einem ganzseitigen Zeitschrifteninserat für *Wyborowa*-Wodka aus Polen, «dem Land, in dem der Wodka geboren wurde». (USA)

31 «Grâce au rhum *Bacardi* vous réussissez toujours!» Annonce de magazine sur page double pour la promotion d'une marque de rhum. Polychrome. (GER)
32 «Moi, je suis naturel.» Annonce de magazine pour les cigars *Agio* de la Havane qui sont fabriqués de vrais tabac cubain. (NLD)
33 «Pas mal, demain c'est le jour de Noël.» Annonce de magazine présentant une bouteille de whisky *Dimple* presque vide. Polychrome. (GER)
34 Annonce de magazine – presque en grandeur nature – présentant une vue typique de l'Europe orientale afin de souligner l'origine du vodka *Wyborowa*. (USA)

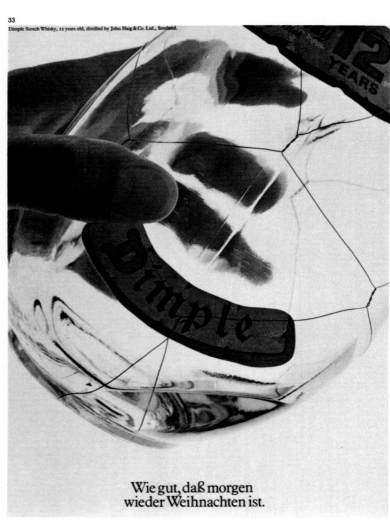

"Out of Belgrade,
we drank Wyborowa vodka with lunch
and dreamily watched the Balkans
speed by."

35 Photograph in the actual size of the transparency for use in advertising the popular table water *Dr. Pepper*. (USA)
36—38 Examples from a campaign with an unchanging line of copy in which typically atmospheric shots of romantic situations by Sarah Moon are used to promote *Mateus Rosé*, a light Portuguese wine. All in full colour. (GBR)
39 Full-colour magazine advertisement appealing to a sense of filial piety in the interests of the upper-price-bracket Scotch whisky *Chivas Regal*. (USA)
40 "To our partnership!" Trade magazine advertisement offering *Burg Weisenau* German champagne to retailers. (GER)

35 Photographie aus einem Inserat für das in Amerika bekannte Tafelwasser *Dr. Pepper*. (USA)
36—38 Mehrfarbige Zeitschrifteninserate für *Mateus Rosé*, einen leichten, erfrischenden Wein aus Portugal, mit an frohe Stunden erinnernden Aufnahmen. (GBR)
39 Ganzseitiges Zeitschrifteninserat für den 12 Jahre alten schottischen Whisky *Chivas Regal*. «Du kannst Deinem Vater nie genug danken für alles, was er für Dich getan hat. Aber Du kannst es wenigstens versuchen.» (USA)
40 Mehrfarbiges Fachzeitschrifteninserat, das sich an Wiederverkäufer von Sekt aus der Kellerei Burg Weisenau richtet. (GER)

35 Photo d'une annonce pour la promotion d'une eau de table très populaire aux Etats-Unis. (USA)
36—38 Exemples d'une campagne publicitaire dont le texte reste inchangé. Les photos de Sarah Moon présentant des vues nostalgiques sont employées pour la promotion d'un vin léger provenant du Portugal. Toute la série est en couleur. (GBR)
39 Annonce de magazine s'adressant aux enfants afin qu'ils remercient leur père pour tout ce qu'il a fait pour eux en lui faisant cadeau d'une bouteille du whisky écossais *Chivas Regal*. (USA)
40 «A notre amitié.» Annonce qui a paru dans la presse professionnelle et qui s'adresse aux détaillants. Promotion pour le champagne allemand *Burg Weisenau*. (GER)

36

35

37

You can never thank your father enough for everything he's done for you. But you certainly can try.

39

Remember with Mateus Rosé
The light refreshing wine from the people of Portugal

38

Auf unsere Partnerschaft!...

40

PHOTOGRAPHER / PHOTOGRAPH / PHOTOGRAPHE:

35 Phil Marco
36–38 Sarah Moon
39 Chuck Lamonica
40 Rainer Schlegelmilch

DESIGNER / GESTALTER / MAQUETTISTE:

35 Phil Marco
36, 37 Mike Trumble
38 Chris Conway
39 Mike Lawlor
40 Heinz Kroehl

ART DIRECTOR / DIRECTEUR ARTISTIQUE:

36, 37 Mike Trumble
38 Chris Conway
39 Mike Lawlor
40 Heinz Kroehl

AGENCY / AGENTUR / AGENCE – STUDIO:

35 Young & Rubicam International Inc.
36–38 J. Walter Thompson Co. Ltd.
39 Doyle Dane Bernbach, Inc.
40 Kroehl Design Gruppe

Advertisements
Inserate
Annonces

37

41

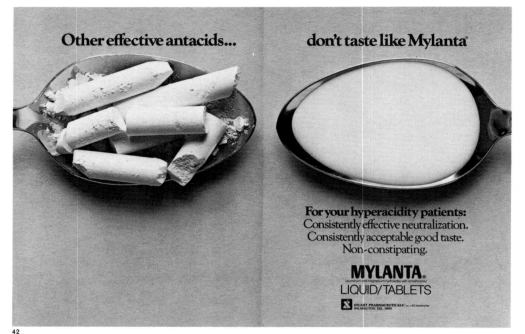

42

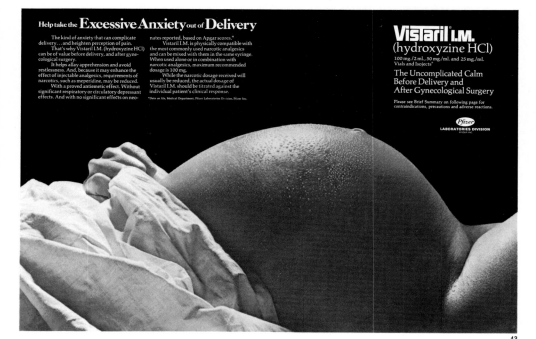

43

Advertisements / Inserate
Annonces

41 Double-spread trade magazine advertisement for *Sinequan*, a *Pfizer* hypnotic with an antidepressant effect. Carmine flower petals. (USA)
42 Double-spread trade magazine advertisement on a pale greenish-blue ground for *Mylanta*, a hyperacidity neutralizer with a pleasant taste made by Stuart Pharmaceuticals. (USA)
43 Full-colour double-spread advertisement in trade magazines for *Vistaril*, a *Pfizer* sedative for use in childbirth. (USA)
44, 45 From a series of black-and-white magazine advertisements for *Aspirin plus C*, a Bayer antidote for headaches, here for the reveller and the grass widower. (GER)
46 One-and-one-third-page advertisement in full colour for *Aspirina C*, a *Bayer* medicinal orange drink for children. (ITA)
47 Black-and-white magazine advertisement for *Slender*, a slimming diet food made by Carnation Co. (USA)

41 Doppelseitiges Zeitschrifteninserat für ein Schlafmittel, das auch gegen Depressionen wirkt. Karminrote Blütenblätter. (USA)
42 In Blau- und Grautönen gehaltenes Zeitschrifteninserat für das angenehm einzunehmende Medikament *Mylanta*. Doppelseitig. (USA)
43 Doppelseitiges Zeitschrifteninserat für *Vistaril*, ein Medikament gegen Angstzustände vor und während der Entbindung. Mehrfarbig. (USA)
44, 45 Schwarzweisse Inserate für *Aspirin plus C* in Form von Brausetabletten. (GER)
46 Eineindrittelseitiges, vierfarbiges Zeitschrifteninserat für die neue, Vitamin C enthaltende Brausetablette *Aspirina C junior* mit Orangengeschmack, für Jugendliche. (ITA)
47 Schwarzweisses Inserat für *Slender*-Diätkost. «Mein Mann findet, dass mir Dicklichkeit ganz gut steht.» (USA)

41 Annonce sur page double pour un sédatif à effet antidépresseur. Pétales en rouge cramoisi. (USA)
42 Annonce de magazine professionnel sur page double en faveur d'un produit pharmaceutique pour le traitement de l'hyperchlorhydrie. Sur fond bleu verdâtre. (USA)
43 Annonce parue dans la presse professionnelle. Pour la promotion de *Vistaril*, un sédatif qu'on emploie avant et pendant l'accouchement. En couleur. (USA)
44, 45 D'une série d'annonces en noir-blanc pour l'*Aspirin plus C*, un produit contre les maux de tête – les illustrations se réfèrent particulièrement aux fêtards et aux veufs à titre temporaire. (GER)
46 Annonce de magazine sur une page et un tiers pour *Aspirina C*, une boisson médicinale à l'arôme d'orange pour les enfants. (ITA)
47 Annonce de magazine en noir et blanc pour *Slender*, un régime amaigrissant de Carnation Co. (USA)

PHOTOGRAPHER / PHOTOGRAPH / PHOTOGRAPHE:

41 Peter Vaeth
42 Carmine Macedonia
43 Studio Hiro
44, 45 Ben Oyne
46 Philip Jude
47 Lamb & Hall

DESIGNER / GESTALTER / MAQUETTISTE:

41, 42 Len Obsatz
43 Frank Wagner
44, 45 Ute Vach/Ben Oyne

ART DIRECTOR / DIRECTEUR ARTISTIQUE:

41, 42 Len Obsatz
43 Frank Wagner
44, 45 Ute Vach
46 Elvezio Ghidoli
47 Bob Rainwater

AGENCY / AGENTUR / AGENCE – STUDIO:

41–43 Sudler & Hennessey, Inc.
44, 45 Leo Burnett
46 Young & Rubicam Italia S.p.A.
47 Erwin Wasey, Inc.

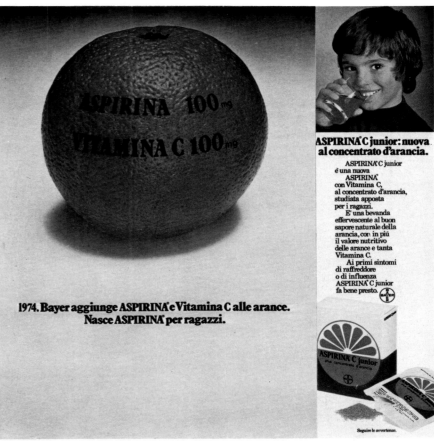

51

48 "*Ducolax* solves this problem without tears." Magazine advertisement for a *Boehringer* purgative. (GER)
49 *Roche* institutional advertisement placed in magazines. Black on blue, white copy. (CAN)
50–52 Complete double-spread advertisement and two examples of the full-page colour photographs from a series placed in medical magazines for the psychotherapeutic drug *Thorazine* made by Smith Klein & French Laboratories. Each advertisement refers to a different attribute of the product. (USA)
53, 54 Double-spread advertisements in Spanish for *Camyña*, a *Boehringer* pharmaceutical for use against acne. Black and white with red strip at the bottom. (GER)
55 Magazine advertisement for *Crest* toothpaste for the prevention of cavities. Full colour. (USA)

48 Zeitschriftenanzeige für ein von *Boehringer* entwickeltes Präparat gegen Verstopfung. Schwarz, Rot. (GER)
49 Zeitschriftenanzeige von *Roche*. Schwarz auf blauem Hintergrund, weisse Schrift. (CAN)
50, 52 Doppelseitiges Zeitschrifteninserat und zwei Beispiele der ganzseitigen Farbaufnahmen aus einer Serie, die in medizinischen Fachzeitschriften für das psychotherapeutische Präparat *Thorazine* von Smith Klein & French wirbt. Jede Anzeige verweist auf eine bestimmte Eigenschaft dieses Produkts. (USA)
53, 54 Doppelseitige Zeitschriftenanzeigen in Spanisch aus einer Serie für ein pharmazeutisches Produkt gegen Akne. Schwarzweiss mit rotem Streifen am untern Rand. (GER)
55 Zeitschriftenanzeige für *Crest*-Zahnpasta zur Verhütung von Karies. Mehrfarbig. (USA)

48 «*Ducolax* résoud le problème sans larmes.» Annonce de magazine pour un purgatif. (GER)
49 Annonce de magazine de *Roche*. Noir sur fond bleu, texte en blanc. (CAN)
50–52 Annonce de magazine complète sur page double et deux exemples des photos couleurs. Eléments tirés d'une série parue dans la presse médicale pour un produit psychothérapeutique. Chaque annonce se réfère à une caractéristique particulière de ce produit. (USA)
53, 54 Annonces sur pages doubles, en langue espagnole, en faveur d'un produit pharmaceutique pour le traitement d'acnés. Noir et blanc, avec bande rouge au bas de la page. (GER)
55 Annonce de magazine pour la pâte dentifrice *Crest* qui maintient la santé générale des dents. Polychrome. (USA)

48

49

50

53

54

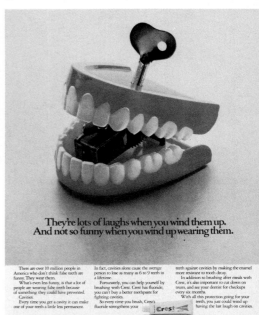

55

Advertisements

Inserate

Annonces

56, 57 Photograph in size of actual reproduction and complete advertisement placed in medical journals for *Ornade*, a treatment for colds. When the encircled area is scratched, it gives off the genuine odour of the pharmaceutical. (USA)
58 "Winter is a hard trial for your skin." Double-spread advertisement in full colour (yellow pullover) for a range of *Lancaster* beauty creams. (FRA)
59 Double-spread magazine advertisement for *Mary Quant* cosmetics specially developed to combat the effects of air pollution in the modern city. Colour photograph. (GBR)
60 Double-spread advertisement for *Mary Quant* eye cosmetics. Full colour. (GBR)
61 Magazine advertisement for a new range of matching lipsticks and nail varnishes by *Max Factor*. Red nails and lips, red ground. (GBR)

56, 57 Originalgrosse Werbephotographie und ganzes, in Fachzeitschriften erschienenes Inserat für *Ornade*, ein pharmazeutisches Produkt, das bei Erkältungen die Entzündung der Nasenschleimhäute lindert, so dass der Geruchsinn intakt bleibt. (USA)
58 Doppelseitiges, mehrfarbiges Zeitschrifteninserat für *Lancaster*-Hautpflegemittel. «Der Winter stellt an Ihre Haut grosse Anforderungen.» (FRA)
59 Doppelseitiges Zeitschrifteninserat für *Mary-Quant*-Kosmetik. «Es ist, als gönnten Sie Ihrer Haut eine Woche auf dem Lande.» Mehrfarbig. (GBR)
60 Mehrfarbiges Zeitschrifteninserat für *Mary-Quant*-Augenkosmetik. Doppelseitig. (GBR)
61 Ganzseitiges Zeitschrifteninserat für farblich aufeinander abgestimmte Lippenstifte und Nagellacke von *Max Factor*. Mehrfarbig. (GBR)

56, 57 Photo en grandeur originale et annonce complète, publiée dans les périodiques médicaux en faveur d'un produit pour le traitement de refroidissements. (USA)
58 Annonce de magazine sur page double pour une gamme de produits cosmétiques *Lancaster* pour la peau. Polychrome, pullover en jaune. (FRA)
59 Annonce de magazine sur page double pour une gamme de produits cosmétiques de *Mary Quant*, développés particulièrement pour traiter les éffets néfastes de la pollution dans les villes modernes. Photographie en couleur. (GBR)
60 Annonce de magazine sur page double pour des produits cosmétiques pour les yeux. (GBR)
61 Annonce de magazine pour une nouvelle gamme de rouges à lèvres et vernis à ongles assortis. Ongles et lèvres rouges sur fond rouge. (GBR)

58

59

60

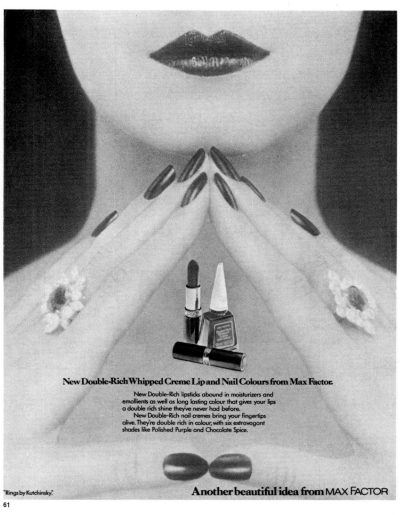

PHOTOGRAPHER / PHOTOGRAPH / PHOTOGRAPHE:

56, 57 Phil Marco
58 Guy Bourdin
60 Brian Duffy

DESIGNER / GESTALTER / MAQUETTISTE:

56, 57 A. Neal Siegel
59, 60 Bob Marchant

ART DIRECTOR / DIRECTEUR ARTISTIQUE:

56, 57 A. Neal Siegel
59, 60 Bob Marchant

AGENCY / AGENTUR / AGENCE – STUDIO:

56, 57 Smith, Kline & French Laboratories, Adv. Dept.
59, 60 Aalders Marchant & Smith Ltd.

57

61

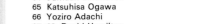

PHOTOGRAPHER / PHOTOGRAPH:

62 Takayuki Ogawa
63 Noriaki Yokosuka
64 Jurriaan Eindhoven
65 Katsuhisa Ogawa
66 Yoziro Adachi
67, 68 David Hamilton

DESIGNER / GESTALTER / MAQUETTISTE:

62 Atsutoshi Saisho
63 Isamu Hanauchi
65 Akihiko Kinbara
66 Ikuo Amano
67, 68 Robert Ricci

ART DIRECTOR / DIRECTEUR ARTISTIQUE:

62 Takushi Mizuno
63 Makoto Nakamura
64 Béla Stamenkovits
65 Akihiko Kinbara
66 Tatsushiro Inuyama

AGENCY / AGENTUR / AGENCE – STUDIO:

64 KVH/CDP
65 Botsford Ketchum International Inc.

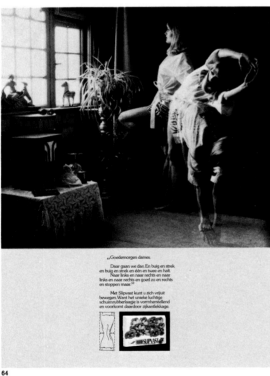
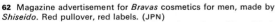

62 Magazine advertisement for *Bravas* cosmetics for men, made by *Shiseido*. Red pullover, red labels. (JPN)
63 Magazine advertisement for the *Shiseido* perfume *More*. Black and white, yellow bottle. (JPN)
64 Full-page newspaper advertisement for *Slipvast* sanitary towels with a reference to morning exercises. (NLD)
65 Magazine advertisement in colour for *Bonne Bell* cosmetics. (JPN)
66 Newspaper advertisement for *MG5 Galac*, a range of cosmetics for men made by the Shiseido Cosmetics Co. (JPN)
67, 68 Photograph and complete magazine advertisement (red ground) for *farouche*, a new Nina Ricci perfume. (SWI)

62 Ganzseitiges Zeitschrifteninserat für *Bravas*-Herrenkosmetik. Pullover und Textband in Rot. (JPN)
63 Zeitschrifteninserat für *More*-Parfum. Schwarzweiss-Photographie mit gelber Flasche. (JPN)
64 Ganzseitiges Zeitungsinserat für *Slipvast*-Damenbinden. (NLD)
65 Ganzseitiges Zeitschrifteninserat für *Bonne-Bell*-Kosmetikartikel. Mehrfarbig. (JPN)
66 Schwarzweisses Zeitungsinserat für eine Reihe von Herren-Kosmetikartikeln, *MG5 Galac*. (JPN)
67, 68 Mehrfarbige Photo und ganzes Zeitschrifteninserat auf rotem Grund für das neue Parfum *farouche* von *Nina Ricci*. (SWI)

62 Annonce de magazine pour les produits cosmétiques *Bravas* pour hommes. Pullover rouge, étiquettes rouges. (JPN)
63 Annonce de revue pour *More*, un parfum de *Shiseido*. Noir et blanc, flacon en jaune. (JPN)
64 Annonce de journal sur page entière pour les serviettes hygiéniques *Slipvast*, avec référence à la gymnastique du matin. (NLD)
65 Annonce de magazine en couleur pour des produits cosmétiques. (JPN)
66 Annonce de journal pour *MG5 Galac*, une gamme de produits cosmétiques pour hommes. (JPN)
67, 68 Photo et annonce de magazine complète (fond rouge) pour *farouche*, un nouveau parfum de *Nina Ricci*. (SWI)

Advertisements

Inserate

Annonces

67

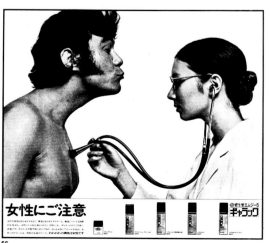
68

45

The Swiss word for fashion flair. Tissot.

Advertisements
Inserate
Annonces

PHOTOGRAPHER / PHOTOGRAPH / PHOTOGRAPHE:

69, 70 Barney Edwards/Vic Pinto
71 Guy Bourdin
72, 73 Michael O'Neill

DESIGNER / GESTALTER / MAQUETTISTE:

69, 70 Chris Albert

ART DIRECTOR / DIRECTEUR ARTISTIQUE:

69, 70 Chris Albert
72, 73 Dennis d'Amico

71

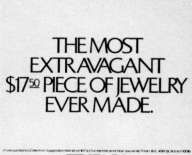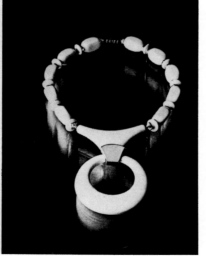

72

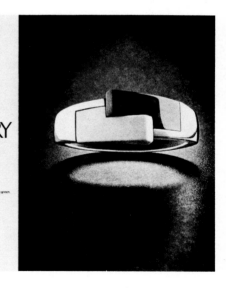

73

AGENCY / AGENTUR / AGENCE – STUDIO:

69, 70 LAP Advertising Ltd.
72, 73 Sacks, Tarlow and Rosen

69, 70 Detail of the photography in actual size and complete magazine advertisement for *Tissot* watches, here underlining their fashion appeal. (GBR)
71 Double-spread magazine advertisement for a *Charles Jourdan* shoe. Black shoe on dark paving, coloured ice cream, blue sky. (FRA)
72, 73 Double-spread magazine advertisement for *Trifari* jewellery, drawing attention to its reasonable prices in spite of its "extravagant" appearance. The campaign won a gold award for photography at The One Show, New York, 1975. (USA)

69, 70 Photographie in Originalgrösse und ganzes Zeitschrifteninserat für eine Reihe modisch-eleganter *Tissot*-Damenuhren. (GBR)
71 Doppelseitiges Zeitschrifteninserat für Schuhe von *Charles Jourdan*. Schwarzer Schuh auf dunklem Pflaster, Cornet mit mehrfarbigem Eis, blauer Himmel. (FRA)
72, 73 Doppelseitige Zeitschrifteninserate für extravaganten und doch preiswerten Schmuck. Die farbigen Aufnahmen erhielten an der One Show 75 (Ausstellung des Art Directors Club) in New York eine Goldmedaille. (USA)

69, 70 Détail de la photo en grandeur nature et annonce de magazine complète pour les montres *Tissot*. (GBR)
71 Annonce de magazine sur page double pour les chaussures *Charles Jourdan*. Chaussure noire sur pavé foncé, glace en couleur, ciel bleu. (FRA)
72, 73 Annonces de magazine sur pages doubles pour les bijoux *Trifari*, soulignant les prix raisonnables malgré les formes «extravagantes». Cette campagne publicitaire de *Trifari* a remporté une médaille d'or pour la photographie lors du One Show, New York, 1975. (USA)

PHOTOGRAPHER / PHOTOGRAPH / PHOTOGRAPHE:

74 Bob Gothard
75, 76 Ryszard Horowitz
77, 78 John Thornton
79, 80 Jordi Gomez

DESIGNER / GESTALTER / MAQUETTISTE:

77, 78 John Harris

ART DIRECTOR / DIRECTEUR ARTISTIQUE:

74 Nick Evans
75, 76 Fred Donoher
77, 78 John Harris
79, 80 Albert Chust

AGENCY / AGENTUR / AGENCE – STUDIO:

74 David Macauley Advertising
75, 76 Fieldcrest
77, 78 Royds
79, 80 M. M. L. B.

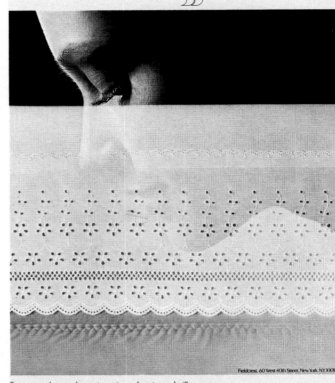

the Lasting Impressions of *Fieldcrest®*

Trousseau Lace, elegant no-iron sheets and pillowcases.

75

74

D into B won't go.

Do you know what size bra you should be wearing?

Most women don't.

The Berlei Anthropometric Survey is showing that the majority of women today are wearing the wrong size bra. To the detriment of our looks, our comfort and even our health.

What is the Berlei Anthropometric Survey?

The Berlei survey is looking at the shape of the modern British woman. To discover, among other things, why so many D sized busts are being caged in C sized bras.

And why so many A's find their way into B cups.

Part of the reason is that women's shape is perceptibly changing with every decade. Yet no one knows exactly how or why. So Berlei are helping a team of independent scientists to conduct a vast anthropometric survey of British women.

Previously, there has only been one large scale look at women's figures. Berlei sponsored that too. Now the second Berlei Anthropometric Survey is painstakingly measuring 6,000 British women in 33 ways. Not only around their bust and hips, but also around their thighs, around their arms and across their shoulders. And at the same time asking intimate questions about their diet, the Pill, their medical history and their family.

How we will benefit

Berlei need all this knowledge to help them design more comfortable, more controlling and more flattering bodywear. Because they insist that their bras and girdles mould to, and control, every line, curve and fold of woman as she is today.

And they'll need all this knowledge to help us understand our bodies all the more. Because it's already obvious that we need to know more about ourselves.

Especially when it comes to measuring for a bra.

Measuring for a Berlei bra

Below you see a Berlei Criss Cross non-slip bra as it should look when properly fitted. Giving a beautiful and comfortable bustline.

A Berlei Criss Cross non-slip can do the same for you – if you know your correct fitting.

To find this, measure yourself around your back and front, just underneath your bust. This gives you the size of your frame. And if you add 5″ to that, you arrive at your bra size. So if your frame measures 31″, you need a 36″ bra.

A guide to choosing your cup size

To discover your cup size, you now need to take your overall bust measurement. Place the tape around your back so that it is level with a point two inches above where your breast joins the chest wall. Holding it firmly, bring it around the front over your nipples – even if you have to angle it downwards to do so.

Your cup size depends on the difference between your bra size and this overall bust measurement.

If it is 1″, choose an A cup.
If it is 2″, choose a B cup.
If it is 3″, choose a C cup.
If it is 4″, choose a D cup.
If it is 5″, choose a DD cup.

From the Non-Slip range

And if you find all this a little complicated, you'll be pleased to know that Berlei is one manufacturer who still trains sales assistants to measure and fit bras.

Berlei

The Berlei Anthropometric Survey. The last word on women.

the Lasting Impressions of *Fieldcrest®*

Freestyle Directions, a new bed and bath collection by Missoni. Stripes, florals, and dots in easily coordinated colors and textures.
76

74 Newspaper advertisement on the subject of finding the right fit in *Berlei* bras. D and B are two of the five cup sizes. Black and white. (GBR)
75, 76 Magazine advertisements in somewhat muted colours from a campaign for the *Fieldcrest* range of bed linens and bath towels. (USA)
77, 78 Magazine advertisements from a campaign for *Lirelle* fabrics made by *Courtaulds*, drawing attention to their "old-fashioned", quality. Fig. 77 chiefly pink and brown, fig. 78 chiefly brown and green shades. (GBR)
79, 80 Magazine advertisements from a series for Italian shoes designed by *Bruno Colombo*. Shoes in full colour on blue and green backgrounds. (SPA)

There's a certain old-fashioned quality about Lirelle this spring.

There's a certain old-fashioned quality about Lirelle this spring.

77

78

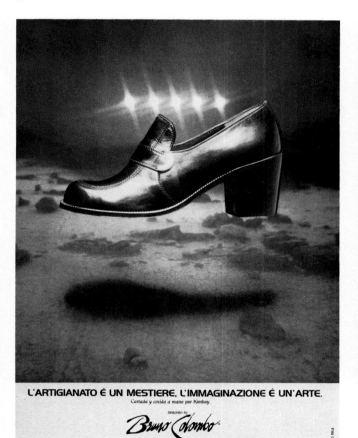

L'ARTIGIANATO É UN MESTIERE, L'IMMAGINAZIONE É UN'ARTE.
Cortada y cosida a mano por Kimbay.

DESIGNED BY
Bruno Colombo

QUANDO BRUNO COLOMBO DISEGNA SCARPE, LE DISEGNA COSÌ.
Cortada y cosida a mano por Kimbay.

DESIGNED BY
Bruno Colombo

79

80

74 Ganzseitiges Zeitungsinserat für *Berlei*-Büstenhalter mit Hinweis auf die verschiedenen Masse der Schalen A bis D. Schwarzweiss. (GBR)
75, 76 Aus einer Serie ganzseitiger Zeitschrifteninserate für neue Farben und Muster der *Fieldcrest*-Bettwäsche. Mehrfarbig. (USA)
77, 78 Aus einer Serie mehrfarbiger Zeitschrifteninserate für *Lirelle*-Stoffe, die eine besondere «altmodische Qualität» aufweisen. (GBR)
79, 80 Aus einer Serie Zeitschrifteninserate für Schuhe von *Bruno Colombo*, die in Handarbeit hergestellt werden. Farbaufnahmen auf blauem und grünem Hintergrund. (SPA)

74 Annonce de journal pour la détermination correcte d'un soutien-gorge *Berlei*. D et B se réfèrent à des bonnets de dimensions différentes. Noir et blanc. (GBR)
75, 76 Annonces de magazine en teintes atténuées, tirées d'une campagne publicitaire pour les draps et linges *Fieldcrest*. (USA)
77, 78 D'une série d'annonces de magazine pour les tissus *Lirelle* de *Courtaulds*, avec référence à leur qualité «surannée». La fig. 77 en rose et brun prédominants, la fig. 78 en teintes brunes et vertes prédominantes. (GBR)
79, 80 D'une série d'annonces de magazine pour les chaussures italiennes créées par *Bruno Colombo*. Chaussures en couleurs sur fonds bleu et vert. (SPA)

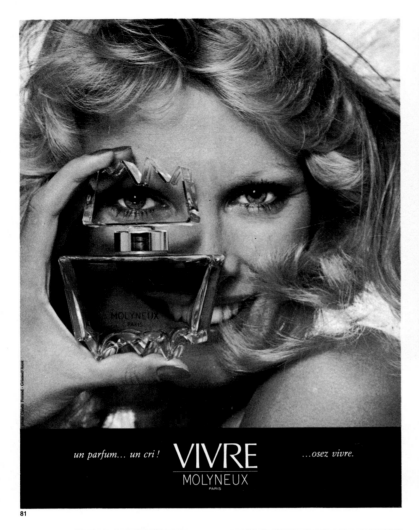

un parfum... un cri! **VIVRE** ...osez vivre.
MOLYNEUX
PARIS

81

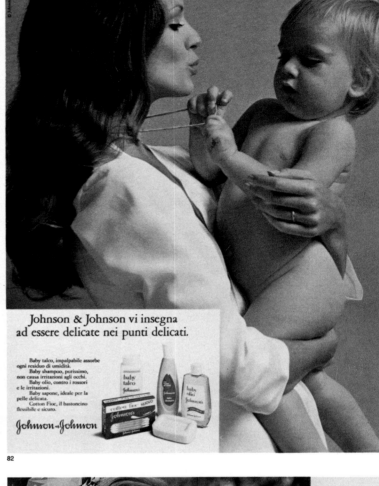

Johnson & Johnson vi insegna
ad essere delicate nei punti delicati.

82

Détendez-vous.
Voici Lifting Base
Anti-Rides.

Harriet
Hubbard
Ayer

84

« Madame Rochas »
de Rochas

un parfum, pour toute une vie

85

PHOTOGRAPHER / PHOTOGRAPH / PHOTOGRAPHE:

81 Claude Ferrand
82 Luciano Ferri
83 Fresco Photographics
84 Bill King
85 Patrick Demarchelier
87 Wolfgang Klein

DESIGNER / GESTALTER / MAQUETTISTE:

81 Claude Ferrand
83 Heinz Grunwald
87 Wolfgang Klein

ART DIRECTOR / DIRECTEUR ARTISTIQUE:

81 Claude Ferrand
83 Heinz Grunwald
84 Bruno Sutter
87 Werner Hammer

AGENCY / AGENTUR / AGENCE – STUDIO:

81 Grizeaud
82 Young & Rubicam Italia S.p.A.
83 Neish, Tutt, Grunwald
84 Feldman Calleux Associés
85 Impact S.A.

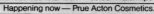

The eyecatchers

The latest dusty Prue Acton shades
to take fashion colours right to your eyes.
Fabulous tones from the darkest denim to the palest softest cashmere.
And for the fabulous total look — colour-match lips and nails.
Happening now — Prue Acton Cosmetics.
The eyecatchers

Prue
Acton

The latest eye shadows
The Denims (Blue eyes)
The Cashmeres (Brown eyes)
The Shetlands (Dark brown eyes)
The Tweeds (Green eyes)

83

Whisper your love without words with a Max Factor fragrance.

Hypnotique Primitif Chontrelle Exuberance Jonquille Electrique
More beautiful ideas from MAX FACTOR

86

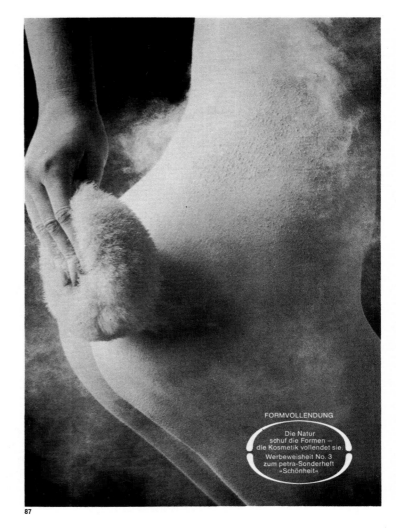

FORMVOLLENDUNG

Die Natur
schuf die Formen —
die Kosmetik vollendet sie.
Werbeweisheit No. 3
zum petra-Sonderheft
»Schönheit«

87

81 Magazine advertisement in full colour for the *Molyneux* perfume *Vivre*. (FRA)
82 "*Johnson & Johnson* teaches you to be delicate in the delicate places." Magazine advertisement for baby care products. Full colour. (ITA)
83 Magazine advertisement for *Prue Acton* eye cosmetics. Figure in delicate hues. (AUL)
84 Double-spread magazine advertisement in full colour for a *Harriet Hubbard Ayer* anti-wrinkle beauty cream. (FRA)
85 Double-spread magazine advertisement for the *Madame Rochas* range of perfumery products. Black and white. (FRA)
86 Magazine advertisement in pale yellow-brown shades listing the names of the *Max Factor* range of perfumes. (GBR)
87 Space promotion advertisement for a special issue of the women's magazine *Petra* devoted to cosmetics. Lilac pink shades. (GER)

81 Ganzseitiges Zeitschrifteninserat für das Parfum *Vivre* von *Molyneux*. Mehrfarbig. (FRA)
82 Mehrfarbiges Zeitschrifteninserat für Baby-Pflegemittel von *Johnson & Johnson*. (ITA)
83 Ganzseitiges Zeitschrifteninserat für *Prue Acton*-Augenkosmetik. Vorwiegend in den Farbtönen Beige, Grün und Rosa. (AUL)
84 Doppelseitiges Zeitschrifteninserat für *Harriet-Hubbard-Ayer*-Hautpflegemittel gegen Runzeln. Mehrfarbig. (FRA)
85 Doppelseitiges, schwarzweisses Zeitschrifteninserat für *Madame Rochas*, «ein Parfum für ein ganzes Leben». (FRA)
86 In Braun- und Beigetönen gehaltenes Zeitschrifteninserat für *Max-Factor*-Kosmetikartikel. «Erkläre deine Liebe wortlos durch *Max-Factor*-Düfte.» (GBR)
87 Anzeige zur Inseratenwerbung für ein Kosmetik-Sonderheft der Zeitschrift *Petra*. Lila Töne, weisse Schrift. (GER)

81 Annonce de magazine en couleur pour le parfum *Vivre* de *Molyneux*. (FRA)
82 «*Johnson & Johnson* vous apprend d'être délicat en certains endroits délicats.» Annonce de magazine en faveur des produits pour bébés. En couleur. (ITA)
83 Annonce de magazine en faveur de produits cosmétiques pour les yeux. Figure en teintes atténuées. (AUL)
84 Annonce de magazine sur page double pour une crème antirides de *Harriet Hubbard Ayer*. Polychrome. (FRA)
85 Annonce de magazine sur page double pour une gamme de produits de parfumerie de *Madame Rochas*. Noir et blanc. (FRA)
86 Annonce de magazine en tons jaunes et bruns atténués avec une liste dans laquelle figurent les noms de toute la gamme des parfums de *Max Factor*. (GBR)
87 Annonce de magazine s'adressant aux annonceurs potentiels pour un numéro spécial de la revue féminine *Petra*, numéro qui est consacré entièrement aux produits cosmétiques et à la beauté. Teintes rose lilas. (GER)

Advertisements / Inserate / Annonces

89

90

88

Room for a little one

Towards the end of your pregnancy, your baby
and your tummy will need a little extra support.
Your legs, too, are carrying several extra pounds
and it's very important to care for them
as well as you possibly can.
Supp-hose make two kinds of
maternity tights; Mother's Lib which
are very sheer and flattering and
Supp-hose Special which
are slightly heavier.
Both styles have an expanding
panel which comes right up
and over the baby –
growing as you grow.
Supp-hose Maternity tights
will help to keep your legs
pretty and healthy
throughout your pregnancy.

ELBEO
Maternity tights

88 Magazine advertisement for *Elbeo* maternity tights to provide support for the legs during pregnancy. Full-colour illustration. (GBR)
89, 90 Magazine advertisements starring women who have "become legends" for *Blackglama* mink coats. (USA)
91 Magazine advertisement for *Gill* medicated soap. In full colour on pale blue ground. (SAF)
92 Magazine advertisement for *Gala* nail polish in 24 "sensational" colours. Fingers and nails in colour. (GBR)
93 "When you shower with *Duschfrisch,* you're less frowzy at once." Magazine advertisement for a liquid soap. (GER)
94 Double-spread centre-fold magazine advertisement in full colour for *Protein 21* shampoo. (AUL)
95 Double-spread magazine advertisement for *Pierre Cardin* tights, which are available in assorted sizes. Illustration in full colour. (GBR)

88 Mehrfarbiges Zeitschrifteninserat für elastische *Elbeo*-Strumpfhosen während der Schwangerschaft. (GBR)
89, 90 Ganzseitige Zeitschrifteninserate für *Blackglama*-Wildnerz aus Amerika. Schwarzweiss. (USA)
91 Mehrfarbiges, ganzseitiges Zeitschrifteninserat für flüssige *Gill*-Seife zum Schutz gegen Infektionen. (SAF)
92 Ganzseitiges Zeitschrifteninserat für *Gala*-Nagellack in 24 «sensationellen» Farben. Mehrfarbig. (GBR)
93 Ganzseitiges Zeitschrifteninserat für die flüssige Badeseife *Duschfrisch.* Mehrfarbig. (GER)
94 Doppelseitiges Zeitschrifteninserat für *Protein 21*, ein Haarwaschmittel für empfindliche Haare. (AUL)
95 Doppelseitiges, farbiges Zeitschrifteninserat für Strumpfhosen von *Pierre Cardin*, die in verschiedenen Grössen erhältlich sind. «Sobald alle Frauen gleich gross sind, werde ich gleich grosse Strumpfhosen machen!» (GBR)

88 Annonce de magazine pour les collants de santé *Elbeo* spécialement faits pour les femmes enceintes. Illustration en couleur. (GBR)
89, 90 D'une série d'annonces de magazine pour les fourrures de vison de *Blackglama*. (USA)
91 Annonce de magazine pour *Gill,* un savon médicinal contre les infections. Polychrome sur fond bleu pâle. (SAF)
92 Annonce de magazine pour les vernis à ongles *Gala*, en vente en 24 couleurs «sensationnelles». Doigts et ongles en couleur. (GBR)
93 «Prenez une douche avec *Duschfrisch* et vous vous sentez plus frais tout de suite.» Annonce de magazine pour la promotion d'un savon liquide. (GER)
94 Annonce de magazine sur page double pour le shampooing *Protein 21*. En couleur. (AUL)
95 Annonce de magazine sur page double pour les collants *Pierre Cardin*, en vente aux tailles assorties. (GBR)

**Advertisements / Inserate
Annonces**

Put your finger-tips under this page. See what we mean by Drawing Attention?

Grab yourself some attention, with Gala Nail Polish.
In 24 sensational colours, about 35p.
Mix-and-match with Gala Supersmooth lipstick, in 24 toning shades, about 40p.

GALA
of London

91

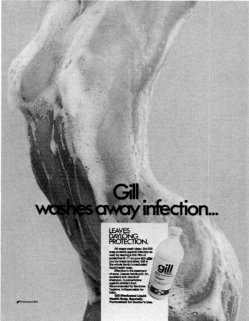

Gill washes away infection...

LEAVES DAYLONG PROTECTION.

All soaps wash clean. But Gill soap protects against infection as well, by leaving a thin film of protective B-11 on your skin after you've rinsed and dried. Gill is the whole family's medicated soap.

Effective in the treatment of acne. Leaves hands soft, an excellent anti-dandruff shampoo. A preventative against athlete's foot. Recommended for feminine hygiene. Indispensable for baby.

Gill Medicated Liquid Health Soap. Specially Formulated for Doctor's Use.

gill

92

How could a beautiful girl like Nerida Piggin possibly love our homely little bottle?

The answer's simple.
She doesn't.
But she does have a great deal of respect for what's inside it.
You might say that there's nothing particularly unique or unusual in a product containing protein.
And we'd be forced to agree.
We'd also be forced to point out that Protein 21 shampoo contains an expensive protein that can actually help repair split ends and damaged hair with regular use.

Which means Protein 21 isn't cheap. But it also means that it works so well for Nerida Piggin that she's prepared to overlook the bottle's appearance.
And now she tells us she loves Protein 21.

Naturally, we're delighted.
But whenever we look at the bottle, we can't help wondering if Nerida Piggin isn't confusing love with gratitude.
Protein 21. It's available at chemists.

94

Wenn man mit Duschfrisch duscht, ist man gleich nicht mehr so muffig.

Duschfrisch ist der kompakte Ball, der nicht aus der Hand glitscht, der lustig ist, der nicht aufweicht, der nicht einrollt, der nicht einrocknet, der den Ball behält bis zum letzten Tropfen.
Denn Duschfrisch ist flüssig.
Es verteilt sich ganz leicht auf der Haut.
Es ist schön kühl auf der Haut, es prickelt fröhlich auf der Haut. Es desodoriert die Haut, und es pflegt die Haut.
Denn schließlich kommt Duschfrisch von Dulgon.

duschfrisch
NEU DEOAKTIV

Duschfrisch:
deoaktiv.

**Besser duschen.
Länger frisch.**

93

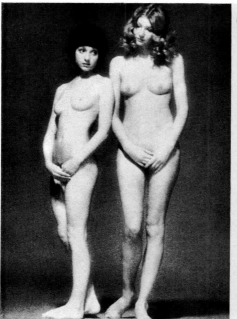

'WHEN THEY MAKE ONE-SIZE WOMEN, I'LL MAKE ONE-SIZE TIGHTS.'
Pierre Cardin, Frenchman.

Novel thought number one.
Not every woman has the same hip size. Not every woman has the same thigh size. Not every woman has the same length leg.
Novel thought number two.
A woman who is 5'5" tall, with 33"hips and slim thighs, obviously needs different sized tights from a woman who is 5'5" tall, with 42"hips and full thighs.
Just as obviously, no standard 'medium' or 'one-size' fitting can fit both women equally well. It has to be an uncomfortable compromise for one, the other, or both.
Which brings us to Pierre Cardin.
Pierre Cardin's tights aren't a compromise. They aren't 'one-size'. They aren't 'small', 'medium', or 'long'.
Instead, they are made in just about every combination of height, hip and thigh size. To fit just about every size of woman.
From 4'11" and 31½"hips to 4'11"and 41"hips.
From 5'9" and 33½"hips, to 5'9" and 50"hips.
Plus everything in between.

THEY FIT AS NO OTHER TIGHTS CAN.
Because Pierre Cardin's tights are made specifically for your height, for your hips, for your thighs, they fit as no other tights can.
They fit around the crotch. They fit around the hips. They fit around the thighs.
And because they fit, they are comfortable.
Obviously though, comfort alone isn't enough. Your tights should also do something for your legs. So Pierre Cardin's tights come in eight shades, and two deniers.
Needless to say, all eight shades are extremely fashionable. Which is only to be expected when you remember who designed them.

HOW TO FIND YOUR COLOUR.
To find out which of Pierre Cardin's tights fit you exactly, use the 'Cardinoscope' that you find in every store that sells Pierre Cardin tights. (There's a store list on this page.)
The 'Cardinoscope' is an ingenious little wheel that has height measurements on the outside, hip measurements on the inside.
All you do is turn the wheel until you match your hip size to your height.
The 'Cardinoscope' will then show you which colour coded tights to buy for your height, your hips, and your thigh size.

For example, if you are 5'6" tall with 35"hips and slim thighs, then the Cardin tights that are made for you come in the yellow box.
Once you know your colour, you will never again have a problem finding tights that fit.

THE PRICE MAY COME AS A SURPRISE.
By now, you're probably thinking that Pierre Cardin's tights cost a fortune.
After all, they're made to fit. They're imported from France. They're extremely fashionable. They're designed by Pierre Cardin.
So how much can they cost?
We're happy to tell you that they cost no more than the better brand 'one-size' tights. About 50p for the 17 denier. About 70p for the 15 denier.
It's a small price to pay for tights that really fit.

'MADE-TO-MEASURE TIGHTS' FROM NO ONE ELSE BUT PIERRE CARDIN.

95

53

97

96

98

Advertisements

Inserate

Annonces

96 Magazine advertisement for timeless *Richard-Ginori* tableware, here shown in white and dark blue. (ITA)
97, 98 "Your daily beauty parlour." Complete double-spread advertisement and detail of the colour photography for *Villeroy & Boch* bathrooms. (GER)
99 Black-and-white newspaper advertisement for *Tessa* furniture. (AUL)
100, 101 "For this and the next hundred winters." Detail of the colour photography (tableware in brown and blue shades) and complete magazine advertisement for timeless tableware designed by *Richard-Ginori* (see also Fig. 96). (ITA)

96 Ganzseitiges Zeitschrifteninserat für modernes Tafelgeschirr von *Richard-Ginori*. Aufnahme in Blau und Weiss. (ITA)
97, 98 Doppelseitiges, mehrfarbiges Zeitschrifteninserat für eine reiche Auswahl an Fliesen für Badezimmer und Wohnräume der keramischen Werke *Villeroy & Boch*. (GER)
99 Schwarzweisses Zeitungsinserat für *Tessa*-Sitzmöbel. (AUL)
100, 101 Farbaufnahme und ganzes Zeitschrifteninserat für *Richard-Ginori*-Tafelgeschirr, dessen Modell *Caldo* «für diesen und die nächsten hundert Winter passt». Siehe auch Abb. 96. (ITA)

96 Annonce de magazine pour la vaisselle *Richard-Ginori* aux formes et dessins qui restent. Blanc et bleu foncé. (ITA)
97, 98 «Votre petit salon de beauté de tous les jours.» Annonce sur page double et détail de la photo couleur pour des salles de bain. (GER)
99 Annonce de journal en noir et blanc pour les meubles *Tessa*. (AUL)
100, 101 «Pour cet hiver et les cent autres qui suivent.» Détail de la photo en couleur (vaisselle en tons bruns et bleus) et annonce de magazine complète pour la vaisselle créée par *Richard-Ginori* aux formes et dessins qui restent (voir aussi la fig. 96). (ITA)

100

99

101

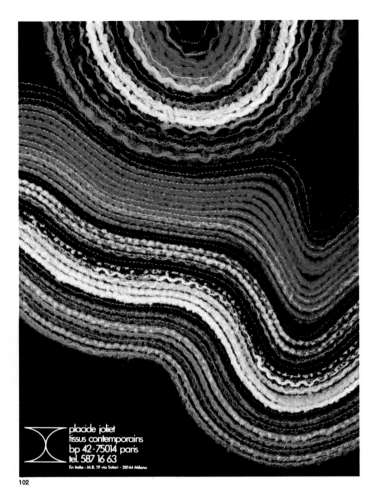

102

103

102 Magazine advertisement for contemporary fabrics from *Placide Joliet*. (FRA)
103 Magazine advertisement for *American Olean* tiles that are supplied in pregrouted sheets. Black tiles, orange soap. (USA)
104, 105 From a series of magazine advertisements in full colour for *Lenox Crystal* hand-blown glassware. (USA)
106 Magazine insert for *Dayco* offset blankets. Full colour. (GBR)
107, 108 "A hundred-year-old silversmith's tradition."—"Distinguishing marks of the cultivated table." From a series of magazine advertisements for R & B cutlery. The design shown in Fig. 107 dates from 1874, when the company was founded. Reproduction in shades of brown. (GER)

102 Zeitschriftenanzeige für moderne Gewebe von *Placide Joliet*. (FRA)
103 Zeitschriftenanzeige für Fliesen, die in zusammenhängenden Platten geliefert werden. Schwarze Fliesen, orange Seife. (USA)
104, 105 Beispiele aus einer Serie mehrfarbiger Zeitschriftenanzeigen für mundgeblasene Glaswaren von *Lenox Crystal*. (USA)
106 Zeitschriftenbeilage für Gummitücher für Offset-Druckwalzen. Mehrfarbig. (GBR)
107, 108 Beispiele aus einer Serie von Zeitschriftenanzeigen für R & B-Bestecke. Das in Abb. 107 gezeigte Modell stammt aus dem Jahr 1874, dem Gründungsjahr dieser Firma. Illustration in Brauntönen. (GER)

102 Annonce de magazine pour les tissus à la mode de *Placide Joliet*. (FRA)
103 Annonce de magazine pour les carreaux qui sont livrés déjà jointoyés en bandes. Carreaux noirs, savon orange. (USA)
104, 105 D'une série d'annonces de magazine en couleur pour des articles en verre soufflé à la main. (USA)
106 Encart de magazine pour des revêtements de caoutchouc pour les cylindres à imprimer. Polychrome. (GBR)
107, 108 «La tradition séculaire de l'orfèvrerie.» – «Les caractéristiques distinctives de la table soignée.» D'une série d'annonces de magazine pour l'argenterie R & B. La pièce présentée sous fig. 107 a été créée en 1874, l'année de la fondation de cette société. Reproductions en tons bruns. (GER)

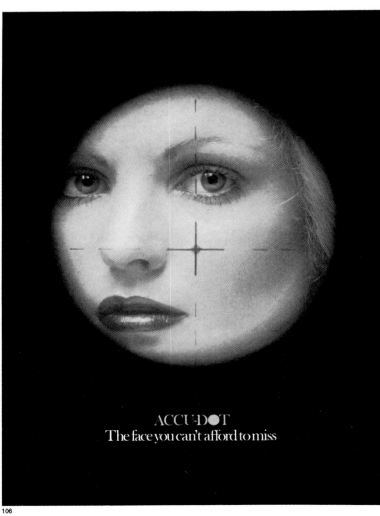

106

Advertisements / Inserate
Annonces

Iced Tea by Lenox

Crystal, hand-blown and hand-cut, with the same breed of artistry that gives Lenox China its stature the world over.

LENOX CRYSTAL
TRENTON, N.J. 08605

104

Lemon Ice by Lenox

Hand-blown, hand-finished lead crystal, created with the same breed of artistry that gives Lenox China its stature the world over.

LENOX CRYSTAL
TRENTON, N.J. 08605

105

PHOTOGRAPHER / PHOTOGRAPH:

102 Pierre Berdoy
103 Charles Garoner
104, 105 Jim Vicari
106 Roger Alexander
107, 108 Klaus P. Ohlenforst

DESIGNER / GESTALTER:

102 Agence Hautefeuille
103 Larry Rosengren
104, 105 Alexander Mohtares
107, 108 Werner Würdinger

ART DIRECTOR:

103 Larry Rosengren
104, 105 Alexander Mohtares
106 Colin Axon
107, 108 Werner Würdinger

AGENCY / AGENTUR / AGENCE:

102 Agence Hautefeuille
103 Lewis & Gilman, Inc.
104, 105 Chirurg & Cairns
106 Axon Garside & Co. Ltd.
107, 108 Gottschling &
         Würdinger GmbH & Co.

Hundertjährige Silberschmiedetradition

Alt-Kopenhagen geht zurück auf einen Entwurf aus dem Jahre 1874, dem Gründungsjahr der Firma Robbe & Berking. R&B hat diesen Entwurf mit behutsamem Feingefühl und Stilempfinden überarbeitet. Alt-Kopenhagen ist ein klassisches Besteck. Frei von modischen Einflüssen. Zeitlos wie ein edles, wertvolles Schmuckstück. Jedes einzelne Besteckteil trägt auf der Rückseite eine andere kunstvoll geprägte Filigrangravur. Die Gravuren stellen Gewürzkräuter dar. Thymian auf der Tafelgabel, Safran auf dem Tafellöffel. Rosmarin auf der Dessertgabel usw. Alt-Kopenhagen gibt es in der neuen, besonders strapazierfähigen 150-g-Massiv-Versilberung und natürlich in Echtsilber. Sie finden es in guten Fachgeschäften. Wenn Sie sich über weitere R&B-Juwelierbestecke informieren möchten – schreiben Sie an: Robbe & Berking, 239 Flensburg, Zur Bleiche 47.

R&B
Juwelierbestecke

107

Erkennungszeichen anspruchsvoller Tischkultur.

Zuviele Bestecke lassen Konzessionen an Moden, Trends, an die Fertigungstechnik oder einfach nur schlechten Geschmack erkennen. Zwischen modisch und modern, zwischen zeitbedingt und zeitlos bestehen Unterschiede. Menschen, die sich für R&B-Juwelierbestecke entscheiden, kennen diese Unterschiede. Die vollkommene Harmonie von Form, Dekor, Material und Funktion machen jedes R&B Juwelierbesteck zu einem kleinen Meisterwerk der Silberschmiedekunst. Juweliere in aller Welt sind sich einig, daß sie zu den schönsten Bestecken überhaupt zählen. Das abgebildete Modell „R&B-Spaten" gibt es in der neuen, hochwertigen 150-g-Massiv-Versilberung und natürlich in Echtsilber. Sie finden es in guten Fachgeschäften. Wenn Sie sich über weitere R&B Juwelierbesteck informieren möchten – schreiben Sie uns: Robbe & Berking, 2390 Flensburg, Postfach 765.

R&B
Juwelierbestecke

108

INNOVATING.

IT LED TO DILOFLO™ 60. THE PERFORMANCE CHEMICAL THAT GIVES YOU INCREASED CEMENT THROUGHPUT. SAVES FUEL.

Diloflo 60 dispersant helps you boost mill output while it dramatically cuts wet processing's biggest expense. Fuel.

Sprayed into cement slurry in the ball mill, Diloflo 60 makes a lot less water do a lot more work. Lets you actually replace some of the slurry water with higher solids and still keep viscosity low. And the less water in your slurry, the less heat you need to dry it. Down goes fuel consumption, up goes cement output. Up by as much as 6%.

So Diloflo 60 pays off tangibly. In higher output. In less fuel.

And that's more power to you. From us.

For technical information and samples of Diloflo 60, get in touch with the Process Industries Department, Diamond Shamrock, Process Chemicals Division, 350 Mt. Kemble Ave., Morristown, N.J. 07960. (201) 267-1000.

Diamond Shamrock

109

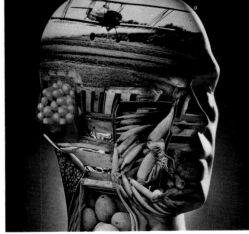

CREATIVITY.

IT LED TO THE AGRIMUL® SERIES OF PERFORMANCE CHEMICALS THAT GIVE YOUR PRODUCT SHELF LIFE STABILITY, EXCELLENT SPONTANEITY AND DISPERSIBILITY.

The Agrimuls are complementary dispersing agents from Diamond Shamrock, specifically designed for preparation of stable high quality, "flowable" systems. They're compatible with a broad range of toxicants and permit your flowable to be easily prepared at ambient temperature. Flowables prepared with Agrimul F-100 and F-200

exhibit excellent shelf life and freeze-thaw characteristics. These Agrimuls are designed to impart better spontaneity and dispersion properties to formulations in use dilution concentration.

For technical information and samples of Agrimul F-100 and F-200, get in touch with the Process Industries Dept., Diamond Shamrock, Nopco Chemical

Division, 350 Mt. Kemble Ave., Morristown, N.J. 07960. (201) 267-1000.

Diamond Shamrock

110

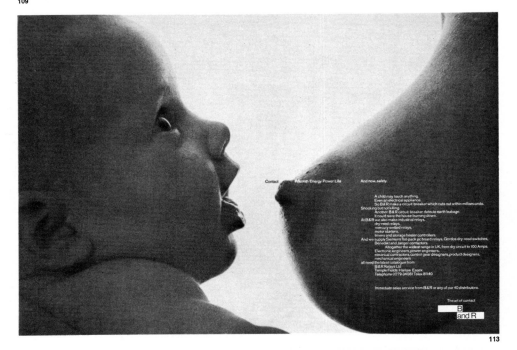

113

114

109 Double-spread magazine advertisement with colour illustration for a *Diamond Shamrock* dispersant used in cement manufacture. (USA)
110–112 Two advertisements from a series for *Diamond Shamrock*, with detail of the photography for one of them. The series gives examples of "creativity"—here a dispersant for use in agricultural insecticides and a wire-drawing lubricant. (USA)
113, 114 Black-and-white double-spread trade magazine advertisements on "contacts" for B & R Relays Ltd. (GBR)

109 Doppelseitige Zeitschriftenanzeige mit Farbaufnahme für ein chemisches Produkt von *Diamond Shamrock,* das für die Zementherstellung verwendet wird. (USA)
110–112 Aus einer Serie von Zeitschriftenanzeigen für *Diamond Shamrock* und Detail der Farbaufnahme einer Anzeige. Die Serie zeigt Beispiele zum Thema «Kreativität» – hier ein chemischer Zusatz für landwirtschaftliche Insektizide und ein Schmiermittel für die Drahtzieherei. (USA)
113, 114 Doppelseitige Fachzeitschriftenanzeigen über «Kontakte» für B & R Relays Ltd. Schwarzweiss. (GBR)

109 Annonce de magazine sur page double en faveur d'un dispersant de *Diamond Shamrock* qu'on utilise dans la production du ciment. Illustration en couleur. (USA)
110–112 Deux annonces figurant dans une série pour *Diamond Shamrock* et détail de la photo de l'une d'elles. Toute la série est consacrée à la «créativité» – les deux exemples reproduits ici se réfèrent à un dispersant utilisé pour des insecticides et à un lubrifiant de tréfilerie. (USA)
113, 114 Annonces professionnelles, pages doubles, de B & R Ltd., se référant aux «contacts». Noir et blanc. (GBR)

PHOTOGRAPHER / PHOTOGRAPH / PHOTOGRAPHE:

109–112 Seymour Mednick
113, 114 Steve Slayford

DESIGNER / GESTALTER / MAQUETTISTE:

109–112 Jack Taylor
113–114 Peter Eaton

ART DIRECTOR / DIRECTEUR ARTISTIQUE:

109–112 Jack Taylor
113, 114 Peter Eaton

AGENCY / AGENTUR / AGENCE – STUDIO:

109–112 Gray & Rogers, Inc.
113, 114 Evenett & Desoutter

111

112

115

occhi felici

la lente corneale morbida
Galiflex

116

ART DIRECTOR / DIRECTEUR ARTISTIQUE:

117 Ron Shew
118, 119 Horst Blachian
120, 121 Chris Gregory/Cathy Heng
122 Ozzie Hawkins
123 Tony Oliveto/Art Harris

AGENCY / AGENTUR / AGENCE – STUDIO:

115, 116 GPM
117 McCann-Erickson Europe S.A.
118, 119 Young & Rubicam Italia S.p.A.
120, 121 Roe Humphries
122 J. Walter Thompson Co.
123 Young & Rubicam International, Inc.

Advertisements
Inserate
Annonces

115, 116 ''Happy eyes.'' Detail of the photography and complete magazine advertisement for *Galiflex* soft contact lenses. (ITA)
117 Trade magazine advertisement for *Stauffer* agricultural chemicals. Green trade mark. (SWI)
118, 119 Two double-spread black-and-white magazine advertisements from a series for *Brionvega* radios and recording equipment. (ITA)
120, 121 Double-spread trade magazine advertisements in full colour from a series for *Stanley* forged garden tools. (GBR)
122 Double-spread trade magazine advertisement for *7up* table waters. (USA)
123 Double-spread magazine advertisement about the ''green revolution'' for *Union Carbide*. (USA)

117

Comunicazione aperta

Brionvega rr126, rr130 fo/st Hi-Fi *(dan, dan, dan DAAA)*

118

119

PHOTOGRAPHER / PHOTOGRAPH / PHOTOGRAPHE:

115, 116 Carlo Vajenti
117 Anthony Blake
118, 119 Luciano Muratori
120, 121 David Thorpe
122 Fred Brodersen
123 Carl Fischer/Steve Horn

DESIGNER / GESTALTER / MAQUETTISTE:

117 Ron Shew
122 Ozzie Hawkins

EVERY GARDEN TOOL WE MAKE,
WE PUT OUR HEADS ON THE BLOCK.

STANLEY

120

EVERY GARDEN TOOL WE MAKE,
WE PUT OUR HEADS ON THE BLOCK.

STANLEY

121

LET FOUNTAIN 7 UP TURN YOUR
SALES AND PRO FITS UNSIDE UP

122

We're expecting a few extra people
for dinner tonight.

UNION CARBIDE
Today, something we do
will touch your life.

123

115, 116 «Glückliche Augen.» Farbphotographie und ganzes Inserat für die biegsame Kontakt-linse *Galiflex 287.* (ITA)
117 Schwarzweisses Fachzeitschrifteninserat mit grüner Firmenmarke für Düngemittel der Stauf-fer Chemical Europe S.A. (SWI)
118, 119 Doppelseitige, schwarzweisse Zeitschrifteninserate für *Brionvega*-Radioapparate, Kas-settenrekorder und Stereo-Anlagen. (ITA)
120, 121 Doppelseitige, farbige Fachzeitschrifteninserate für geschmiedetes Gartengerät. (GBR)
122 Doppelseitiges, mehrfarbiges Zeitschrifteninserat für das Erfrischungsgetränk *7up.* (USA)
123 Doppelseitiges Zeitschrifteninserat über die «grüne Revolution», für *Union Carbide.* (USA)

115, 116 «Le regard heureux.» Détail de la photographie et annonce de magazine complète pour les verres de contact en matière plastique souple. (ITA)
117 Annonce de magazine pour des produits chimiques agricoles. Marque verte. (SWI)
118, 119 Deux annonces de magazine figurant dans une série publicitaire pour les radios et articles électriques de *Brionvega.* Noir et blanc. (ITA)
120, 121 Annonces de magazine professionnel tirées d'une série pour des outils de jardin en fer forgé. En couleur. (GBR)
122 Annonce de magazine sur page double pour l'eau minérale *7up.* (USA)
123 Annonce de magazine sur page double sur le thème de la «révolution verte». (USA)

124 Double-spread trade magazine advertisement for an *Armstrong* flooring material, showing the types of boot and shoe it has to stand up to. Full colour. (GBR)
125 Double-spread magazine ad on the hidden virtues of the *Volkswagen*. Black and white. (USA)
126 Double-spread trade magazine advertisement for *Fruehauf* chemical tanks of stainless steel, inviting customers to come and see them. Illustration in shades of green. (USA)
127 Announcement of a 60-minute TV programme sponsored by *Xerox* on America's obsessive desire to look young. Black and white. Silver award in the 1975 One Show, New York. (USA)
128 Magazine advertisement for *Islander* yachts. The one shown won an important race. Yacht in colour on black ground, white type matter. (USA)
129, 130 Detail of the photography and complete trade magazine advertisement for *Amchem* low-temperature metalworking chemicals for people who ''don't have money to burn''. (USA)

124 Doppelseitiges, mehrfarbiges Fachzeitschrifteninserat für einen strapazierfähigen Fussboden-belag aus *Arlon.* (GBR)
125 Doppelseitiges, schwarzweisses Zeitschrifteninserat für den *Volkswagen,* mit Hinweis auf seine normalerweise unsichtbaren Qualitäten. (USA)
126 Doppelseitiges, farbiges Zeitschrifteninserat für *Fruehauf*-Tanks aus rostfreiem Stahl. (USA)
127 «Das Streben nach Jugend.» Schwarzweisses Zeitschrifteninserat für ein Fernsehprogramm von *Xerox* über die Sucht vieler Amerikaner, jung auszusehen. Silbermedaille an der Ausstellung The One Show 75, New York. (USA)
128 Ganzseitiges, mehrfarbiges Zeitschrifteninserat für *Islander-41*-Segeljachten. (USA)
129, 130 Werbephotographie in Originalgrösse und ganzes Inserat für Chemikalien zur Metall-bearbeitung, die Dollars sparen helfen. (USA)

124 Annonce de magazine professionnel sur page double pour le matériel de pavage *Armstrong* présentant les différentes sortes de souliers et de bottes auxquels il doit résister. (GBR)
125 Annonce de magazine sur page double vantant les vertus cachées de la VW. Noir-blanc. (USA)
126 Annonce de magazine professionnel sur page double pour les réservoirs en acier inoxydable qui sont utilisé pour le stockage de produits chimiques. Tons verts. (USA)
127 Annonce d'un programme télévisé, patronné par *Xerox.* Il traite des Américains et de leur effort – presque obsédé – de garder un air jeune. Médaille d'argent du One Show 1975. (USA)
128 Annonce de magazine pour les yachts *Islander.* Celui qui est reproduit ici a gagné une compéti-tition importante. Yacht en couleur sur fond noir, texte en blanc. (USA)
129, 130 Détail de la photo et annonce de magazine professionnel pour des produits chimiques utilisés dans l'usinage des métaux «lorsqu'on n'a pas d'argent à brûler». (USA)

AGENCY / AGENTUR / AGENCE – STUDIO:

124 Batten, Barton, Durstine & Osborn Ltd.
125 Doyle Dane Bernbach, Inc.
126 D'Arcy, MacManus & Masius
127 Needham, Harper & Steers
128 Semper/Moser & Associates
129, 130 Lewis & Gilman, Inc.

SEARCH OUR SOUL

Before you invest in a tank, you ought to know what you're getting into. Take ours, for instance. The Fruehauf SS Chemical Tank Trailer. Inside, pure stainless steel. Outside, too. Which means you get a 100% stainless steel tank. And a stronger structure to boot.

Like the outer rings. They're not just strapped on. They're welded right to the vessel. Stainless steel rings, continuously welded. The rings you see inside are proof. They're tell-tale weld marks. Not exactly pretty. But they tell you that your tank is more collapse resistant. More durable. And that's what a tank is all about.

Now about cleaning. Everyone has different needs. So we make it easy. You can have one of three choices. Three degrees of smoothness. The one you see is standard. It's deburred, brushed and snag-proof. Or you can have it ground flush. Even polished.

Then there's everything from separately mounted light boxes to a Fruehauf design manhole. All great features that add up to a smarter investment today.

See for yourself. Come on in and search our soul.
That's why you're way ahead with Fruehauf behind you.

FRUEHAUF

126

Advertisements
Inserate
Annonces

From Amchem: Low-temperature chemicals that can pay for themselves.

Boy, do you need them now.

130

129

131

WE SELL MORE CARS THAN FORD, CHRYSLER, CHEVROLET AND BUICK COMBINED.

MATCHBOX.

LESNEY PRODUCTS CORP. 141 W. COMMERCIAL AVENUE, MOONACHIE, NEW JERSEY, (201) 935-3800. A "MATCHBOX" QUALITY PRODUCT.

132

135

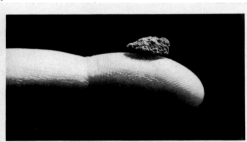

This is all it takes to stop a 40-ton truck.

That's right, a piece of dirt.
Lodged in the piston area of an off-the-road hauler's disk brakes, that little bit of dirt could freeze the piston actuating the braking pads. Causing a skid, or even leading to ultimate loss of braking power.

At best, it would leave a valuable unit inoperable until the brakes are disassembled and cleaned. At worst, it could cause a serious accident.

Of course, haulers and other heavy construction equipment have rubber boots to keep dirt and stones out.

But the boots take a terrific beating from the materials they are meant to keep out.

And temperatures in the brake boot area often soar to 325°F, making heat resistance another prime requirement.

If not regularly replaced, the brakes are soon left without protection.

We have a tough synthetic rubber called Epcar® EPDM that can withstand this punishment of temperature, dirt and flying stones.

And we have other problem solving materials.

Like rubbers that take the heat of today's new engines. A vinyl resin to coat nylon and polyester with adhesion two and three times that of other vinyls.

It's all imaginative thinking from BFG Chemical.

For more information write B.F. Goodrich Chemical Company, Dept. BWI-10, 6100 Oak Tree Boulevard, Cleveland, Ohio 44131.

B.F. Goodrich Chemical Company
B.F. Goodrich

131 Double-spread magazine advertisement pointing out the good qualities of the *Honda* for "getting away". Full colour. (USA)
132 Double-spread magazine advertisement for Lesney Products Corporation, makers of matchbox model cars. The ad won a gold award at the 1975 One Show, New York. (USA)
133 Double-spread trade press advertisement for USS Chemicals, here about plasticizers as used in paints. (USA)
134 Black-and-white magazine advertisement for *Sony* with a reference to future television developments. (GBR)
135 Advertisement about a tough synthetic rubber for disc brakes developed by B.F. Goodrich, Inc. (USA)

131 Doppelseitiges, mehrfarbiges Zeitschrifteninserat für *Honda*-Motorräder, deren Fahreigenschaften von Bankräubern, aber auch von der Polizei geschätzt werden. (USA)
132 Doppelseitiges Zeitschrifteninserat für Spielzeugautos, von denen mehr verkauft werden, als von den vier führenden Automarken der USA zusammen. Goldmedaille, One Show 75, New York. (USA)
133 Doppelseitiges Zeitschrifteninserat für Weichmacher. (USA)
134 Ganzseitiges Inserat für *Sony*-Apparate. Es zeigt die künftige Entwicklung der Fernsehgeräte. (GBR)
135 Zeitschrifteninserat des Chemieunternehmens *Goodrich* über einen neuen synthetischen Gummi für Scheibenbremsen. «Dies reicht, um einen 40-Tonnen-Lastwagen anzuhalten.» (USA)

131 Annonce sur page double vantant la *Honda* et les qualités exceptionnelles qu'elle possède en ce qui concerne le démarrage. (USA)
132 Annonce de magazine sur page double pour un fabricant d'autos-jouets. Médaille d'or du One Show 1975 à New York. (USA)
133 Annonce de magazine professionnel sur page double pour USS Chemicals, en faveur des plastifiants utilisés dans la fabrication de peintures. (USA)
134 Annonce de magazine en noir et blanc pour *Sony* avec référence au développement technique dans le domaine des téléviseurs. (GBR)
135 Annonce pour un caoutchouc synthétique particulièrement dur pour disques de freins mis au point par *Goodrich*. (USA)

PHOTOGRAPHER / PHOTOGRAPH / PHOTOGRAPHE:

131 Carl Furuta
132 Cailer/Resnick
133 Marini, Climes & Guip, Inc.
134 John Thornton
135 Jan Czyrba

DESIGNER / GESTALTER / MAQUETTISTE:

131 Norm Friant
132 Allan Beaver
133 Len Moser
134 John O'Driscoll

ART DIRECTOR / DIRECTEUR ARTISTIQUE:

131 Norm Friant
132 Allan Beaver
133 Len Moser
134 John O'Driscoll
135 Don Ozyp

AGENCY / AGENTUR / AGENCE – STUDIO:

131 Grey Advertising, Inc.
132 Levine, Huntley, Schmidt
133 David W. Evans Agency
134 Batten, Barton, Durstine & Osborn Ltd.
135 Griswold-Eschleman Co.

Advertisements / Inserate Annonces

An enthusiastic testimonial for our micro computers from someone who doesn't even know what they are.

136

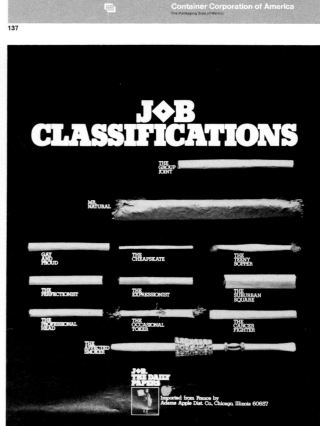

137

Weyerhaeuser is paper, too.
Sometimes you can't see that for the trees.

139

JOB CLASSIFICATIONS

140

136 Magazine advertisement for *Olivetti* micro-computers, here for use in insurance. (GBR)
137 Magazine advertisement for the Container Corporation of America about their packaging "space programme". Red ground. (USA)
138 Black-and-white advertisement for a *Ronson* battery shaver. (GBR)
139 Colour magazine advertisement for *Weyerhaeuser* papers. (USA)
140 Magazine advertisement for *Job* cigarette papers imported from France, with a pun on the name. (USA)
141 Magazine advertisement in predominantly brown shades for *Rowney* oil colours for artists. (GBR)
142 Trade magazine advertisement for *Colt* ventilation to prevent the hot, stuffy conditions in factories that sap workers' energy. (GBR)
143 "We let the horn sound in honour of the day." Magazine advertisement in full colour for a supplier of hunting equipment. (DEN)

136 Ganzseitiges, mehrfarbiges Zeitschrifteninserat für Mikro-Computer der Firma *Olivetti,* hier im Einsatz in Versicherungen. (GBR)
137 Ganzseitiges Zeitschrifteninserat der Container Corporation of America für ihr Packungs-Programm. Schwarzweiss auf Rot. (USA)
138 Schwarzweisses Inserat für *Ronson*-Batterie-Rasierapparate. (GBR)
139 Ganzseitiges, mehrfarbiges Inserat einer Papierfabrik für ihr Angebot an Papiersorten für jeden Zweck. (USA)
140 Ganzseitiges Zeitschrifteninserat für *Job*-Zigarettenpapier. (USA)
141 Ganzseitiges, mehrfarbiges Zeitschrifteninserat für *Rowney*-Künstler-Ölfarben, die in zwei Preislagen angeboten werden. (GBR)
142 Ganzseitiges, schwarzweisses Fachzeitschrifteninserat für *Colt*-Klimaanlagen, die verhüten, dass die Arbeiter schlapp machen. (GBR)
143 Mehrfarbiges Fachzeitschrifteninserat für Jagdgeräte. «Das Horn erklinge zu Ehren des Tages.» (DEN)

"It has come to my notice that there's a battery shaver what is as powerful as the plug-in variety."

The Ronson RS65 is the battery shaver in question.

It has a motor as powerful as the mains model.

So you get the same number of cutting strokes per minute.

It has the same foil shaving head to give you the same close, comfortable shave.

It even has an identical long-hair trimmer.

What it hasn't got is a flex.

Instead, four HP7 batteries give you up to four weeks' shaving.

So you'll be able to keep that handsome, clean-shaven look even when you're out on manoeuvres.

OK, lovely boys? **RONSON**

138

Rowney oil colour–the best at any price.

There are two qualities of oil colour made by Rowney – their Artists' professional quality, the finest in the world, where quality and permanence are upheld regardless of cost – and their Georgian Oil Colours specially formulated for economy where some of the more expensive pigments are replaced by

modern, tested and permanent alternatives.

Rowney have used their 180 years experience to the benefit of both qualities and with new advances in paint technology, traditional colours can be used alongside new bright saturated reds and intense olives.

Rowney Artists' professional

quality and Georgian have a uniform consistency which enables a painter to progress from one to the other, or work with both on the same palette.

George Rowney & Company Limited PO Box 10 Bracknell Berks RG12 4ST

Rowney (Canada) Limited Concord Ontario

141

At around 90°F, workers evaporate.

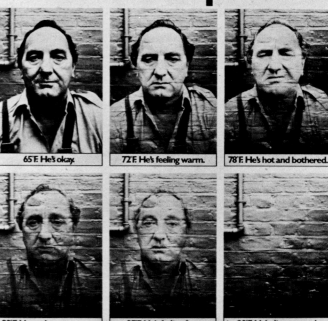

It's a sad fact of life that the 'Disappearing Workers' actually exist in large numbers throughout Britain.

And if you're in any doubt about it, try spending an hour or two on the factory floor one sunny afternoon.

The chances are, you'll find that a number of employees aren't to be seen. And of those who are, many will be present in body but not in spirit.

It's quite simply, the hot, sweltering atmosphere caused by bad ventilation. It's unpleasant to walk around in, it's damned near impossible to work in. And if you subject a man to these conditions, his will to work dies.

His productivity drops like a stone, his attitude to management takes a very fast turn for the worse. In his eyes, you actually become the cause of his misery – for it's an industrial fact he can only work at his best at a temperature of 60°F to 72°F.

So what's to be done about it? The answer that over 60,000 British companies have found is to call us at Colt.

We carry out a detailed survey at your factory, then report in full and without charge, showing how the right use of ventilation can create healthier, safer, altogether better working conditions (and, incidentally, help to keep you within the Act).

It can only do good for your company's profits – and even the taxman shoulders a fair share of the capital outlay.

Write or phone. It's the one sure way you have of making a very real problem disappear.

Colt International Limited (Heating, Ventilation and Industrial Access). Havant, Hants. Havant 6411. Telex 86219.

People work better in Colt conditions.

142

Vi la'r hornet gjalde i dagens anledning.

Petersen Bach · Aalborg

143

144

145

PHOTOGRAPHER / PHOTOGRAPH:

144 Melvin Sokolsky
145 Neish, Tutt, Grunwald
146–149 Phil Marco

DESIGNER / GESTALTER:

144 Lee Epstein
145 Jim Passmore
146, 147 Phil Marco

144 Double-spread magazine advertisement for a *Polaroid* film that supplies both a positive print and a negative. Black and white. (USA)
145 Full-colour trade magazine advertisement for *Gadsden* steel cans for packaging fruit and vegetables. (AUL)
146, 147 Full-page illustrations in full colour for double-spread trade magazine advertisements (see Figs. 148 and 149) about the high quality of printing and reproduction obtainable with *Westvaco* papers. (USA)
148, 149 Complete double-spread magazine advertisement and detail of the photography in actual ad size for *Westvaco* papers. (USA)

144 Doppelseitiges Zeitschrifteninserat für einen neuen *Polaroid*-Film, der ein Positiv- und ein Negativbild liefert. (USA)
145 Ganzseitiges Zeitschrifteninserat eines Herstellers von Konservendosen für Obst und Gemüse. Mehrfarbig. (AUL)
146, 147 Mehrfarbige Aufnahmen für Inserate, die die hervorragenden Reproduktionsmöglichkeiten auf *Westvaco*-Feinpapier demonstrieren sollen. (USA)
148, 149 Doppelseitiges Fachzeitschrifteninserat der *Westvaco*-Papierfabrik und Detail einer Aufnahme, womit auf die verschiedenen Papiersorten hingewiesen wird. Siehe auch Abbildungen 146 und 147. (USA)

146

147

144 «Nous ne nous sommes jamais rendus compte qu'un produit *Polaroid* pourrait avoir tant de qualités négatives.» Annonce de magazine sur page double pour une pellicule *Polaroid* qui produit à la fois des épreuves positives ainsi que des négatifs. Noir et blanc. (USA)
145 Annonce de magazine professionnel en couleur pour une marque de boîtes en acier pour les fruits et les légumes. (AUL)
146, 147 Illustrations sur page entière (en couleur) pour des annonces de magazine professionnel sur pages doubles (voir les figs. 148 et 149) se référant à la haute qualité de reproduction grâce aux papiers *Westvaco*. (USA)
148, 149 Annonce de magazine sur page double et détail de la photographie en grandeur nature en faveur des papiers *Westvaco*. (USA)

ART DIRECTOR / DIRECTEUR ARTISTIQUE:

144 Lee Epstein
145 Heinz Grunwald
146, 147 Ted McNeil

AGENCY / AGENTUR / AGENCE – STUDIO:

144 Doyle, Dane Bernbach, Inc.
145 Neish, Tutt, Grunwald
146, 147 McCaffrey & McCall, Inc.

148

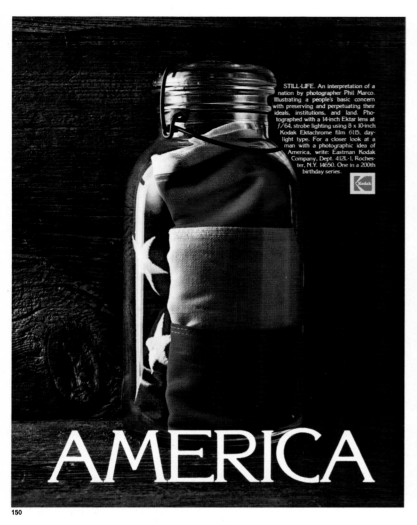

150

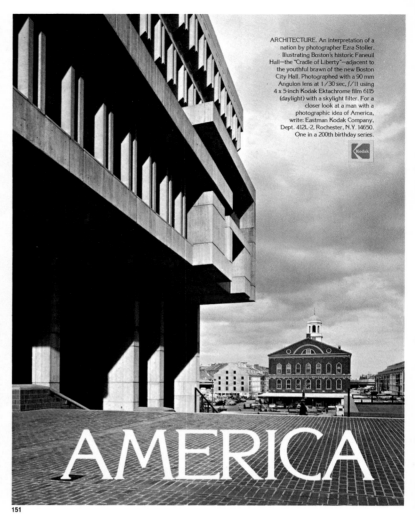

151

150–152 Examples from a series of full-page magazine advertisements with shots by well-known photographers, issued by *Kodak* on the occasion of the American Bicentennial. These three illustrate the American wish to preserve the national heritage, traditional and modern architecture in Boston, and the love of music embodied in the Preservation Hall Jazz Band of New Orleans. (USA)
153–156 From a series of magazine advertisements for *Kodak* films as a means of recording some of the highlights of family life—here children spending a first night in a tent, learning to dance and to tie one's own shoes, and the experience of fatherhood. (USA)

150–152 Anlässlich des 200jährigen Bestehens der Vereinigten Staaten von Amerika beauftragte *Kodak* namhafte Photographen, für eine Inseratenserie in Fachzeitschriften typische Beispiele des amerikanischen Lebens festzuhalten. Abb. 150 versinnbildlicht den Wunsch vieler Amerikaner, das nationale Erbe zu bewahren; 151 stellt ein historisches Gebäude in Boston einem Neubau gegenüber, während 152 eine Jazzband aus New Orleans zeigt. (USA)
153–156 Aus einer Serie von Zeitschrifteninseraten für *Kodak*-Filme. Sie halten wichtige Geschehnisse im Leben des einzelnen fest: Kinder verbringen die erste Nacht im Zelt; sie versuchen ihre ersten Tanzschritte; die Vaterschaft; das Kind lernt, sich die Schuhe selbst zu binden. (USA)

150–152 Exemples figurant dans une série d'annonces de magazine sur pages entières, série qui présente des prises de vue de photographes de renom. *Kodak* a fait paraître cette série dont les sujets se réfèrent entièrement aux Etats-Unis à l'occasion du Bicentenaire de ce pays. Les trois illustrations: les efforts entrepris par les Etats Unis afin de préserver le patrimoine national; l'architecture traditionnelle et moderne à Boston; l'amour de la musique personnifiée par le Preservation Hall Jazz Band de la Nouvelle Orléans. (USA)
153–156 Eléments d'une série d'annonces de magazine pour les films *Kodak* promus en tant que moyen pour retenir les points culminants de la vie familiale – les enfants qui passent leur première nuit dans la tente, les enfants qui aprennent à danser et à lacer leurs souliers, les sentiments qu'éprouve l'homme devenu père. (USA)

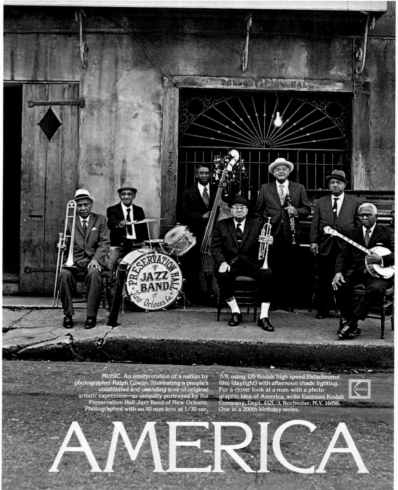

152

A man just can't be sheltered by his folks forever.
Someday, he's got to pack up, go out into the world and
spend a whole night in Eddie's backyard next door.

Kodak film. For the times of your life.

153

Standing close together is hard enough to learn.
And then they ask you to move your feet.

Kodak film. For the times of your life.

154

There are more
than 40 million fathers
in America. And yet,
sometimes you're
the only one.

Kodak film.
For the times of
your life.

155

There comes a day in
every man's life when
he must face up to the
inevitable truth that
it's time to learn to tie
his own shoes.

Kodak film.
For the times of
your life.

156

PHOTOGRAPHER / PHOTOGRAPH / PHOTOGRAPHE:

150 Phil Marco
151 Ezra Stoller
152 Ralph Cowan
153–156 Tom McCarthy

DESIGNER / GESTALTER / MAQUETTISTE:

150 Phil Marco
151, 152 Seth Fagerstrom
153–156 Fred Kittel

ART DIRECTOR / DIRECTEUR ARTISTIQUE:

150–152 Seth Fagerstrom
153–156 Fred Kittel

AGENCY / AGENTUR / AGENCE – STUDIO:

150–152 Rumrill-Hoyt, Inc.
153–156 J. Walter Thompson Co.

157

159

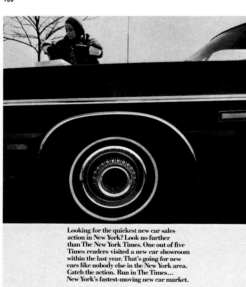

160

158

157, 158 "You're better than they think." Detail of the photography (full colour) and complete double-spread magazine advertisement about a new women's magazine called *brava* offering lots of creative ideas. (ITA)
159 Newspaper advertisement for *Baird & Warner* about luxury condominium homes. (USA)
160 Newspaper space promotion advertisement for *The New York Times,* addressed to new car dealers. (USA)
161–163 From a series of space promotion advertisements placed in newspapers by the magazine *Psychology Today*— here about rage, delinquency and defeat. (USA)
164 Double-spread space promotion ad for the *Chicago Tribune,* whose readers buy "41 new cars an hour". (USA)

PHOTOGRAPHER / PHOTOGRAPH / PHOTOGRAPHE:

157, 158 Giac Casale
159 Michael Ditcove
160 Duane Michals
161–163 Mike Levins/Michael Rougier
164 Jim Oberhofer

DESIGNER / GESTALTER / MAQUETTISTE:

160 Arnold Kushner
161–163 Herb Stein

157, 158 Photographie und doppelseitiges Zeitschrifteninserat für die neue Frauenzeitschrift *brava.* Mehrfarbig. (ITA)
159 Ganzseitiges Zeitungsinserat einer Immobilienfirma für luxuriöse Eigentumswohnungen. (USA)
160 Ganzseitiges Zeitungsinserat, das auf die *New York Times* als bestes Organ für Autoinserate hinweist. (USA)
161–163 Aus einer Schwarzweiss-Serie zur Inseratenwerbung in einer Zeitschrift über Psychologie. Die Photos zeigen einige psychologische Fälle: Wut, Jugendkriminalität, Versagen beim Sport. Ganzseitig. (USA)
164 Doppelseitiges Fachzeitschrifteninserat zur Werbung von Inserenten für die *Chicago Tribune,* deren Leser «pro Stunde 41 Autos kaufen». (USA)

157, 158 Détail de la photo en couleur et annonce de magazine sur page double pour la promotion d'une nouvelle revue féminine – *brava* – qui offre nombre d'idées créatives. (ITA)
159 Annonce de journal de *Baird & Warner* pour des appartements en copropriété. (USA)
160 Annonce de journal promotionnelle pour le *New York Times,* qui s'adresse aux concessionnaires de voitures. (USA)
161–163 D'une série d'annonces promotionnelles en faveur du magazine *Psychology Today* – les reproductions se réfèrent à la rage, à la délinquance et à la défaite. Noir-blanc. (USA)
164 Promotion pour le journal *Chicago Tribune* dont les lecteurs achètent «chaque heure 41 nouvelles voitures». (USA)

Vent it or prevent it?

Rage. How well do we understand it?

Should we bottle it up? Or let it all hang out? Is there a way to channel and control it? Or can it be converted to creative purposes?

All of us are afflicted by rage and perhaps that's why there are so many ideas about handling rage. Everyone seems to have his own solution, his own approach, his own theory. Fine.

What are the facts?

Right now a handful of specialists are looking for them—in labs and classrooms, on the couch and in encounter sessions, all over the country. Whatever the freshest,

the latest, and the most germane facts, you'll find them presented in depth in PSYCHOLOGY TODAY.

We can guarantee that kind of authority because it's the authority itself who writes the story—not a third-party layman. It's not slick and suave or short and punchy—just thorough. That's why PSYCHOLOGY TODAY isn't always easy to read.

But it's just this kind of reading that attracts 4½ million men and women every month—people who want to understand themselves, their families, their friends, their business associates—today's world. People who look beyond the who and the what of current events and want

to know the why of the human condition—even if the answers sometimes are tough to take.

Not surprisingly, most of them are among the bright and quick under-35 group. They're better educated, in better jobs, with better incomes. Inquisitive, acquisitive.

psychology today
The human experience—and the why behind it.

161

By chance or by choice?

Delinquency. How well do we understand it?

Bad kids come from bad neighborhoods. Right? They have no choice. Bad homes. Turned off by education. Dropping out of school into the street. But what about the kids from the suburbs and comfortable homes, shooting up and ripping off? What gives?

Crazy kids: everybody reads about them, everybody knows about them. Why can't they do what they're supposed to? We all have our theories about what made them go wrong and how to set them straight. It's obvious.

But what are the facts?

Youthful rage, adolescent alienation and protest among the young are, thankfully, subjects of continuing concern

among seasoned professionals and on-the-spot observers today. The more they work, analyze and observe, the more they see how subtle and complex the problem of delinquency is.

To share the experts' findings is our job, whatever the subject matter sensitivity. And we publish the experts' findings in their own words—it's the best way for you to know fully all they've come to know. That's also why PSYCHOLOGY TODAY isn't always easy to read.

But it's just this kind of reading that attracts 4½ million men and women every month—people who want to understand themselves, their families, their friends, their business associates—today's world. People who look

beyond the who and the what of current events and want to know the why of the human condition—even if the answers sometimes are tough to take.

Not surprisingly, most of them are among the bright and quick under-35 group. They're better educated, in better jobs, with better incomes. Inquisitive, acquisitive.

psychology today
The human experience—and the why behind it.

162

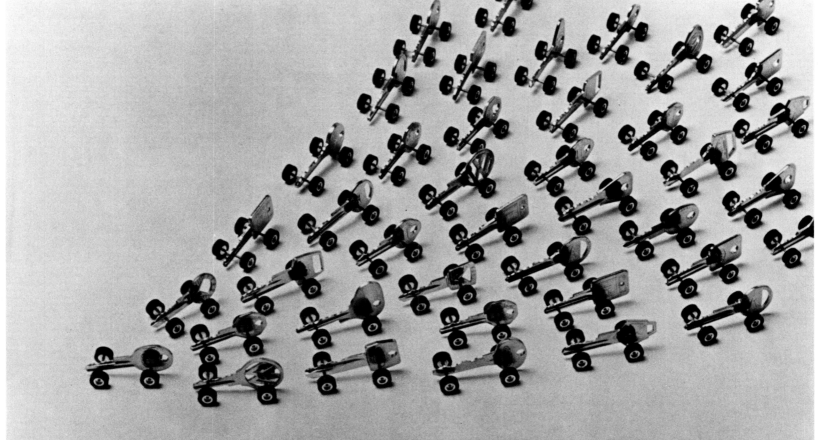

Lack of talent or lack of desire?

Defeat. How well do we understand it?

Did he lose because he lacked the athlete's skills? Or because he was afraid to win? How can a whole team have an "off day"? Or suddenly come alive, click, win? Is losing just a case of physical failure? Or a case of attitude?

A lot of people care about the answers—and think they have them. Pet theories and folk myths abound about everything, from how the body's chemistry works to how a psyche yourself up—and your opponent out.

What are the facts?

We don't think we have all the answers, but we do know who's asking the right questions: the professionals, trained and experienced, who are studying, researching,

interviewing, watching. Learning. Their findings are what we publish—first-hand, eye-witness reports from the men and women who literally know what they're talking about.

Because there's a kind of person who wants to know what the specialist knows, we let the experts speak for themselves. No quick summaries here. No digests. No slants toward a particular audience. Just the words of an authority, exploring his specialty in depth. That's why PSYCHOLOGY TODAY isn't always easy to read.

But it's just this kind of reading that attracts 4½ million men and women every month—people who want to understand themselves, their families, their friends, their business associates—today's world. People who

look beyond the who and the what of current events and want to know the why of the human condition—even if the answers sometimes are tough to take.

Not surprisingly, most of them are among the bright and quick under-35 group. They're better educated, in better jobs, with better incomes. Inquisitive, acquisitive.

psychology today
The human experience—and the why behind it.

163

ART DIRECTOR / DIRECTEUR ARTISTIQUE:

157, 158 Gino Motta
159 Lester Teich/Mahl Craft
160 Andrew Kner
161–163 Herb Stein
164 Andy Shomsky

AGENCY / AGENTUR / AGENCE – STUDIO:

157, 158 Young & Rubicam Italia S.p.A.
159 Nader-Lief
161–163 Ziff Davis Publishing Co.
164 Marvin H. Frank & Co.

The Tribune Crowd. Their pick-up speed on new cars is 41 an hour.

In Chicago, the Tribune Crowd buys 41 new cars an hour. 6,967 a week. 30,192 a month. 362,298 a year. In short, the Tribune Crowd makes 70% of Chicago's new car purchases.

But their drive for goods doesn't brake there. Because Chicago Tribune readers register as the largest (and most affluent) Chicago newspaper audience. Tribune advertisers register more mileage per ad dollar in foods, furniture, clothing, travel, books—just about anything.

If you want to accelerate your sales, Chicago's fastest moving newspaper, the Tribune, is the option to choose. In Chicago, nobody else comes close.

Chicago Tribune
A step ahead of the times.

164

165 Army recruiting advertisement playing on the attraction of belonging to a regiment. Gold award in the D&AD exhibition. (GBR)
166 Newspaper announcement of a new television series about a policewoman. (AUL)
167 "Previously an old person was usually a poor person too. Not any more." From a series of newspaper advertisements about projects to help the aged organized by the *Winterthur* insurance company to mark its jubilee. (SWI)
168, 169 Newspaper advertisements opposing housing discrimination in Cleveland. (USA)
170 Advertisement for the BBDM agency offering a booklet about marketing in the recession. (USA)
171 Double-spread magazine advertisement in full colour to encourage saving with the Halifax Building Society. (GBR)

165 Rekrutierungsinserat der englischen Armee, worin die Vorteile der Regimentszugehörigkeit gepriesen werden. (GBR)
166 Zeitungsinserat für ein australisches Fernsehprogramm, «Die Polizistin». (AUL)
167 Ganzseitiges, schwarzweisses Zeitungsinserat der *Winterthur*-Versicherungsgesellschaft, die anlässlich ihres 100jährigen Bestehens neue Projekte für die Altersfürsorge aufstellte und «Modelle für das dritte Leben» schuf. (SWI)
168, 169 Ganzseitige Zeitschrifteninserate mit einem Aufruf, die Wohnbedingungen der Minoritäten von Cleveland zu verbessern. (USA)
170 Schwarzweisses Inserat einer amerikanischen Werbeagentur, die eine Broschüre über Marketing in Zeiten der Rezession anbietet. (USA)
171 Doppelseitiges, mehrfarbiges Zeitschrifteninserat der Bausparkasse *Halifax*. (GBR)

165 Annonce de recrutement pour les forces armées où les avantages d'un régiment sont passés en revue. Médaille d'or de l'exposition D&AD. (GBR)
166 Annonce de presse pour une série TV consacrée à une femme policière. (AUL)
167 Elément d'une série d'annonces de journal présentant un projet d'assistance sociale pour les âgés, projet que la compagnie d'assurances *Winterthur* a mis sur pied à l'occasion du centenaire de la compagnie. (SWI)
168, 169 Annonces de presse contre la discrimination dans le domaine du logement. (USA)
170 Annonce pour l'agence publicitaire BBDM offrant une brochure sur le marketing en période de récession. (USA)
171 Annonce de magazine sur page double de la Halifax Building Society exhortant les gens à épargner davantage. En couleur. (GBR)

One day, my boy, all this could be yours.

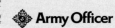

165

168

This family suffers from the disease that kills entire cities.

Cleveland, Ohio. Isn't it a wonderful place to raise a family?

169

Legs like this should be against the law.

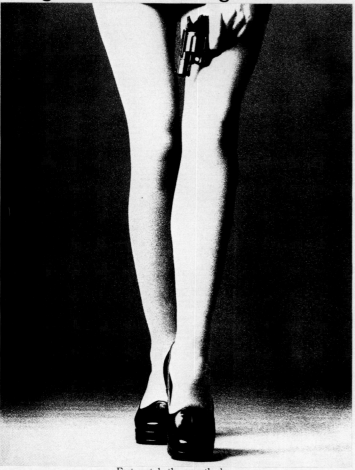

Fortunately they are the law.
Angie Dickinson is Sgt. Pepper Anderson in "Police Woman" a new series
starting on Channel Seven at 9 o'clock tonight.

166

Früher war ein alter Mensch meist auch ein armer Mensch.
Heute nicht mehr.

Heute ist ein alter Mensch meist auch ein einsamer Mensch. Gegen solche Not helfen auch wachsende Altersrenten und Altersheime nicht viel.

Diesen besonderen Altersproblemen hat sich die «Winterthur» in ihrem Jubiläumsjahr zugewandt. Sie will einen wesentlichen Beitrag zu ihrer Lösung leisten.

Unter dem Titel «Modelle für das dritte Leben» verwirklicht die «Winterthur» vier Projekte:

– eine Lern- und Begegnungsstätte, die alt und jung zu gemeinsamem Tun vereinigt;

– den Bau von altersgerechten und altersfreundlichen Wohnungen inmitten einer gemischten Siedlung;

– die Planung von Dienstleistungen, die es den Betagten erleichtern sollen, in ihrer liebgewordenen Umgebung zu bleiben;

– einen Wettbewerb zur Gewinnung von zukunftsweisenden Ideen für das Zusammenleben von jung und alt.

Diese vier Projekte werden zur Zeit in Winterthur realisiert.

Sie sind so angelegt, dass sie durch Änderung der Vorgaben für andere schweizerische Gemeinden anwendbar sind.

Am 10. Juni begeht die «Winterthur» ihr Jubiläum.

Bei diesem Anlass wird das «Winterthur»-Modell der Öffentlichkeit vorgestellt werden.

winterthur
versicherungen

Möchten Sie mehr über das «Winterthur»-Modell wissen? Wir haben eine kleine Informationsschrift verfasst, die wir Ihnen auf Verlangen gerne zustellen. Winterthur Versicherungen, Postfach 250, 8401 Winterthur.

167

Happy New Year.

Compared to this recession, few economic downturns have been so widely heralded, with such cordial acceptance by the experts.

Still, in the face of it all, we think the times are ripe for improving your business, just as we've been improving ours.

Not necessarily with "business as usual." (When has business ever been "usual?") But by preparing for change, being alert to it, responsive to it, and acting accordingly.

Sure. A lot of companies are going to lose money.

But some companies will make more than ever.

Some will panic, stumble, retrench, and shrink. Others will toughen and expand.

We believe that the smart businessman must accept changing economic climates as readily as he accepts the changing seasons.

And we have prepared a booklet that can help you deal with the changes ahead.

It's called "Marketing for Profit in a Business Recession."

We are not, obviously, presuming to solve your problems with a single brochure.

But we are offering to share some workable strategy that can help you live through 1975 more comfortably.

If you're in marketing or management, you should have a copy. And a smile on your face.

Simply attach the coupon to your letterhead.

To:
W. S. Browning
BBDM, Inc.
233 E. Ontario St.
Chicago, Illinois 60611

Yes, please send me free and without obligation a copy of your new brochure entitled "Marketing for Profit in a Business Recession."

Name
Title
Company
Address
City _____ State ___ Zip

BBDM

BBDM Advertising, 233 E. Ontario St., Chicago (312) 943-8445

We serve the following companies: Victor Comptometer, Sherwood Electronics, Honda, IMC, McGuire and Cleo, Zenith, Henry M. Goodman Furniture Stores, Cleveland Jackson Furniture Mfg., Franklin Picture Frames, Hawthorn Mellody Dairy, Mellody Lane Foods, International Harvester Trucks, Projex, Clean Coal Fuel Shop, Amoco Chemicals Corporation, Stetson Discount Stores, Elgin Watch.

170

It makes sense, while you're a working girl, to save for the kind of life you really want.

Being able to get what you want out of life, that's what independence is all about. And a special dream is even more special when you achieve it for yourself. Ask any girl. You can do it too.

By saving with the Halifax, where your money is safe, and always earning steady interest. You can withdraw it easily too. (And, at almost all Halifax branches, that goes for lunch times and Saturday mornings.)

Wherever you are in the country, you can be sure of finding a branch or agency of the Halifax nearby.

Call in. It takes only minutes to open an account.

HALIFAX
BUILDING SOCIETY
Member of The Building Societies Association
It's good to know it's there

171

Advertisements

Inserate

Annonces

172 Announcement of a drug addiction programme on WVON Television. (USA)
173, 174 Double-spread magazine advertisement in full colour about the beaches of South Carolina, and detail of the photography. Silver award in the 1975 One Show, New York. (USA)
175 "As Swiss we know a thing or two about holiday countries." Double-spread magazine advertisement about inclusive tours offered by the *Swissair* airline. Black and white. (GER)
176, 177 Double-spread magazine advertisements in full colour in which *Singapore Airlines* vaunt the qualities of their hostesses. (GBR)

172 Schwarzweiss-Inserat mit Ankündigung einer Fernsehsendung über Rauschgift. «Dieses kleine Päckchen kann in die Sklaverei zurückführen.» (USA)
173, 174 Mehrfarbiges Zeitschrifteninserat und Aufnahme als Werbung für den unverdorbenen Sandstrand in South Carolina. Silbermedaille der One Show 75 in New York. (USA)
175 Doppelseitiges, schwarzweisses Zeitschrifteninserat der *Swissair* mit Hinweis auf die alles einschliessenden Ferienarrangements dieser Luftfahrtgesellschaft. (GER)
176, 177 Doppelseitige, mehrfarbige Zeitschrifteninserate der *Singapore Airlines*, die auf die gute Betreuung durch ihre Hostessen verweisen. (GBR)

172 Annonce d'un programme TV consacré à la drogue. (USA)
173, 174 Annonce de magazine sur page double et détail de la photo. «Voici ce qu'on trouve sur nos plages» – c'est-à-dire les plages de la Californie du Sud. Polychrome. Médaille d'argent du One Show 1975, New York. (USA)
175 «Etant Suisses, nous connaissons les pays de vacances.» Annonce de magazine, double page, concernant les voyages tout compris de la compagnie aérienne *Swissair*. Noir et blanc. (GER)
176, 177 Annonces de magazine sur page double par lesquelles *Singapore Airlines* vantent les qualifications de leurs hôtesses de l'air. Polychrome. (GBR)

These are the things that litter our beaches. Not beer cans, paper cups and candy wrappers.

173

Grüezi mitenand.

Als Schweizer verstehen wir was von Ferienländern.

175

Travellers must be content

SINGAPORE AIRLINES

176

172

Heroin. Roughly a quarter gram is all you need to get started on a lifetime of misery. In no time at all you can become the property of some pusher—a twisted puppet with a wound that never heals.
While other radio stations are dishing out glib chatter, the Black Giant is spreading the truth about drug addiction. In high schools, playgrounds and on the air – 24 hours a day.
More than a million people listen to the Black Giant to find out what's happening. And every time we save a kid from dope, the giant feels a little taller.
When you're Chicago's Black Giant, you do more than just spin records. WVON 1450 AM
24-HOUR HEROIN HOTLINE 800-368-5363

THIS LITTLE PACKET CAN BRING BACK SLAVERY.

PHOTOGRAPHER / PHOTOGRAPH / PHOTOGRAPHE:

172 John Cascarano
173, 174 Phil Marco/Ralph Holland
175 Feico Derschow
176, 177 John Thornton

DESIGNER / GESTALTER / MAQUETTISTE:

172 Russ Slaughter
173, 174 Michael Winslow
176, 177 Fay Davis

174

You're as
young as you feel

SINGAPORE AIRLINES

177

ART DIRECTOR / DIRECTEUR ARTISTIQUE:

172 Russ Slaughter
173, 174 Michael Winslow
175 Jürgen Pilger
176, 177 Fay Davis

AGENCY / AGENTUR / AGENCE – STUDIO:

172 Hurvis, Binzer & Churchill, Inc.
173, 174 McKinney & Silver
175 GGK Werbeagentur
176, 177 Batey Advertising

Advertisements / Inserate / Annonces

178

This aircraft is a perfectly safe piece of equipment. Until an amateur gets hold of it.

A sudden down-draft. Clear air turbulence. An unexpected thermal. They're all phenomena that usually scarcely ripple the cocktails in the first class cabin of your aircraft. But on the week-end they could really do a number on your ski kite or your sailplane. And you.

Which is just one more reason we offer professional airline pilots occupational disability insurance—from $25,000 up to $75,000—and we pay the benefit in one tax-free "lump sum," after the specified waiting period, if you're ever permanently prevented from flying for your airline for medical reasons. What's more, we've got an Aerospace Medical Specialist on our staff who has logged many years of experience helping grounded pilots get the lift they need. For information.

write Harvey W. Watt. P.O. Box 20787, Atlanta, Ga. 30320. Or call us at 767-7501. If you're outside the state of Georgia, call us toll-free (800) 241-6103. **Aviation Insurance Agency**

179

One of these days, like tomorrow or next weekend, you could get knocked right out of the saddle. And right out of flying status, too. That's why we offer pilots like yourself

occupational disability coverage from $25,000 to $75,000. If you're permanently prevented from flying for a living. But since we know that flying is your life, we'll do everything humanly possible to help get you back in the saddle again. Our Pilot

"lump sum" after the specified waiting period. Is designed to do just that. It's headed up by an Aerospace Medical Specialist with many years of experience in getting pilots back up to 492 knots in a hurry.

Recertification Program is designed to do just that. It's headed up by an Aerospace Medical Specialist with many years of experience in getting pilots back up to 492 knots in a hurry.

For details, write Harvey W. Watt, P.O. Box 20787, Atlanta Airport, Atlanta, Georgia 30320. Or call us at 767-7501. If you're located outside Georgia, call our toll-free number: (800) 241-6103.

A 26-knot vehicle can be a lot more dangerous than the 492-knot job you fly for a living.

Aviation Insurance Agency

182

Grounded.

Another ALPA Member Service

Your landings may be going just great, but unless you've thought about your insurance needs lately, then your own wheels may be stuck to the ground.

Let's talk unpleasantness for a minute: Income Protection. At 32,000 feet the need for it may seem pretty remote when all that's ahead is your future and smooth flying. But most disabilities don't occur in the cockpit. As a rule, they happen on the ground. When you least expect them.

If the big bird has to take off without you, don't let your monthly income do the same. ALPA's "Extended Total Disability Insurance" will help keep

you and your income together. For example, if you were totally disabled at 40, the policy would pay you $90,000 in addition to Loss of License benefits by the time you were 60!

We at ALPA want to keep you in the blue and your income out of the red. Mail the postage paid card to us today. We'll send you full information at once. Remember: You must be an ALPA member and 37 years or younger to qualify. Act today.

183

Grounded.

Another ALPA Member Service

A raft is a great thing to have when water's coming at you in all directions. And that's what it feels like when Loss of License strikes. Suddenly, there's a sea of bills to be coped with, and no one's around to help. That is, unless you were smart enough to join ALPA's Loss of License Insurance Plan. It's the best friend a professional pilot can have when the going gets rough.

We don't make any money on insurance. We offer it as your professional association because our sole interest is your future as a pilot—in the cockpit or out. And remember: You must be an ALPA member and 37 years or

younger to qualify. Be careful that the sands of time don't catch up with you.

Should one day you find yourself beached for a short time or forever, ALPA's Loss of License will take care of you. It covers temporary disabilities as well as the permanent ones. Which ever way it goes, ALPA will keep you on your own two feet. There's no reason why you shouldn't be allowed to walk away from financial disaster. ALPA's Loss of License plan will let you take those steps.

Mail the reply card today. We'll send you full facts. And no obligation, ever.

178, 179 Full-colour magazine advertisements from a series about the insurance offered to professional airline pilots by Aviation Insurance Agency. (USA)
180, 181 Detail of the photography and complete advertisement for *Singapore Airlines,* underlining the qualities of their hostesses. (SWI)
182–184 From a series of full-colour magazine advertisements about the insurance offered to professional pilots by Air Line Pilots Association. (USA)
185 Advertisement for The Elliot Organization, Inc., offering help in handling the less successful products and services. (USA)

178, 179 Ganzseitige Zeitschrifteninserate einer Versicherungsgesellschaft, bei der sich Berufspiloten versichern lassen können. (USA)
180, 181 Ausschnitt und ganzes schwarzweisses Zeitungsinserat der *Singapore Airlines.* «Unsere Art, mit Menschen umzugehen.» (SWI)
182–184 Mehrfarbige Zeitschrifteninserate einer Gesellschaft, die Berufspiloten für den Fall des Verlustes ihrer Pilotenlizenz versichert. (USA)
185 «Schicken Sie uns Ihren Hund.» Ganzseitiges Zeitschrifteninserat einer Organisation, die sich für Betriebsberatung und Umsatzförderung empfiehlt. (USA)

180

Grounded.

Another ALPA Member Service

Happy Birthday to you! We hope only that you haven't lighted your thirty-eighth candle yet. Not that there's anything wrong with being 38—at least, not if you're covered with ALPA's Loss of License Insurance program. Because the program is offered only to professional pilots who are 37 years of age or younger. And who are ALPA members, too. After 37, it's just a lot of pie in the sky.

We want to keep your career as bright as your candles. You've devoted too much time to blow it all out at once. Yet that's what can happen if Loss of License hits you. That's why we offer

our insurance program. We make no money on it. We have no salesmen. Your need is our only motivation.

Write us today about the Loss of License program. We'll send you full information. At ALPA, we want all of your birthdays to be happy ones.

Write:

Air Line Pilots Association
Membership Services Department
1625 Massachusetts Avenue, N.W.
Washington, D.C. 20036

184

181

Send us your dog.

Every company has at least one product or service that isn't moving the way it should.

And when there's not enough bucks to promote it the way you think it should be, things get even tougher.

We've built a reputation for turning losers into winners. Often with minimal budgets.

And we'd be happy to show you what we've done in the automotive, building product, liquor, office product, publishing, fibre/floor covering, photographic, chemical, cosmetic, public utilities and bank areas.

Call us, before it eats you out of house and home.

The Elliot Organization, Inc.
358 West 20 Street, New York, New York 10011 212 741-1690

185

PHOTOGRAPHER / PHOTOGRAPH:

178 Randy Miller
179 Richard Hoflich
180, 181 John Ashenhurst
182—184 Mike Mitchell
185 Norman Sanders

DESIGNER / GESTALTER / MAQUETTISTE:

178, 179 Jerry Sullivan
180, 181 John Ashenhurst
182—184 Jack Beveridge

ART DIRECTOR / DIRECTEUR ARTISTIQUE:

178, 179 Jerry Sullivan
180, 181 Fay Davis
182—184 Jack Beveridge
185 Ken Carson

AGENCY / AGENTUR / AGENCE – STUDIO:

178, 179 Cole Henderson Drake, Inc.
180, 181 Batey Advertising
182—184 Beveridge & Associates, Inc.
185 The Elliot Organization, Inc.

178, 179 Annonces de magazine en couleur tirées d'une série concernant une assurance offerte aux pilotes professionnels. (USA)
180, 181 Détail de la photo et annonce complète de *Singapore Airlines,* vantant les qualifications de leurs hôtesses de l'air. (SWI)
182—184 Eléments d'une série d'annonces de magazine en couleur concernant une assurance de l'Air Line Pilots Assoc. offerte aux pilotes professionnels. (USA)
185 Annonce de l'Elliot Organization, Inc., qui offre son assistance quant à la promotion de produits ou services moins réussis. (USA)

Advertisements / Inserate

Annonces

2

Booklets

Folders

Catalogues

Invitations

Programmes

Broschüren

Faltprospekte

Kataloge

Einladungen

Programme

Brochures

Dépliants

Catalogues

Invitations

Programmes

186 Colour illustration on a double gatefold for an article on the ropes used for logging.
From a publication of the Exxon Chemical Company. (USA)
187 Full-page illustration in full colour from a brochure on "superior building" issued by the
Züblin building company. (SWI)
188, 189 Detail of the photography and complete cover of a booklet on the Limburgerhof,
an agricultural research station of BASF. (GER)
190, 191 Detail of the cover photograph in actual size and complete cover of a booklet about
A/S Aug. Laursen, printers and lithographers. The apples replace the three coloured circles of the
company's trade mark. (DEN)

186 Farbige Illustration einer Doppel-Innenklappe für einen Artikel über Seile zum Festbinden der
Baumstämme beim Flössen. Aus der Firmenzeitschrift eines Chemie-Unternehmens. (USA)
187 Ganzseitige, mehrfarbige Illustration aus der Broschüre «Überlegen bauen» der General-
unternehmung Ed. Züblin & Cie. AG, Zürich. (SWI)
188, 189 Photoausschnitt und ganzer Umschlag einer Broschüre über die landwirtschaftliche
Versuchsstation Limburgerhof der BASF AG, Ludwigshafen. (GER)
190, 191 Farbaufnahme in Originalgrösse und ganzer Umschlag einer Broschüre der Druckerei
A/S Aug. Laursen. Die drei Äpfel stehen für die drei Farbkreise des Firmenzeichens. (DEN)

186 Photographie en couleur (page à deux replis) illustrant un article sur les cordes qu'on utilise
pour le flottage du bois. Illustration figurant dans une publication de l'Exxon Chemical
Company. (USA)
187 Illustration sur page entière figurant dans une brochure consacrée à la «construction
réfléchie». Brochure publiée par *Züblin,* une entreprise de construction. (SWI)
188, 189 Détail de la photo et couverture d'une brochure consacrée au Limburgerhof, un centre
de recherches agricoles de la BASF. (GER)
190, 191 Détail de la photo de couverture en grandeur nature et couverture complète d'une
brochure consacrée aux activités d'un lithographe-imprimeur. Les pommes remplacent
les trois cercles polychromes qui constituent la marque de l'entreprise. (DEN)

187

186

188

PHOTOGRAPHER / PHOTOGRAPH / PHOTOGRAPHE:

186 Harald Sund
187 René Groebli
188, 189 Dieter Gnade
190, 191 Poul Ib Henriksen

DESIGNER / GESTALTER / MAQUETTISTE:

188, 189 Hans Maurer/Johannes Wolf
190, 191 Hans Wienberg

ART DIRECTOR / DIRECTEUR ARTISTIQUE:

186 John J. Conley
188, 189 Wolfgang Görlach
190, 191 Hans Wienberg

AGENCY / AGENTUR / AGENCE – STUDIO:

187 H. R. Abächerli
188, 189 BASF, Grafisches Büro
190, 191 Aug. Laursen A/S

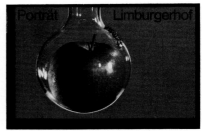

189

191

190

**Booklets / Prospekte
Brochures**

192

192 Cover in roughly actual size of a booklet about a *Corning* solar energy collector of new design. (USA)
193 Detail of the cover of a booklet about a new IBM computer-based bridge system for ships. Reddish ship and sky, yellow sun. (USA)
194 *Kodak* folder showing the shot "Broken Doll". It was taken to illustrate an article on a girl who blew herself up. A picture of the decaying door of an old truck was superimposed on a shot of the model's face. Yellowish shades. (USA)
195 Cover of a *Ciba-Geigy* booklet about a method of dyeing acrylic yarns. Yellow liquid, greenish ground. (SWI)
196 Photograph from the booklet *Nikon World* showing the wake of a boat in front of Norwegian cliffs. Shades of blue. (USA)
197 Double spread from a *Polaroid* booklet addressed to retailers. Portrait in colour (red hat) on a black ground. (USA)

The IBM Maritime Applications/Bridge System   ...a matter of course

193

**Booklets / Prospekte
Brochures**

"Broken Doll" came about as a speculative assignment to illustrate a magazine article on the Weatherman girl who blew herself up in New York's Greenwich Village a few years ago.
The problem, according to photographer Robin Perry, "was to take a photograph of a real girl and show her blown up, without being too gruesome."
So Perry photographed Sandy Adams in his Waterford (Connecticut) studio, using High Speed EKTACHROME Film in a 35mm slr with umbrella-reflected strobe. Next, he went looking for a jagged piece of yellow or pink metal or plastic to shoot and combine with Sandy's pretty face. He eventually found the decaying door of an old truck which he photographed on High Speed EKTACHROME Film on an overcast day. Working on a light table, he matched transparencies until he found the right combination. Then he had a dye transfer print made by Berkey K & L Laboratories in New York. The result is what Perry calls an assemblage, as distinguished from a sandwich. The difference, he says, is preplanning.
A prolific writer and lecturer, Perry has had one-man shows in Amsterdam, Antwerp, Brussels, Cologne, London, Paris, and around the U.S.

IMAGINATION DOES IT—
with Kodak products.

194

195

196

But the main difference this year is SX-70 film.

1. SX-70 Model 2 opens up a vast new market with its lower price. Your SX-70 film business will dramatically increase.
2. You'll have 6-month dating on all Christmas SX-70 film shipments.

197

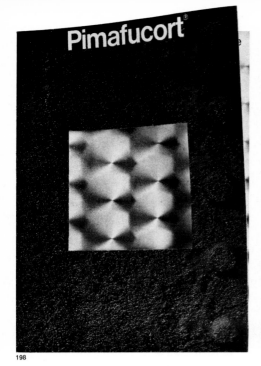

198

199

Booklets / Prospekte / Brochures

PHOTOGRAPHER / PHOTOGRAPH / PHOTOGRAPHE:

198, 199 Kroehl Design Gruppe
200, 201 José Baquès
202, 203, 203a Miguel Martinez

DESIGNER / GESTALTER / MAQUETTISTE:

198, 199 Heinz Kroehl/Peter Offenberg
200, 201 José Baquès
202, 203, 203a Ramón Roda

ART DIRECTOR / DIRECTEUR ARTISTIQUE:

198, 199 Heinz Kroehl/Peter Offenberg
200, 201 José Baquès
202, 203, 203a Ramón Roda

AGENCY / AGENTUR / AGENCE – STUDIO:

198, 199 Kroehl Design Gruppe
200, 201 Estudio Baquès
202, 203, 203a Industrias Graficas PAUTA

200

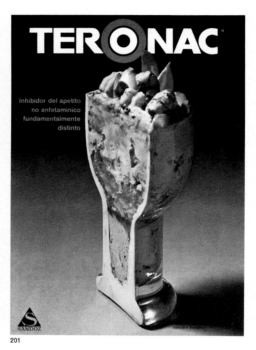

201

198, 199 Cards sent to doctors to promote *Pimafucost,* a medicament for the treatment of skin affections. From a series contrasting a rough surface on the cover with a fine surface in the cut-out. (GER)
200, 201 Full-colour covers of two folders sent to doctors on the *Sandoz* pharmaceutical product *Teronac,* which promotes slimming by inhibiting the appetite. (SPA)
202, 203, 203a Inside spread of a large folder, panel and detail of one of the outside panels in actual size, for a *Cromoarte* photoengraving system making use of lasers as a light source. Full-colour photographs on a black ground. (SPA)

198, 199 Aus einer Serie Werbekarten an Ärzte für *Pimafucost,* ein Mittel gegen Hautkrankheiten. Die rauhe Oberfläche kontrastiert mit der im ausgestanzten Quadrat sichtbaren glatten Oberfläche. (GER)
200, 201 Mehrfarbige Umschläge zweier Faltprospekte für die Ärzteschaft als Werbung für *Teronac,* ein appetithemmendes Präparat der Firma *Sandoz.* (SPA)
202, 203, 203a Innenseiten eines dreiteiligen Faltprospekts und originalgrosse Teilaufnahme der Rückseite für ein Clichierverfahren, das Laserstrahlen als Lichtquelle benützt. Mehrfarbige Photographien auf schwarzem Grund. (SPA)

198, 199 Cartes pour le corps médical présentant *Pimafucost,* un médicament des dermatoses. Série qui contraste une surface rugueuse (couverture) avec une surface fine (découpure). (GER)
200, 201 Couvertures polychromes de deux dépliants destinés au corps médical. Publicité pour un produit pharmaceutique de *Sandoz,* un produit d'amaigrissement qui dompte l'appétit. (SPA)
202, 203, 203a Pages intérieures d'un dépliant grand format et détail d'un panneau extérieur (grandeur nature). Publicité pour un système de photogravure utilisant les lasers en tant que source de lumière. Photos en couleur sur fond noir. (SPA)

202

204

PHOTOGRAPHER / PHOTOGRAPH / PHOTOGRAPHE:

204–206 Peter Schudel
207, 208 Robert Rich

DESIGNER / GESTALTER / MAQUETTISTE:

204–206 Norbert Rämisch
207, 208 Kramer/Miller/Lomden/Glassmann

ART DIRECTOR / DIRECTEUR ARTISTIQUE:

204–206 Lothar F. Kümper
207, 208 Alan J. Klawans

AGENCY / AGENTUR / AGENCE – STUDIO:

207, 208 Smith, Kline & French Laboratories, Advertising Dept.

204–206 Full-page illustration and two double spreads in colour from a booklet marking the centenary of Haarmann & Reimer GmbH, suppliers of flavouring matters and perfumes. The references are to scents (Fig. 204), spices (Fig. 205) and fresh fruits (Fig. 206). (GER)
207, 208 Full-page colour illustrations from a booklet on the psychotherapeutic drug *Thorazine*. The face on the blocks is built up with advancing treatment. (USA)

204–206 Illustration und Doppelseiten aus der Festschrift zum 100jährigen Bestehen von Haarmann & Reimer GmbH, Riech- und Geschmackstoffe. Abb. 204 bezieht sich auf Duftstoffe; 205 auf Gewürze; 206 auf Früchte. (GER)
207, 208 Ganzseitige, mehrfarbige Illustrationen aus einem Prospekt für *Thorazine*, das mithelfen soll, das Realitätsbewusstsein des Patienten wieder herzustellen. (USA)

204–206 Illustration sur pleine page et deux pages doubles d'une brochure publiée lors du centenaire de Haarmann & Reimer GmbH. Les illustrations se réfèrent aux parfums (fig. 204), aux épices (fig. 205) et aux fruits frais (fig. 206). (GER)
207, 208 Illustrations d'une brochure pour un produit psychothérapeutique. Les cubes reconstituant le visage symbolisent le progrès du traitement. (USA)

205

206

207

208

209

210

209 Folder containing a case history sent to doctors. For *Tetrex*, a pharmaceutical against infections. (USA)
210 Detail of a card sent by *Roche* to wish doctors pleasant holidays. Shells on red ground. (BEL)
211 Folder about *Dociton,* an ICI product for the treatment of high blood pressure. Figure in colour. (GER)
212 "Don't forget gloss." Cover of a *Schering* folder about a product used in nickel plating. Green ground. (GER)
213 Cover of a small booklet about *Artifort* furniture design and manufacture. Brown shades. (NLD)
214, 215 Double spreads from a *Corning* catalogue showing Christmas-tree decorations from the 1975 collection. (USA)

209 Mappe mit einer Krankengeschichte; an Ärzte gerichtete Werbung für ein Mittel gegen Infektionen. (USA)
210 Ausschnitt aus einer von *Roche* an Ärzte versandten Werbekarte mit Wünschen für die Ferien. Muscheln auf rotem Grund. (BEL)
211 Faltprospekt für *Dociton,* ein Mittel der ICI Pharma, Plankstadt, gegen zu hohen Blutdruck. (GER)
212 Umschlag eines Faltprospekts der Schering AG, Berlin, über das Vernickeln von Stahlrohrmöbeln. (GER)
213 Umschlag eines kleinformatigen Prospekts für einen Gestalter und Hersteller von Sitzmöbeln. (NLD)
214, 215 Doppelseiten aus einem Katalog für Christbaumschmuck von *Corning.* (USA)

209 Dépliant contenant un dossier médical. Elément de publicité pour le corps médical présentant *Tetrex,* un produit pharmaceutique contre les infections. (USA)
210 Détail d'une carte que *Roche* a adressée aux médecins afin de leur souhaiter de bonnes vacances. Coquilles sur fond rouge. (BEL)
211 Dépliant pour *Dociton,* un produit d'ICI pour le traitement de l'hypertension. Figures en couleur. (GER)
212 «N'oubliez pas le lustre.» Couverture d'un dépliant *Schering* présentant un produit qu'on utilise pour les revêtements de nickel. (GER)
213 Couverture d'une petite brochure pour les meubles créés et fabriqués par *Artifort.* Tons bruns. (NLD)
214, 215 Pages doubles figurant dans un catalogue de *Corning.* Il présente la collection 1975 des articles de décoration de Noël. (USA)

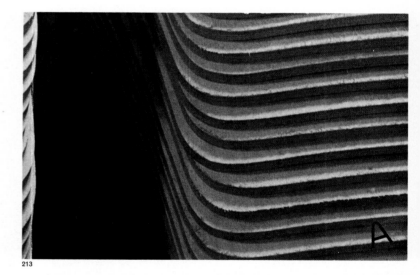

213

214

Booklets / Prospekte / Brochures

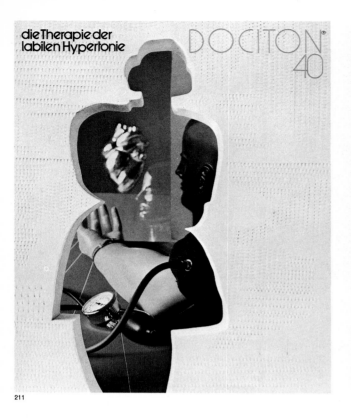

die Therapie der labilen Hypertonie DOCITON 40

211

...vergiß Glanz nicht

212

215

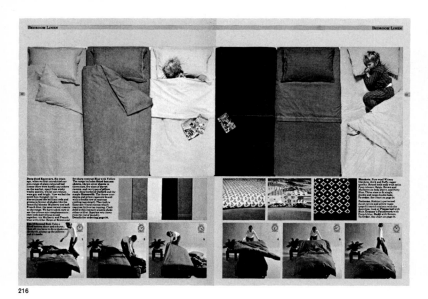

216

217

KITCHEN EQUIPMENT   KITCHEN EQUIPMENT

1/Salt jar. Stoneware. With cork stopper. 4½" × 4". **Buy from shops only. £1·10**

2/Plywood barrels. With close-fitting knob topped lids. One stencilled Flour another Pasta and a third plain, for beans perhaps, or rice or biscuits. 8½" diam. **Buy from shops only. Each £1·52**

3/Linen barrel. Huge. With leather strap handled lid. 24" × 18½". **Buy from shops only. £4·43**

4/Spaghetti jars. Handmade. 22" high. **Buy from shops only. £3·05**

5/Kitchen utensil jar. Stoneware. 5" × 4½". **Buy from shops only. 55p**

6/Tin canisters. Drum shape. Two sizes. 2lb and 4lb.
Small 2lb
N1748 blue, N1764 brown
N1756 yellow. **55p**
Large 4lb
N1705 blue, N1721 brown
N1713 yellow. **65p**

7/Knife rack. Wood. Screws to wall. 15½" long.
N0468 **£1·32**

8/Magnetic knife rack.
N5192 **£1·52**

9/Folding wine rack. Wood. Holds up to 10 bottles wine. 15½" × 22" × 7".
N9141 **£1·42**

10/Wine rack. Wood and metal frame. Packed flat ready for assembly at home. Two sizes.
N3887 13" × 16½" × 9", holds 16 bottles. **£2·30**
N3879 9" × 16½" × 9", holds 12 bottles. **£1·92**

11/Dripping jars. Stoneware. Two 1lb jars, one for pork the other beef dripping. And one 2lb size, simply marked dripping. **Buy from shops only. Pork or beef 49p. Dripping 63p**

12/Cutlery box. Wooden, red baize lined. 2½" × 9½" × 13½".
N7971 **£1·55**

13/Salt hood. Stoneware. Store for cooking salt. 8" high. **Buy from shops only. £1·62**

14/Oil and vinegar bottles. Cork tops. 6" tall. **Buy from shops only. Each 16p**

15/Stoneware store jars. Buff coloured body with darker brown top-dipped shoulder and lid. 4 sizes. **Buy from shops only.** ½lb, 1lb, 3lb and 7lb. **52p, 65p, £1·10 and £1·80**

16/Tin bread bin. Enamelled tin. 12½" × 11½" × 9".
N3240 **£3·35**

17/Wooden salt box. Hinged lid. 7½" × 4½" × 4½".
N7998 **£1·55**

18/Spice racks. Beechwood. Can be screwed to wall. Sold without jars. Two sizes. Both 2" deep.
N0433 11¾" × 15¼" **£1·67**
N0441 6½" × 15¼" **£3·79**

19/Spice jars. Glass. Airtight stoppers. 4½" tall. **Buy from shops only. 25p**

20/Bread crock. Hand thrown earthenware. 13½" × 11". **Buy from shops only. £4·15**

74

75

220

Booklets / Prospekte / Brochures

92

PHOTOGRAPHER / PHOTOGRAPH:

216, 219 Rowland Sherman
217, 220 Malcolm Robertson
218 Chris Thompson
221, 222 Ilmari Kostidinen

DESIGNER / GESTALTER / MAQUETTISTE:

216–220 Conran Associates
221, 222 Pekka Martin

ART DIRECTOR / DIRECTEUR ARTISTIQUE:

216–220 Stafford Cliff/John White
221, 222 Pekka Martin/Riitta Markkanen

AGENCY / AGENTUR / AGENCE – STUDIO:

216–220 Conran Associates
221, 222 SEK Advertising Ltd.

218

219

221

216–220 Three double spreads and one page, all in full colour, from the large and generously illustrated catalogue of *Habitat* household products for 1975. The pictures relate to bed linen (Fig. 216), tableware (Fig. 217), special articles available in the Conran Shop, London (Fig. 218), kitchen utensils (Fig. 219) and storage receptacles (Fig. 220). (GBR)
221, 222 Complete double spread and full-page illustration in actual size from a booklet about cocktails issued by Oy Alko AB, a government monopoly company for spirits. (FIN)

216–220 Drei mehrfarbige Doppelseiten und Seite aus einem umfangreichen Katalog für Wohnbedarfsartikel. Die Illustrationen beziehen sich auf Bettwäsche (216), Tafelgeschirr (217), Spezialartikel, die in einem besondern Ladengeschäft in London erhältlich sind (218), Küchengeräte (219) und Lebensmittelbehälter (220). (GBR)
221, 222 Doppelseite und ganzseitige Illustration in Originalgrösse aus dem Prospekt einer Firma, die das Staatsmonopol für alkoholische Getränke hat. (FIN)

216–220 Trois pages doubles et l'une des pages d'un catalogue grand format présentant la collection des articles de ménage de *Habitat.* Les illustrations se réfèrent à la linge (fig. 216), à la vaisselle (fig. 217), aux articles spéciaux qui sont en vente au Conran Shop, Londres (fig. 218), aux ustensiles de cuisine (fig. 219) et aux récipients de cuisine (fig. 220). (GBR)
221, 222 Double page et illustration pleine page (grandeur nature) d'une brochure consacrée aux cocktails. La brochure a été publiée par une compagnie finlandaise détenant le monopole d'état des spiritueux. (FIN)

222

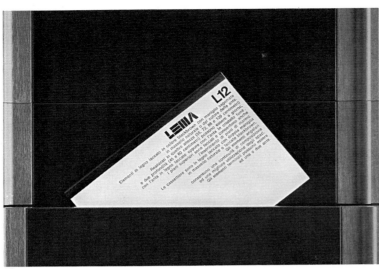

DESIGN ARCHITETTO ANGELO MANGIAROTTI

223

PHOTOGRAPHER / PHOTOGRAPH:

223 Antonini E. M.V. Corradi
224, 225 Theo Cockerell
226 Romylos Parissis
227 Patrice Tourenne
228 Richard Waldron

DESIGNER / GESTALTER:

223 Giampietro Geretti
224, 225 Roger Denning
226 Andreas Georgiades
227 Claude Gauthereau
228 Richard Waldron

224

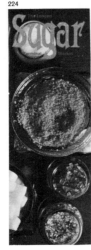

225

ART DIRECTOR / DIRECTEUR ARTISTIQUE:

223 Ennio Lucini
224, 225 Roger Denning
226 Andreas Georgiades
227 Serge Rouland
228 Richard Waldron

AGENCY / AGENTUR / AGENCE – STUDIO:

223 Studio Elle
224, 225 Roger Denning
226 Creative Shop
227 DCI-Agal Publicité
228 Deburgh Graphics

226

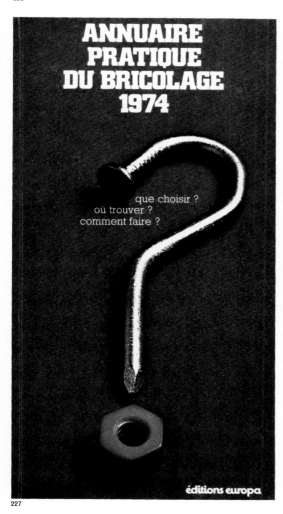

227

228

223 Double spread from a catalogue of *Lema* modular furniture. Left-hand page in colour. The right-hand page shows the designer and architect Angelo Mangiarotti. (ITA)
224, 225 Front cover of a tall booklet about the London sugar terminal market and detail of the complete cover photograph. (GBR)
226 Detail of a point-of-sale showcard. The die-cut circle opens to reveal a Father Christmas drinking a glass of *Amstel* beer, with season's greetings. (GRE)
227 Cover of a catalogue for handymen. Red nut, white lettering, blue ground. (FRA)
228 Detail of the photography used on a catalogue of *Vestric* sunglasses, made in Italy. The catalogue was sent to retail chemists. Full colour on sand. (GBR)

223 Doppelseite aus einem Katalog für neuzeitliche *Lema*-Möbel. Die linke Seite ist mehrfarbig, die rechte zeigt den Gestalter und Architekten Angelo Mangiarotti. (ITA)
224, 225 Vorderseite und Ausschnitt der Aufnahme, die den Umschlag einer Broschüre über den Londoner Zuckermarkt illustriert. (GBR)
226 Verkaufsständer, dessen Kapseloberteil sich heben lässt, so dass darunter der Weihnachtsmann mit Bierglas und Festtagsgrüssen sichtbar wird. (GRE)
227 Umschlag eines Katalogs für Bastler. (FRA)
228 Ausschnitt der Photo zu einem Katalogumschlag für Sonnenbrillen. Der Katalog wurde an Wiederverkäufer versandt. Mehrfarbig auf Beige. (GBR)

223 Page double d'un catalogue pour les meubles contemporains de *Lema*. La page à gauche est en couleur, celle à droite présente le designer et architecte Angelo Mangiarotti. (ITA)
224, 225 Couverture d'une brochure grand format et détail de la photo de couverture. La brochure est consacrée au marché du sucre de Londres. (GBR)
226 Détail d'une carte publicitaire. Le cercle découpé révèle le père Noël buvant un verre de bière *Amstel*. (GRE)
227 Couverture d'un catalogue s'adressant aux hommes à tout faire. Ecrou rouge, texte blanc sur fond bleu. (FRA)
228 Détail de la photo illustrant la couverture d'un catalogue pour les lunettes de soleil *Vestric*, fabriquées en Italie. Le catalogue est destiné aux droguistes. Polychrome. (GBR)

229

231

Booklets / Prospekte / Brochures

230

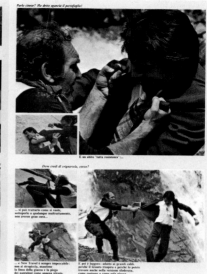

232

229 Double spread in full colour from a booklet introducing BMW Motorsport GmbH, a motor racing enterprise of the BMW company. (GER)
230 Double spread in full colour from a booklet sent to agents and retailers showing examples of the promotion done for *Milus* watches. (SWI)
231–233 Cover, four panels (full colour) and illustration in actual size from a large folder demonstrating in a comics-inspired sequence how a *Facis* suit stands up to wear and tear. (ITA)

229 Doppelseite aus einer mehrfarbigen Broschüre der BMW Motorsport GmbH, Zweigunternehmen der BMW AG. (GER)
230 Doppelseite aus einem mehrfarbigen Prospekt für *Milus*-Wiederverkäufer, mit Angaben über die Werbekampagne der Uhrenfabrik. (SWI)
231–233 Umschlag, Innenseite und originalgrosse Illustration aus einem mehrfarbigen Leporelloprospekt, der in Comics-Manier zeigt, wie widerstandsfähig *Facis*-Anzüge sind. (ITA)

229 Page double en couleur tirée d'une brochure introduisant BMW Motorsport GmbH, une entreprise pour les courses d'autos. (GER)
230 Page double en couleur d'une brochure destinée aux agents et détaillants. Elle présente des exemples de publicité pour les montres *Milus*. (SWI)
231–233 Couverture, quatre panneaux (en couleur) et illustration d'un dépliant grand format. Sous forme d'une bande dessinée, il met en évidence comment les complets *Facis* résistent à l'usure. (ITA)

PHOTOGRAPHER / PHOTOGRAPH / PHOTOGRAPHE:

230 Pierre-Michel Delessert
231–233 Pietro Gagliardi

DESIGNER / GESTALTER / MAQUETTISTE:

229 Joe Hohn
230 Julien van der Wal
231–233 Silvio Saffirio

ART DIRECTOR / DIRECTEUR ARTISTIQUE:

231 Pietro Gagliardi, Marco Silombria, Silvio Saffirio

AGENCY / AGENTUR / AGENCE – STUDIO:

229 Sportive Werbeproduktion GmbH & Co.
230 Caspari Advertising
231–233 Gagliardi Saffirio Silombria

233

234

235

PHOTOGRAPHER / PHOTOGRAPH / PHOTOGRAPHE:

234, 235 Jerry Friedman
236 B Communications
237 Vic Pinto

DESIGNER / GESTALTER / MAQUETTISTE:

236 B Communications
237 Chris Albert

ART DIRECTOR / DIRECTEUR ARTISTIQUE:

234, 235 Constance von Collande
236 B Communications
237 Chris Albert

AGENCY / AGENTUR / AGENCE — STUDIO:

234, 235 Elizabeth Arden, Inc., Creative Dept.
236 B Communications
237 LAP Advertising Ltd.

234, 235 Rectos of two sheets for company salesmen (Fig. 234 in actual size) presenting "full-spectrum" collections of *Elizabeth Arden* lip make-up and nail varnishes. (USA)
236 Cover of a large folder about *Princess Galitzine* cosmetics for sunbathing beauty care. Full colour, vermilion nails. (ITA)
237 Cover of a folder addressed to watch retailers about the *Tissot* watch collection to go with autumn fashions and the advertising programme supporting it. Blue shades, orange lettering. (GBR)

234, 235 Vorderseite zweier Werbeblätter für Wiederverkäufer (Abb. 234 in Originalgrösse) mit dem ganzen Spektrum von *Elizabeth-Arden*-Lippenstiften und -Nagellacken. (USA)
236 Umschlag eines grossformatigen Faltprospekts über *Princess-Galitzine*-Kosmetik für den Strand. Mehrfarbig, Zehennägel zinnoberrot. (ITA)
237 Umschlag eines mehrfarbigen Prospekts für die Wiederverkäufer von *Tissot*-Uhren mit Wiedergabe der neuesten Modelle und Bekanntgabe des Werbeprogramms. Blautöne, Schrift orange. (GBR)

234, 235 Rectos de deux feuilles destinées aux représentants (fig. 234 en grandeur nature). Elles présentent toute la gamme des rouges à lèvres et vernis à ongles d'*Elizabeth Arden*. (USA)
236 Couverture d'un dépliant grand format pour les produits cosmétiques *Princess Galitzine*, pour les bains de soleil. Polychrome, ongles en vermillon. (ITA)
237 Couverture d'un dépliant qui s'adresse aux magasins qui vendent des montres *Tissot*. Il présente les modèles qui s'assortissent à la collection des modes d'automne. Tons bleus, texte en orange. (GBR)

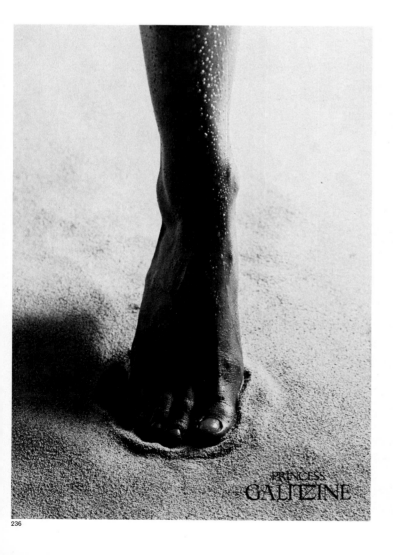

236

237

PHOTOGRAPHER / PHOTOGRAPH / PHOTOGRAPHE:

238–244 Henry Wolf

DESIGNER / GESTALTER / MAQUETTISTE:

238–244 Henry Wolf

ART DIRECTOR / DIRECTEUR ARTISTIQUE:

238–244 Henry Wolf

AGENCY / AGENTUR / AGENCE – STUDIO:

238–244 Henry Wolf

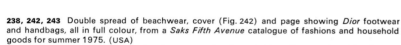

238

239

238, 242, 243 Double spread of beachwear, cover (Fig. 242) and page showing *Dior* footwear and handbags, all in full colour, from a *Saks Fifth Avenue* catalogue of fashions and household goods for summer 1975. (USA)
239–241, 244 Cover and pages showing accessories, household products and watches from a *Saks Fifth Avenue* catalogue for autumn 1974. All in full colour. (USA)

238, 242, 243 Doppelseite mit Strandkleidern, Umschlag (Abb. 242) und Seite mit *Dior*-Schuhen und -Handtaschen aus dem mehrfarbigen Sommerkatalog eines Spezialgeschäfts für Damenmode und Haushaltartikel. (USA)
239–241, 244 Umschlag und Seiten für Modeschmuck, Haushaltartikel und Uhren aus dem mehrfarbigen Herbstkatalog eines Spezialgeschäfts für Damenmode und Haushaltartikel. (USA)

238, 242, 243 Page double consacrée à la nouvelle mode de plage, couverture (fig. 242) et pleine page présentant les souliers et articles en cuir de *Dior*. Eléments figurant dans un catalogue qui présente la collection d'été 1975 des articles de mode et de ménage de la maison *Saks Fifth Avenue*. Entièrement en couleur. (USA)
239–241, 244 Couverture et pages tirées du catalogue d'automne (1974) de *Saks Fifth Avenue*. Il présente la nouvelle collection d'accessoires de mode, d'articles de ménage et de montres. Toutes les illustrations sont en couleur. (USA)

242

Booklets / Prospekte / Brochures

240

241

243

244

246

247

248

PHOTOGRAPHER / PHOTOGRAPH / PHOTOGRAPHE:

245 Larry Willett
246–250 Uwe Ommer
251, 252 Alan Brooking

DESIGNER / GESTALTER / MAQUETTISTE:

245 Ronald Wolin
246–250 M. Pahin
251, 252 Brian Bridge

245

ART DIRECTOR / DIRECTEUR ARTISTIQUE:

245–250 Ronald Wolin
251 252 Brian Bridge

AGENCY / AGENTUR / AGENCE – STUDIO:

245–250 Grey Advertising, Inc.
251, 252 Brian Norman Associates

249

250

251

252

245 Détail du panneau extérieur d'un dépliant consacré à la motocyclette *Honda* à deux temps qui se prête particulièrement aux courses sur un terrain accidenté. En couleur. (USA)
246–250 Couverture (titre en lilas), pages doubles et page figurant dans le catalogue automne/hiver de *Charles Jourdan*. Publicité pour les chaussures, les sacs à main et les accessoires de mode assortis. Toutes les illustrations sont en couleur avec textes en trois langues. (FRA)
251, 252 Couverture et page d'une brochure consacrée au *Mini* de la British Leyland Motor Corp. Les photos couleurs présentent des scènes françaises. (GBR)

245 Vorderseite eines mehrfarbigen Faltprospekts für das Zweitakt-Motorrad *Honda* für Querfeldeinfahrten. (USA)
246–250 Umschlag (Titelschrift violett), Doppelseiten und Seite aus einem Herbst- und Winterkatalog von *Charles Jourdan*, Spezialgeschäft für Damenschuhe und Handtaschen. Mehrfarbig, mit dreisprachigen Legenden in drei verschiedenen Farben. (FRA)
251, 252 Umschlag und Seite einer Broschüre über den von der British Leyland Motor Corp. hergestellten *Mini*-Kleinwagen. Farbaufnahmen französischer Landschaften. (GBR)

245 Detail of the outside of a folder about a *Honda* two-stroke motorcycle for off-road riding. Full colour. (USA)
246–250 Cover (pink title), double spreads and page from a *Charles Jourdan* autumn and winter catalogue of shoes, handbags and accompanying fashions. All in full colour, colour captions in three languages. (FRA)
251, 252 Cover and page of a brochure about the *Mini* made by British Leyland Motor Corp. Colour photographs of scenes in France are used throughout. (GBR)

AIR TREADS, INC.

253

Alling and Cory's distinctive coated papers guarantees "no compromise" of graphics creators' printed expression.

254

258

The night they'd got lost. Sitting and finding the way again by the map-reading light, close together in the warm darkness.

One day they'd taken a picnic to the forest. "You know, it really is a beautiful shape," she'd suddenly remarked, looking at the Spitfire parked across the clearing.

"It most certainly is," he said, looking at her.

And she caught his eye and laughed.

It wasn't very long before they married. There was no point in waiting. From the first, there'd never been any doubts in either of their minds.

Knowing she'd be pleased, he suggested they went on honeymoon in the car.

"You mean you can afford me and the Spitfire?" she said, laughing.

"That's the beauty of it," he replied.

After the Reception, when every last piece of their luggage had gone into the boot, he opened the car door for her.

"What kind of car is this, madam?" he asked.

"Everything we've ever wanted," she said. "Everything we've ever wanted."

259

PHOTOGRAPHER / PHOTOGRAPH / PHOTOGRAPHE:

253 Fred Hunt/Illustrator: James Berry
254 John L. Alexandrowicz
255–257 Günter Derleth
258, 259 John S. Clarke
260, 261 Studio Seekamp

DESIGNER / GESTALTER / MAQUETTISTE:

253 Dan Pruitt
254 Robert Bowden
255–257 Herbert Carl Traue
258, 259 Brian Bridge
260, 261 Manfred Rose

ART DIRECTOR / DIRECTEUR ARTISTIQUE:

253 Tom Wood
254 Robert Bowden
258, 259 Brian Bridge
260, 261 Manfred Rose

AGENCY / AGENTUR / AGENCE – STUDIO:

253 Creative Services, Inc.
254 Robert Bowden
258, 259 Brian Norman Associates
260, 261 CTB

Booklets / Prospekte / Brochures

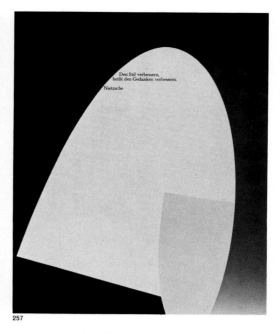

255

256

257

253 Cover of a booklet for Air Treads, Inc., producers of rebuilt aircraft tyres. Bluish tyre, red ground, brown margin. (USA)
254 Inside of a folder about *Alling and Cory* coated papers for high-quality reproduction. Black and white. (USA)
255–257 Pages from a brochure about transparent papers from a supplier in Munich. Each black-and-white photograph is covered by a transparent overlay printed in red. (GER)
258, 259 Double spreads in full colour from a booklet about the *Spitfire*. All the scenes are set in Italy. Yellow car. (GBR)
260, 261 "With *Zanders*, more time for what counts." Detail of the photography and complete cover of a folder about the *Zanders* range of art papers. (GER)

253 Umschlag eines Prospekts für ein Unternehmen, das Flugzeugreifen neugummiert. Bläulicher Reifen, roter Grund. (USA)
254 Innenseite eines Faltprospekts für feines Kunstdruckpapier für anspruchsvolle Reproduktionen. Schwarzweiss. (USA)
255–257 Seiten aus einer Broschüre der 2H-Papier-Grosshandels GmbH, München. Über jeder Schwarzweissaufnahme liegt ein rotbedrucktes Transparentblatt. (GER)
258, 259 Mehrfarbige Doppelseite aus einem Prospekt für *Spitfire*-Automobile. Aufnahmen aus Italien. Auto gelb. (GBR)
260, 261 «Mit *Zanders* mehr Zeit für das, was zählt.» Ausschnitt der Aufnahme und Umschlag eines Faltprospekts für Zanders Feinpapiere GmbH. (GER)

253 Couverture de la brochure d'une maison spécialisée dans la réfection de pneus. Pneu bleu sur fond rouge. (USA)
254 Intérieur d'un dépliant en faveur de papiers couchés pour des reproductions de qualité. Noir et blanc. (USA)
255–257 Pages d'une brochure consacrée aux papiers transparents d'un fabricant munichois. Une feuille transparente, imprimée en rouge, couvre chacune des photos noir-blanc. (GER)
258, 259 Pages doubles en couleur tirées d'une brochure consacrée au *Spitfire*. Photos de scènes italiennes. (GBR)
260, 261 «Avec *Zanders* on a plus de temps pour ce qui compte.» Détail de la photo et couverture qu'elle illustre. Dépliant pour la collection des papiers couchés de *Zanders*. (GER)

260

261

267

262

263

PHOTOGRAPHER / PHOTOGRAPH / PHOTOGRAPHE:

262, 263 Miho
264—268 Flemming Weiland

DESIGNER / GESTALTER / MAQUETTISTE:

262, 263 Miho
264—268 Flemming Weiland/J. Ricken

ART DIRECTOR / DIRECTEUR ARTISTIQUE:

262, 263 Edward Russell, Jr.
264—268 Flemming Weiland

AGENCY / AGENTUR / AGENCE — STUDIO:

262, 263 Miho, Inc.
264—268 Poul Juncher a/s Fotografi

idea

size

finish

264

265

266

262, 263 Cover and double spread from an issue of *Imagination*, a publication of Champion International Corp., papermakers, devoted to the safari. Cover in full colour, lion and cheetah in yellow shades, interleaved text on tinted papers. (USA)
264—268 Four complete pages, with detail of the photography used on one of them, from a large spirally bound booklet issued by A/S Ricken, suppliers of display material. All illustrations in full colour. (DEN)

262, 263 Umschlag (mehrfarbig) und Doppelseite in Gelbtönen aus der Publikation *Imagination* der Papierfabrik *Champion*. Diese Ausgabe ist der afrikanischen Tierwelt gewidmet. Die eingehefteten Textblätter mit Hinweisen auf die abgebildeten Tiere sind auf verschiedenfarbigem Papier gedruckt. (USA)
264—268 Vier ganze Seiten und originalgrosse Aufnahme aus einem grossformatigen, spiralgehefteten Prospekt eines Herstellers von Werbematerial. Mehrfarbig. (DEN)

262, 263 Couverture et page double d'un numéro de la publication *Imagination*, de Champion International Corp. Le numéro est consacré aux safaris. Couverture en couleur, lion et guépard en tons jaunes, texte sur feuilles intercalées. (USA)
264—268 Quatre pages avec détail de l'une des photographies. Eléments figurant dans une brochure grand format, à reliure spirale, publiée par un fabricant de matériel d'exposition. Toutes les illustrations sont en couleur. (DEN)

speed

268

Booklets / Prospekte / Brochures

269

270

PHOTOGRAPHER / PHOTOGRAPH / PHOTOGRAPHE:

269, 270 Peter Jochen Schott
271, 272 Brian Brandt
273 Elliott Erwitt
274 Kai Schmakowski

DESIGNER / GESTALTER / MAQUETTISTE:

269, 270 Peter Mattis
271, 272 Andy Schmid
273 Dawson D. Zaug/Ellen Smith
274 Gerd Zimmermann

ART DIRECTOR / DIRECTEUR ARTISTIQUE:

269, 270 Peter Jochen Schott
271, 272 Andy Schmidt
273 Reginald R. Jones
274 Gerd Zimmermann

AGENCY / AGENTUR / AGENCE:

269, 270 Schott GmbH
271, 272 Andy Schmidt
273 Unigraphics
274 Gerd Zimmermann

269, 270 Detail of the photography and complete magazine insert ("Insiders have known it for a long time ...") for Edelmann packaging. (GER)
271, 272 Two black-and-white double spreads from a catalogue of the well-designed Décor plastic kitchenware and household products made by Brian Davis and Company Pty. Ltd. (AUL)
273 Double spread from a booklet about forest management issued by the manufacturers of Crown Zellerbach papers. The full-colour photograph shows aerial fertilization from a helicopter above Tillamook Forest, Oregon. (USA)
274 Double spread in full colour from a brochure on Viaflex plastic bags for airless infusion in hospitals. (GER)

269, 270 Aufnahme und Vorderseite des Beilageblattes für Carl Edelmann GmbH, Heidenheim, einen Verpackungsgestalter. (GER)
271, 272 Schwarzweisse Doppelseiten aus dem Katalog einer Fabrik für Geschirr und Haushaltartikel aus Plastik. (AUL)
273 Doppelseite aus einem Prospekt über Waldbewirtschaftung einer Papierfabrik. Die mehrfarbige Aufnahme zeigt eine Befruchtung vom Helikopter aus. (USA)
274 Mehrfarbige Doppelseite aus einem Prospekt für Viaflex-Plastikbeutel, die für Infusionen in Krankenhäusern verwendet werden. Hergestellt von Travenol GmbH, München. (GER)

269, 270 Détail de la photographie et encart de magazine où elle figure («Les insiders sont au courant depuis longtemps ...»). Publicité pour les emballages Edelmann. (GER)
271, 272 Deux pages doubles en noir et blanc tirées d'un catalogue consacré aux articles en matière plastique pour la cuisine et le ménage. (AUL)
273 Page double d'une brochure contenant des informations sur la gestion des forêts. Publication d'un fabricant de papiers. Les photographies en couleurs se réfèrent à la fertilisation du Tillamook Forest, Oregon, à l'aide d'un hélicoptère. (USA)
274 Page double en couleur tirée d'une brochure consacrée aux sacs en matière plastique, utilisés pour les infusions à l'hôpital. (GER)

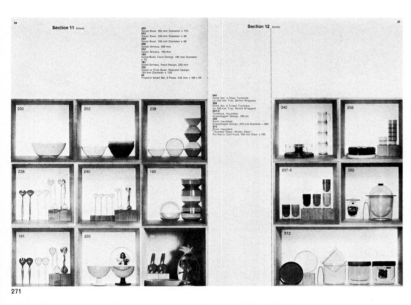

271

272

273

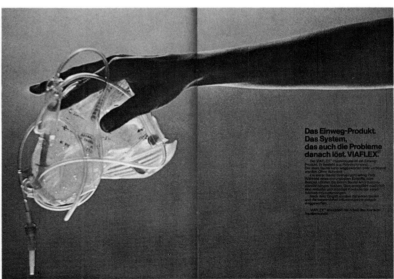

274

275

275 Double spread from a brochure about career opportunities with Radio-Schweiz AG, a telecommunications company. Full-colour photographs on black. (SWI)
276 Colour cover of a booklet on co-operation issued by a farmers' association. (AUS)
277 Page from an issue of *Imagination,* a publication of Champion International Corp., devoted to Hong Kong. The subject is Chinese food. Full colour. (USA)
278, 279 Cover and opening spread of a newspaper-size space promotion insert to attract corporate advertising to the Op-Ed page of *The New York Times.* Black and white. (USA)
280 Double spread from a booklet about career opportunities with Barclays Bank Ltd., here with reference to computer, secretarial and specialist staff. (GBR)

275 Doppelseite aus einer Broschüre der Radio-Schweiz AG mit Auskünften über die Ausbildungs- und Berufsmöglichkeiten bei dieser Firma. Mehrfarbig auf schwarzem Grund. (SWI)
276 Mehrfarbiger Umschlag einer Broschüre über die Gemeinschaftsarbeit des Österreichischen Bauernbundes. (AUS)
277 Seite aus der Publikation *Imagination* der *Champion*-Papierfabrik. Diese Ausgabe ist Hongkong gewidmet und enthält einen Bericht über die chinesische Küche. Mehrfarbig. (USA)
278, 279 Umschlag und Doppelseite aus einer Beilage in Zeitungsgrösse zur Inserentenwerbung für die *New York Times.* Schwarzweiss. (USA)
280 Doppelseite aus einer Broschüre über die Berufsaussichten in einem Bankhaus. Die Seiten beziehen sich auf Computerfachleute und Sekretärinnen. (GBR)

275 Page double d'une brochure consacrée aux possibilités d'avancement dans une compagnie de télécommunications. Photographie en couleur sur fond noir. (SWI)
276 Couverture en couleur de la brochure d'une association de paysans. Publication consacrée à la coopération. (AUS)
277 Page d'un numéro d'*Imagination,* une publication de Champion International Corp. Ce numéro est consacré à Hong-Kong. La photo présente des produits alimentaires chinois. (USA)
278, 279 Couverture et première page double (format de journal) d'un encart promotionnel visant à stimuler la publicité à la page Op-Ed du *New York Times.* Noir et blanc. (USA)
280 Page double d'une brochure sur les possibilités d'avancement auprès de la Barclays Bank. Les photos se réfèrent aux divers domaines d'activités: opérateurs électroniques, secrétaires, employés spécialisés. (GBR)

WIR GEMEINSAM

276

The New York Times Op-Ed Page: America's most efficient corporate advertising showcase.

Booklets
Prospekte
Brochures

278   279

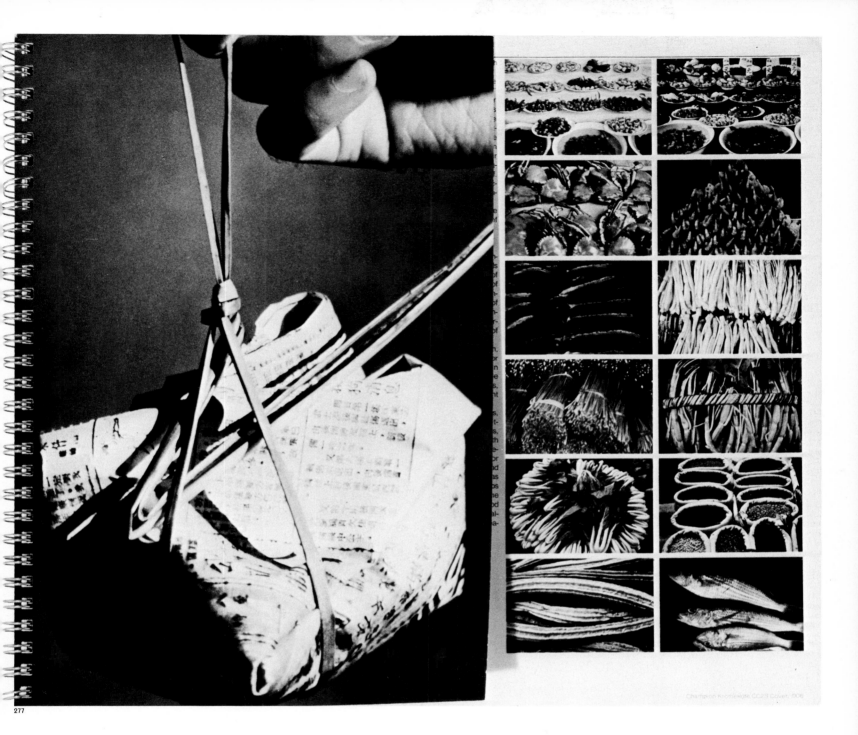

Champion Kromekote, CC2S Cover, 1976

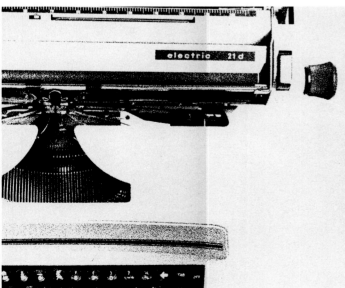

PHOTOGRAPHER / PHOTOGRAPH / PHOTOGRAPHE:

275 Foto Rodo
276 Hans Tropper
277 Miho
278, 279 Al Wegener
280 Michael McDermott

DESIGNER / GESTALTER / MAQUETTISTE:

275 Hermann Eigenmann
276 Karl Neubacher
277 Miho
278, 279 Arnold Kushner
280 Andrew Augustyn

ART DIRECTOR / DIRECTEUR ARTISTIQUE:

275 Hermann Eigenmann
276 Karl Neubacher
277 Miho/Edward Russell, Jr.
278, 279 Andrew Kner
280 Renaud Spencer

AGENCY / AGENTUR / AGENCE — STUDIO:

275 Hermann Eigenmann
277 Miho, Inc.
280 Format Arts Ltd./MRT Studio Ltd.

281

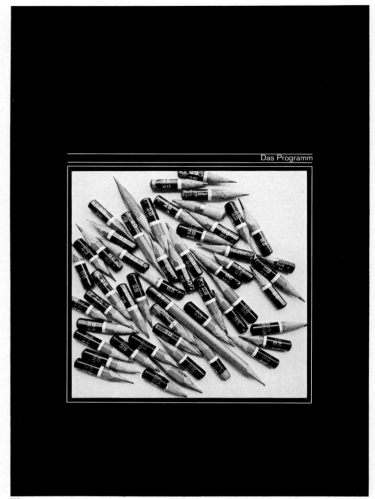

Das Programm

282

281 Page from the programme of the 1974 Edinburgh International Festival. Printed in dark blue and black. (GBR)
282 Intermediate page from a programme of the Bavarian radio authority. Black, blue and white pencil stubs. (GER)
283 Cover of a brochure about tours to Japan organized by *Japan Airlines*. Gold title, blue-green sky and pagoda. (GBR)
284 Page printed in shades of blue from a booklet about Cologne ("Cologne for the Eye"), issued by the city tourist office. (GER)
285, 286 Opening spread, with detail of the photography, from a large brochure about the XXII Olympic Games to be held in Los Angeles in 1980. (USA)

281 Seite aus dem Programmheft für die internationalen Edinburger Festspiele 1974. Dunkelblau und Schwarz. (GBR)
282 Aus einer Serie von Zwischenblättern aus dem Programm des Bayerischen Rundfunks, München. Blau-weiss-schwarze Bleistiftstummel. (GER)
283 Umschlag eines Prospekts für Japanreisen der Luftverkehrsgesellschaft *Japan Airlines*. Titelschrift Gold, Himmel und Pagode blaugrün. (GBR)
284 In Blautönen gehaltene Seite aus dem Photobuch «Köln fürs Auge», herausgegeben vom Verkehrsamt der Stadt Köln. (GER)
285, 286 Erste Doppelseite und Aufnahme aus einer grossformatigen Broschüre über die XXII. Olympischen Spiele 1980 in Los Angeles. (USA)

281 Page figurant dans le programme pour le Festival International 1974 d'Edimbourg. Impression en bleu foncé et noir. (GBR)
282 Page intercalée figurant dans le programme publié par la radiodiffusion-télévision bavaroise. Bouts de crayon en noir, bleu et blanc. (GER)
283 Couverture d'une brochure présentant différents tours du Japon, organisés par la compagnie aérienne *Japan Airlines*. Titre en or, ciel et pagode en bleu vert. (GBR)
284 Page imprimée en tons bleus. Elément d'une brochure consacrée à Cologne («Cologne pour les yeux»). Cette brochure a été publiée par l'office du tourisme de la ville. (GER)
285, 286 Première page double et détail de la photographie qui l'illustre. Eléments d'une brochure grand format consacrée au XXIIe Jeux Olympiques qui auront lieu en 1980 à Los Angeles. (USA)

Booklets / Prospekte / Brochures

Japan
Jaltour
JAL TOUR

283

PHOTOGRAPHER / PHOTOGRAPH / PHOTOGRAPHE:

281 BBC
282 Walter Tafelmaier
283 Michael Boys
284 Heinz Wedewardt
285, 286 Bob Stevens/Don Hale

DESIGNER / GESTALTER / MAQUETTISTE:

281 Hans Schleger and Associates
282 Walter Tafelmeier
283 Robert Custance
284 Heinz Wedewardt
285, 286 James Guerard

ART DIRECTOR / DIRECTEUR ARTISTIQUE:

281 Hans Schleger
283 Neville Eldridge
285, 286 Robert Miles Runyan

AGENCY / AGENTUR / AGENCE – STUDIO:

283 Bloy Eldridge, Ltd.
285, 286 Robert Miles Runyan & Associates, Inc.

284

285

286

113

287

287, 288 Spread and detail of the photography from a brochure about the Rochester Institute of Technology's College of Graphic Arts and Photography, for a fund-raising campaign. (USA)
289 Envelope (printed in red) for a mailer about a learning kit for elementary schools developed by Discovery Workshop. (USA)
290 From a series of folders presenting the work of a printer. The photographer projected a shot of snakeskin on to the body of the model. (SWI)
291 Greetings card with "fruitful wishes" from an agency in Turin. Full colour. (ITA)
292 Programme for a performance of an old Spanish play in Hamburg. Red blood-stain, pale green ground. (GER)
293 Cover of a programme for a play performed in Hamburg. Shades of blue. (GER)

287, 288 Doppelseite und Photographie aus einer Broschüre zur Mittelbeschaffung für die Graphik- und Photographieabteilung des Rochester Institute of Technology. (USA)
289 Umschlag (Rotdruck) zu einem Prospekt über neuartige Lernprogramme und -geräte für Volksschüler. (USA)
290 Aus einer Serie von Faltprospekten für die Offsetdruckerei H. Haller, Zürich. Der Photograph projizierte eine Schlangenhautaufnahme auf den Körper des Modells. (SWI)
291 Karte mit «fruchtbaren» Wünschen einer Werbeagentur. In Mehrfarbendruck. (ITA)
292, 293 Programmumschläge des Hamburger Thalia-Theaters. Abb. 292 für ein altspanisches Bühnenstück, roter Blutfleck, heller Grund. Abb. 293 in Blautönen. (GER)

287, 288 Page double et détail de la photo qui l'illustre. Cette brochure du College of Graphic Arts and Photography du Rochester Institute of Technology a été publiée afin de réunir des fonds. (USA)
289 Enveloppe (imprimée en rouge) d'une brochure au sujet de matériel d'enseignement destiné aux écoles primaires. (USA)
290 D'une série de dépliants présentant le travail d'un imprimeur. La photo de la peau d'un serpent a été projetée sur le corps d'un modèle. (SWI)
291 Carte de vœux d'une agence publicitaire de Turin. En couleur. (ITA)
292 Programme pour la présentation d'une ancienne pièce de théâtre espagnole, mise en scène par le Théâtre Thalia à Hambourg. Tache de sang rouge, fond en vert pâle. (GER)
293 Couverture du programme pour une pièce de théâtre présentée à Hambourg. Tons bleus. (GER)

PHOTOGRAPHER / PHOTOGRAPH / PHOTOGRAPHE:

287, 288 Bob Chebby
289 Ken Korsh
290 Jost Wildbolz
291 Angelo Corrias
292, 293 Holger Matthies

DESIGNER / GESTALTER / MAQUETTISTE:

287, 288 John Kuchera
291 Luciano Graneris
292, 293 Holger Matthies

ART DIRECTOR / DIRECTEUR ARTISTIQUE:

287, 288 John Kuchera
289 Linda Hinrichs
291 Armando Testa
292, 293 Holger Matthies

AGENCY / AGENTUR / AGENCE – STUDIO:

287, 288 Hutchins/Darcy Inc.
289 Hinrichs Design Associates
290 H.R. Abächerli
291 Armando Testa
292, 293 Holger Matthies

288

auguri fruttuosi

291

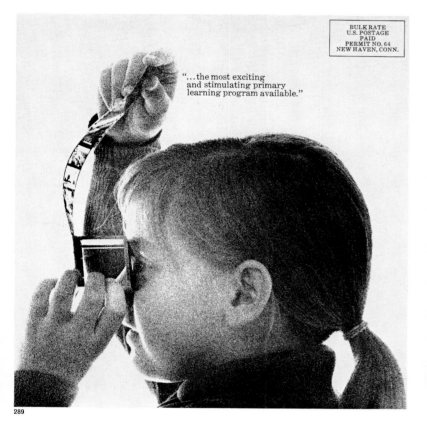

289

290

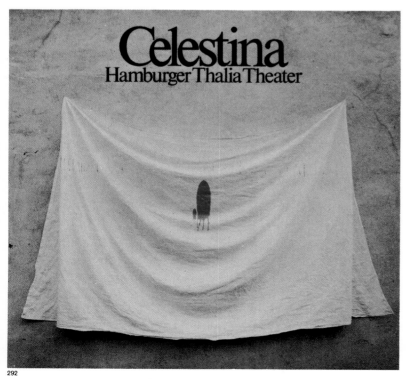

Celestina
Hamburger Thalia Theater

292

Anatol
Hamburger Thalia Theater

293

115

294

294, 295 Photograph and two panels of a sales promotion folder about the audience popularity of the entertainment offered by WABC Television. (USA)
296–300 Cover and four pages in full colour from a series of three direct-mail booklets sent out by Murrie-White & Associates, a design firm. The photographs show various products designed by the company, presented by Chicago's "best" people in their various trades and pastimes. (USA)

294, 295 Photographie und Doppelseite aus einem Faltprospekt mit Angaben über die Beliebtheit der unterhaltenden Programme einer Fernsehanstalt. (USA)
296–300 Umschlag und vier Seiten aus einer Serie von drei Prospekten einer Firma für Packungs-gestaltung. Die Aufnahmen zeigen von ihr entworfene Packungen in den Händen der jeweils in ihrem Beruf oder bei ihren Liebhabereien «Besten» aus Chicago. (USA)

294, 295 Photographie et deux panneaux d'un dépliant promotionnel dans lequel figurent les résultats d'une enquête concernant la popularité des programmes de divertissement diffusés par la TV WABC. (USA)
296–300 Couverture et quatre pages (toutes en couleurs) d'une série de trois éléments de pu-blicité directe distribués par une entreprise spécialisée dans le design industriel. Les photos montrent divers produits conçus par cette entreprise. Les articles sont présentés par les gens de Chicago les plus «qualifiés», soit dans leurs métiers, soit dans leurs activités de loisir. (USA)

PHOTOGRAPHER / PHOTOGRAPH / PHOTOGRAPHE:

294, 295 Robert Colten
297–300 Jean Moss

DESIGNER / GESTALTER / MAQUETTISTE:

294, 295 Diana Graham
296–300 Jim Lienhart

ART DIRECTOR / DIRECTEUR ARTISTIQUE:

294, 295 Mark L. Handler
296–300 Jim Lienhart

AGENCY / AGENTUR / AGENCE – STUDIO:

296–300 Murrie-White & Associates

296

295

MARY LOUISE RAGANO, CHICAGO'S BEST HAIR STYLIST

297

ALEX, CHICAGO'S BEST TRICK DOG

DESIGN & CONCEPT JIM LIENHART   PHOTOGRAPHY JEAN MOSS

298

JIM HIGGINS, CHICAGO'S BEST FIRECHIEF

299

BEN WEINER, CHICAGO'S BEST CAB DRIVER

300

117

301

301 Complete cover of a brochure for a glassworks in Mainz. (GER)
302 New Year's greetings from a compositor. Continents made up of type matter in a composing case symbolize the worldwide importance of typesetting. (GER)
303 Cover of a spirally-bound full-colour booklet about *Uniplant* road construction machines. (GER)
304, 305 Double spread and detail of the photography in actual size from a self-promotion reprint about the photographer. (ITA)

301 Vorder- und Rückseite des Umschlags einer Broschüre der Jenaer Glaswerk Schott & Gen. (GER)
302 Neujahrsglückwunsch des Type Service Leyhausen, Düsseldorf. Die mit Bleilettern dargestellten Erdteile versinnbildlichen die weltweite Bedeutung des Schriftsatzes. (GER)
303 Umschlag einer mehrfarbigen, spiralgehefteten Broschüre für *Uniplant*-Strassenbaumaschinen. (GER)
304, 305 Doppelseite und originalgrosse Photographie aus dem Nachdruck eines Artikels über einen Photographen und Bühnenbildner, den dieser zur Eigenwerbung in Broschürenform herausgab. (ITA)

301 Couverture de la brochure d'une verrerie à Mayence. (GER)
302 Carte de vœux de Nouvel-An d'un typographe. Les continents composés par les caractères d'imprimerie devraient symboliser l'importance de la typographie dans le monde entier. (GER)
303 Couverture d'une brochure, à reliure spirale, consacrée aux machines pour la construction des routes. En couleur. (GER)
304, 305 Page double et détail de la photographie (grandeur nature) figurant dans un tirage à part qu'un photographe a utilisé pour son auto-promotion. (ITA)

302

303

PHOTOGRAPHER / PHOTOGRAPH:

301, 303 Kroehl Design Gruppe
302 Axel Vasco Gnad
304, 305 Serge Lutens

DESIGNER / GESTALTER / MAQUETTISTE:

301, 303 Heinz Kroehl/Peter Offenberg
302 Klaus Winterhager
304, 305 Serge Lutens

ART DIRECTOR / DIRECTEUR ARTISTIQUE:

301, 303 Heinz Kroehl
302 Klaus Winterhager
304, 305 Alberto Piovani

AGENCY / AGENTUR / AGENCE – STUDIO:

301, 303 Kroehl Design Gruppe

serge lutens

304

Booklets / Prospekte
Brochures

306

307

306, 307 Double spread with gatefold, and detail of the right-hand page in actual size, from a brochure about Brenner's Park-Hotel in Baden-Baden, underlining the luxurious accommodation, the social life and the wide spectrum of entertainments in and around the watering-place. (GER)
308, 309 Large colour photographs used for direct-mail self-promotion by Randy Miller, Inc., photographers. Chiefly in shades of brown. (USA)

306, 307 Doppelseite mit Ausleger und Ausschnitt der rechten Seite (in Originalgrösse) eines Prospekts für Brenner's Park-Hotel, Baden-Baden, der auf die luxuriöse Unterkunft und das gesellschaftliche Leben des Kurortes hinweist. (GER)
308, 309 Grossformatige Farbaufnahmen zur Eigenwerbung eines Photo-Studios. Hauptsächlich Brauntöne. (USA)

306, 307 Triple page et détail de la page à droite (grandeur nature). Eléments d'une brochure consacrée à l'Hôtel du Parc à Baden-Baden. Les illustrations se réfèrent aux intérieurs luxueux, à la vie sociale ainsi qu'à la grande variété de divertissements offerts dans la ville même et aux allentours. (GER)
308, 309 Photographies grand format figurant dans une brochure de publicité directe. Autopromotion d'un groupe de photographes. Prédominance de tons bruns. (USA)

Booklets / Prospekte / Brochures

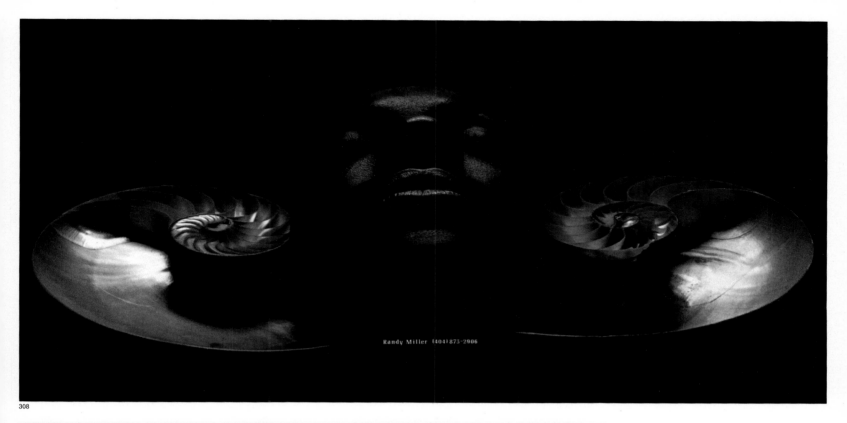

308

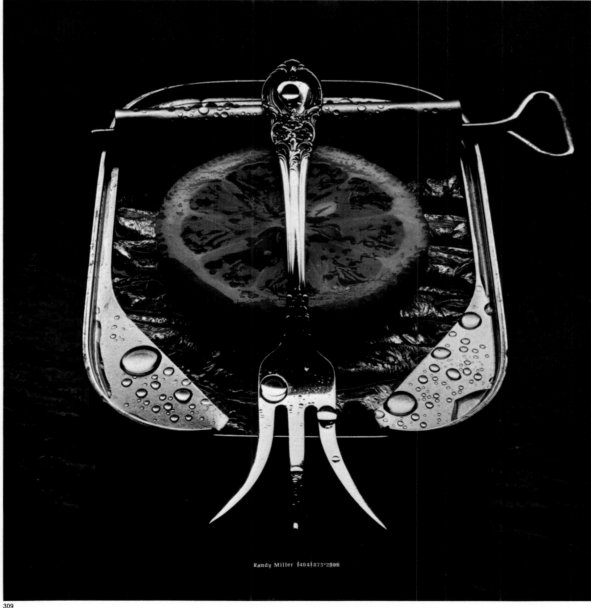

309

PHOTOGRAPHER / PHOTOGRAPH

306, 307 Guido Mangold
308, 309 Randy Miller

DESIGNER / GESTALTER / MAQUETTISTE:

306, 307 Heinz Kroehl/Peter Offenberg
308 Bill Sweeny
309 Randy Miller

ART DIRECTOR / DIRECTEUR ARTISTIQUE:

306, 307 Heinz Kroehl
308 Bill Sweeny
309 Randy Miller

AGENCY / AGENTUR / AGENCE – STUDIO:

306, 307 Kroehl Design Gruppe
308, 309 Randy Miller, Inc.

3

Calendars

Kalender

Calendriers

310

311

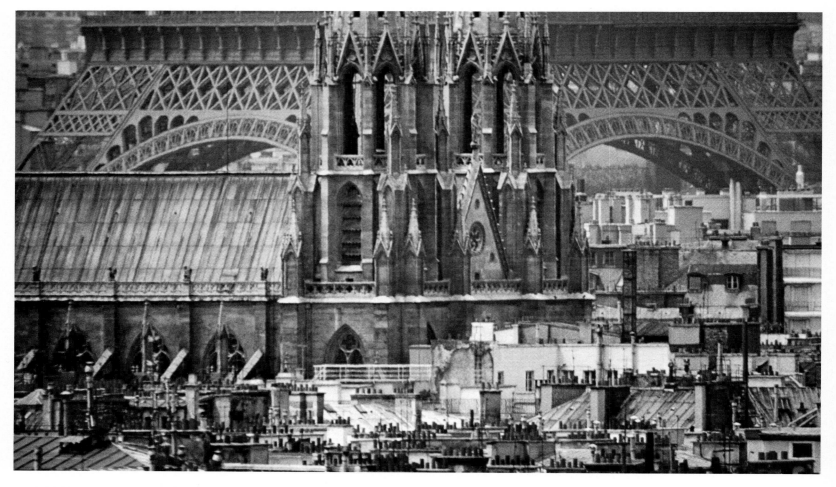

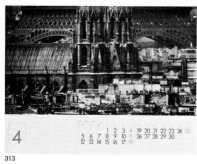

313

310, 311 Two sheets from a large calendar issued by Roberts Graphic Arts, South El Monte, Cal., In the picture of the three nuns, the flair effect around the white has been obtained with a cinematic diffusion lens. In Fig. 311, the photograph is in coarse-grained black and white except for the full-colour reflection in the mirror. (USA)
312, 313 Photograph of Paris in purple and red shades and complete sheet from the *Cityfoto* calendar, which presents twelve cities and provides information on them on the verso. (GER)
314, 315 Detail of an illustration showing multiple reflections of a glass designer and complete spread of a spirally bound calendar published by a glassworks, Vereinigte Glaswerke, Aachen, a German associate of *Saint-Gobain*. (GER)

310, 311 Zwei Monatsblätter aus dem grossformatigen Kalender eines Unternehmens der graphischen Industrie. Bei der Aufnahme der drei Nonnen wurde der helle Saum rund um die weissen Hauben durch ein Diffusionsobjektiv erreicht. Bei Abb. 311 handelt es sich um eine grobkörnige Schwarzweissaufnahme mit Ausnahme des mehrfarbigen Bildes im Spiegel. (USA)
312, 313 Aufnahme von Paris in violetten und roten Tönen und ganzes Monatsblatt aus dem Kunstkalender *Cityfoto* der Accidentia Druck- und Verlags-GmbH, Düsseldorf. Die 12 Blätter sind 12 Städten gewidmet, über die auf der Rückseite nähere Informationen gegeben werden. (GER)
314, 315 Ausschnitt einer Aufnahme mit Spiegelungen und ganzes Blatt aus einem spiralgehefteten Kalender der Vereinigten Glaswerke, der deutschen Gruppe von *Saint Gobain*. (GER)

310, 311 Deux feuilles d'un grand calendrier publié par Roberts Graphic Arts. Dans la photo des trois religieuses, un effet scintillant a été obtenu à l'aide d'un objectif spécial. L'autre illustration est en noir et blanc, à l'exception des réflexions polychromes dans le mirroir. (USA)
312, 313 Photo de la ville de Paris en tons violacés et rouges et feuille qu'elle illustre. Ce calendrier de *Cityfoto* présente douze vues de différentes villes du monde entier; les informations s'y référant se trouvent au verso de chaque feuille. (GER)
314, 315 Détail d'une illustration à réflexions multiples (souffleur de verre) et page double correspondante d'un calendrier à reliure spirale, publié par les verreries Vereinigte Glaswerke, Aachen, une compagnie associée à la verrerie *Saint-Gobain*. (GER)

PHOTOGRAPHER / PHOTOGRAPH / PHOTOGRAPHE:

310, 311 James B. Wood
312, 313 Francisco Hidalgo
314, 315 Hermann Weisweiler

DESIGNER / GESTALTER / MAQUETTISTE:

310, 311 Leo Bestgen
312, 313 Olaf Leu Design
314, 315 Herbert Titz

ART DIRECTOR / DIRECTEUR ARTISTIQUE:

310, 311 Leo Bestgen
312, 313 Olaf Leu
314, 315 Herbert Titz

AGENCY / AGENTUR / AGENCE – STUDIO:

310, 311 Roberts Graphic Arts
312, 313 Olaf Leu Design
314, 315 Herbert Titz

315

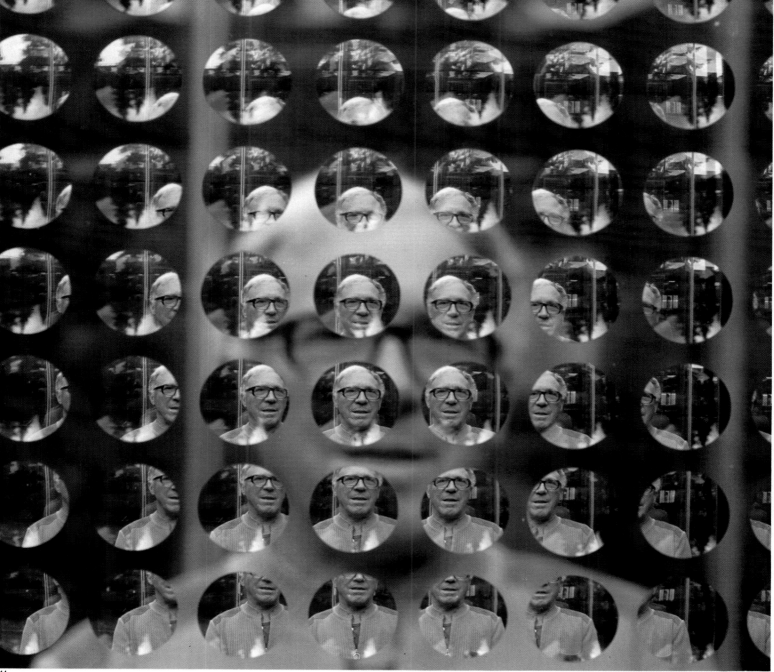

314

Calendars / Kalender / Calendriers

PHOTOGRAPHER / PHOTOGRAPH / PHOTOGRAPHE:

316, 316 a + b Albrecht Ade
317, 318 Umihiko Konishi

DESIGNER / GESTALTER / MAQUETTISTE:

316, 316 a + b Albrecht Ade
317, 318 Hide Gotho

ART DIRECTOR / DIRECTEUR ARTISTIQUE:

316, 316 a + b Albrecht Ade
317, 318 Kaju Yoshida

AGENCY / AGENTUR / AGENCE – STUDIO:

316, 316 a + b Albrecht Ade
    Zanders Feinpapier GmbH, Abteilung Werbung
317, 318 Toppan, Inc.

316, 316a, 316b Detail of a photograph and two complete sheets from a calendar issued by *Zanders*, a paper manufacturer. (GER)
317, 318 Two sheets of a calendar issued by *Pola* cosmetics with fashion shots in subdued colours, each sheet presenting a different product at bottom right. (JPN)

316, 316a, 316b Ausschnitt der Aufnahme und zwei vollständige Blätter aus einem von der Papierfabrik *Zanders* herausgegebenen Kalender. (GER)
317, 318 Zwei Blätter aus dem Kalender einer Kosmetikfirma mit Aufnahmen in zarten Farbtönen. Jedes Zweimonatsblatt zeigt rechts unten ein Produkt der Firma. (JPN)

316, 316a 316b Détail d'une photographie et deux feuilles complètes figurant dans un calendrier de la papeterie *Zanders*. (GER)
317, 318 Deux feuilles d'un calendrier publié par une entreprise de produits cosmétiques. Les feuilles avec des photos de modes en couleurs atténuées présentent chacune, dans la partie inférieure à droite, un produit différent. (JPN)

316a

316b

317

318

319

319–322 Three of the motifs and one complete sheet of a large calendar for the *Roche* sleep-inducing drug *Mogadan,* with relaxed sleepers in various settings. (GER)
323, 324 Photograph in green shades of waves on the Donegal coast, Ireland, from a calendar issued by the marketing division of AEG-Telefunken. (GER)

319–322 Drei Motive und ganzes Blatt eines grossformatigen Kalenders, mit dem Hoffmann-La Roche AG, Grenzach, für das reizabschirmende Schlafmittel *Mogadan* wirbt. (GER)
323, 324 Aufnahme der Brandung an der Donegalküste (Irland) aus dem Kalender der Allgemeinen Elektrizitäts-Gesellschaft AEG Telefunken, Frankfurt. Grüntöne. (GER)

319–322 Trois motifs et l'une des feuilles complètes figurant dans un calendrier grand format pour le somnifère *Mogadan* de Roche. Photos de gens dormant tranquillement dans des environnements divers. (GER)
323, 324 Vue de la côte de Donegal en Irlande avec des vagues en tons verts. D'un calendrier du département du marketing d'une compagnie industrielle. (GER)

320

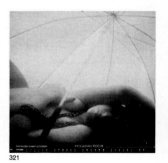

321

323

322

324

PHOTOGRAPHER / PHOTOGRAPH / PHOTOGRAPHE:

319–322 Hans Schweiss
323, 324 Thomas Höpker

DESIGNER / GESTALTER / MAQUETTISTE:

319–322 Hans Schweiss
323, 324 Werner E. Müller

ART DIRECTOR / DIRECTEUR ARTISTIQUE:

319–322 Hans Schweiss
323, 324 Werner E. Müller

AGENCY / AGENTUR / AGENCE – STUDIO:

319–322 Schweiss Gruppe
323, 324 AEG-Telefunken, Zentrale Werbeabteilung

Calendars / Kalender / Calendriers

326

325

327

330

328

329

PHOTOGRAPHER / PHOTOGRAPH:

325 Jay Maisel
326–329 Sarah Moon
330 Alan Boyd

DESIGNER / GESTALTER:

326–330 Arnold Schwartzman

ART DIRECTOR:

326–330 Arnold Schwartzman

AGENCY / AGENTUR / AGENCE:

326–330 Wasey Campbell-Ewald

325 One of the twelve motifs by an American photographer used in a calendar for Caterpillar Tractor Co. (JPN)
326–330 Examples of the photography, complete sheet and cover of a jubilee calendar issued by *Philips* and recalling in highly atmospheric shots some of the events and situations of the last fifty years. (NLD)

325 Eines der Motive eines amerikanischen Photographen, die in einem Kalender für *Caterpillar* erschienen. (JPN)
326–330 Beispiele der Aufnahmen, ganzes Monatsblatt und Deckblatt des Kalenders zum fünfzigjährigen Bestehen von *Philips*. Die Photos und dazwischengebundenen Zeitungsseiten erinnern an Ereignisse der letzten 50 Jahre. (NLD)

325 Détail d'une feuille figurant dans un calendrier pour les tracteurs *Caterpillar*. (JPN)
326–330 Photos, feuille complète et couverture d'un calendrier publié par *Philips* pour célébrer les cinquante ans d'existence. Les photos ainsi que les pages de journaux intercalées évoquent différents événements de cette période. (NLD)

Calendars
Kalender
Calendriers

331

332

331 Wall calendar for *Calanda* beer. Shades of brown and yellow. (SWI)
332–334 Two photographs and one complete sheet from a calendar issued by *Unipart*, a division of British Leyland. Full colour, Fig. 332 chiefly in shades of blue. (GBR)
335 Detail of one of the four sheets from a calendar issued by a photoengraver, Reprocolor/Llovet S.A. The motif symbolizes the great step made in communications from the quill to the electronic age. (SPA)

331 Abreisskalender für Calanda-Bräu, Chur. Braun- und Gelbtöne. (SWI)
332–334 Aufnahmen und ganzes Blatt aus dem mehrfarbigen Kalender einer britischen Automobilfabrik. Abb. 332 in Blautönen. (GBR)
335 Ausschnitt aus einem der vier Blätter des Kalenders einer Clichéanstalt. Das Motiv weist auf die grosse Entwicklung vom Schreibkiel zur elektronischen Übermittlung hin. (SPA)

331 Calendrier mural pour la bière *Calanda*. Tons bruns et jaunes. (SWI)
332–334 Deux photos et feuille complète d'un calendrier d'*Unipart*, une entreprise associée à la *British Leyland*. Toutes les feuilles sont en couleur, la fig. 332 en tons bleus prédominants. (GBR)
335 Détail de l'une des quatre feuilles figurant dans le calendrier d'un photolithographe. Le motif devrait symboliser le grand pas en avant qu'on a fait dans le domaine des communications – de la plume d'oie à l'âge de la communication électronique. (SPA)

PHOTOGRAPHER / PHOTOGRAPH:

331 Dominic Schneider
332–334 Francis Giacobetti
335 Reprocolor Ilovet S.A.

DESIGNER / GESTALTER / MAQUETTISTE:

332–334 Derek Forsyth
335 José Baquès

ART DIRECTOR / DIRECTEUR ARTISTIQUE:

331 Erich Hartmann
332–334 Derek Forsyth
335 José Baquès

AGENCY / AGENTUR / AGENCE – STUDIO:

331 Gisler + Gisler
332–334 Derek Forsyth Graphics Ltd.
335 Estudio Baquès

333

334

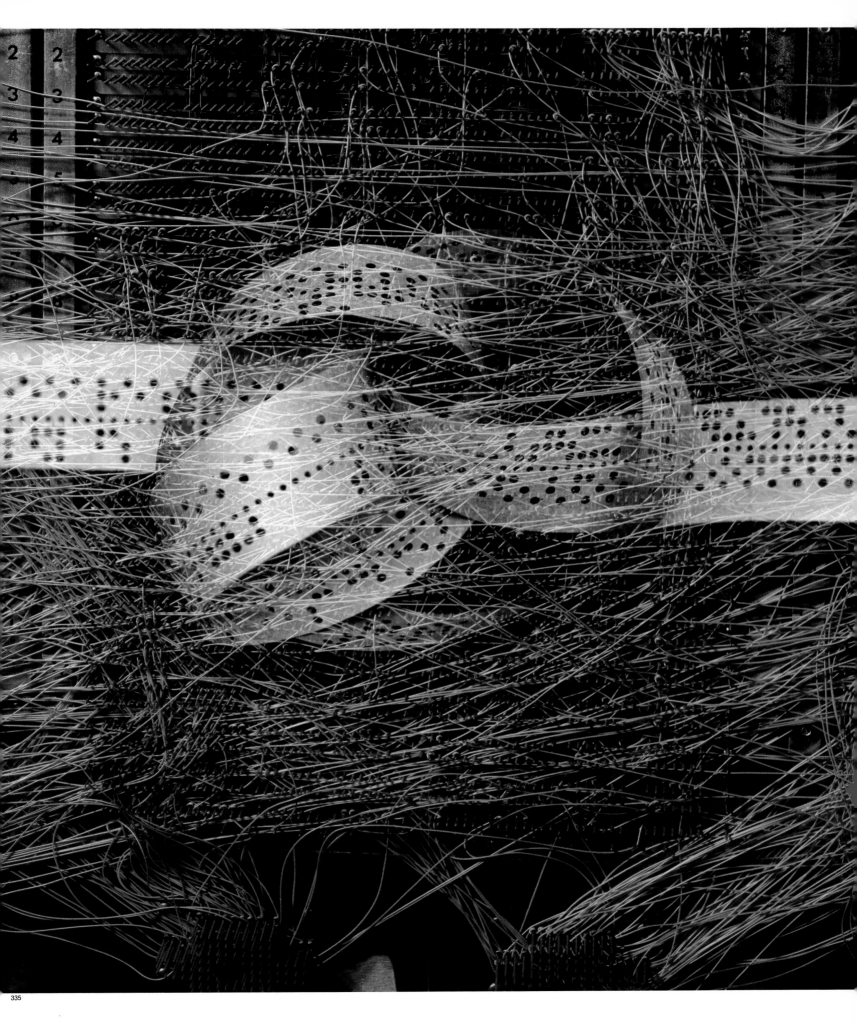

335

336

PHOTOGRAPHER / PHOTOGRAPH / PHOTOGRAPHE:

336, 337 Harald Mante
338, 339 Jorn Freddie

DESIGNER / GESTALTER / MAQUETTISTE:

336, 337 Olaf Leu Design

ART DIRECTOR / DIRECTEUR ARTISTIQUE:

336, 337 Olaf Leu

AGENCY / AGENTUR / AGENCE – STUDIO:

336, 337 Olaf Leu Design

338

337

336, 337 Colour detail in actual size and complete wall calendar for Gebr. Klingspor, photoengravers, Offenbach. It uses examples of photographs taken looking into the sun or towards the light source. (GER)
338, 339 Two sheets from a calendar for SKF ball bearings in which a bearing race is brought into graphic relation with a female model in various poses. Full colour. (SWE)

336, 337 Originalgrosser Ausschnitt und ganzer Wandkalender der Gebr. Klingspor, Clichés und Lithos, Offenbach a. M. Er zeigt Beispiele von Gegenlichtaufnahmen. (GER) ¹
338, 339 Zwei Blätter aus dem Kalender des SKF-Kugellagerwerks. Ein Modell balanciert ein Kugellager auf den verschiedenen Körperteilen. Mehrfarbig. (SWE)

336, 337 Détail en grandeur nature et calendrier mural complet, publié par un atelier de photogravure. Toutes les photos figurant dans ce calendrier ont été prises à contre-jour. Polychromie. (GER)
338, 339 Deux feuilles figurant dans un calendrier de SKF, fabricant de roulements à billes. Série de photos qui présente des roulements à billes en rapport avec un corps féminin en diverses positions. (SWE)

339

PHOTOGRAPHER / PHOTOGRAPH / PHOTOGRAPHE:

340, 342 Georg Gerster
341 Emil Schulthess
343, 344 Peter Vogt

DESIGNER / GESTALTER / MAQUETTISTE:

340–342 Emil Schulthess
343, 344 Atelier Strenger

ART DIRECTOR / DIRECTEUR ARTISTIQUE:

340–342 Emil Schulthess

AGENCY / AGENTUR / AGENCE – STUDIO:

343, 344 Atelier Strenger

■ The photographs shown on this and the following double spread are taken from calendars which won awards in the International Kodak Colour Calendar Contest for 1975. This was the seventh in an annual series of contests organized by Kodak from Stuttgart and intended to show how colour photography has influenced calendar art and how important a part the intelligently conceived and well-illustrated calendar can play in advertising. Some 500 calendars are entered each year in this contest, which is fully international in scope.

340

341

342

Calendars / Kalender / Calendriers

343

340–342 A *Swissair* calendar for 1975 was devoted to the various ways in which people all over the world decorate the outside of their homes. The sheets shown here relate to the gateway to a farmstead in Old Nubia, now submerged under the waters of the Aswan Dam (Fig. 340), modern art on a wall in Sverdlova Street, Kharkov, USSR (Fig. 341), and music by Ravel on the wall of a music shop in Minneapolis (Fig. 342). (SWI)
343, 344 The 1975 *Porsche* calendar consisted of loose interchangeable sheets held between covers of stiff plastic. The car was shown in many settings and situations, all in full colour—here under a cirrus sky (blue car) and in a colourful close-up. (GER)

340–342 Der *Swissair*-Kalender 1975 galt dem Thema «Schmuck von Bauwerken» in der ganzen Welt. Die Monatsblätter zeigen das Tor zu einem Gehöft in Alt-Nubien, Ägypten (Abb. 340), ein modernes Mauerbild in einer Strasse von Charkow, UdSSR (Abb. 341) und eine Notenschrift als Wandschmuck in Minneapolis, USA (Abb. 342). (SWI)
343, 344 Der *Porsche*-Kalender des Jahres 1975 bestand aus zwölf losen Blättern zwischen zwei Platten aus farblosem Plastik. Die Farbaufnahmen zeigen den *Porsche*-Wagen in zwölf verschiedenen Gegenden und Situationen – hier zum Beispiel unter einem Himmel mit Zirruswolken (blauer Wagen) und in einer Nahaufnahme. (GER)

340–342 Le calendrier 1975 de *Swissair* a été consacré aux peintures murales transformant l'aspect des villes dans le monde entier. Les illustrations présentent: le portail d'une ferme en ancienne Nubie, disparue sous les flots du barrage d'Assouan (fig. 340); un tableau monumentale célébrant les cinquante ans d'existence de l'URSS, vue depuis la place Proletarskaya à Kharkov, Ukraine (fig. 341); la partition d'une symphonie de Ravel sur un mur à Minneapolis, USA (fig. 342). (SWI)
343, 344 Ces douze feuilles volantes et échangeables du calendrier 1975 de *Porsche* sont insérées entre deux plaques en matière plastique transparente. Photos couleurs présentant des voitures prises dans des environnements et situations divers. (GER)

344

345

346

PHOTOGRAPHER / PHOTOGRAPH / PHOTOGRAPHE:

345–347 Sabena
348, 349 Hans Feurer/Gerd Spans

DESIGNER / GESTALTER / MAQUETTISTE:

345–347 Rob Buytaert
348, 349 F. G. Boes

ART DIRECTOR / DIRECTEUR ARTISTIQUE:

345–347 Rob Buytaert

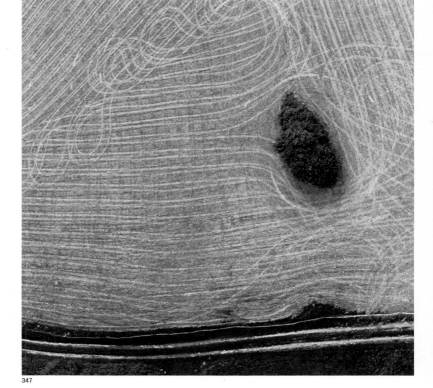

347

345–347 Two photographs and complete sheet from a calendar issued by a photoengraver, Photogravure de Schutter SA, Antwerp, using aerial shots of the patterns left on the landscape by farmers and foresters. (BEL)
348, 349 Cover and sheet of a large and colourful calendar issued by the printers Mohndruck Reinhard Mohn OHG, Gütersloh, and demonstrating a patented binding technique for calendars. The pictures show scantily clad girls engaged in various masculine sports. (GER)

345–347 Zwei Photos und ganzes Blatt aus dem Kalender einer Clichéanstalt. Er zeigt Luftaufnahmen von bewirtschaftetem Land. (BEL)
348, 349 Umschlag und Blatt eines grossformatigen, mehrfarbigen Kalenders des Mohndruck-Kalenderverlags, Gütersloh. Er weist eine neuartige Bindetechnik auf. (GER)

345–347 Deux photos et feuille complète d'un calendrier publié par un photolithographe à Anvers. Il est entièrement illustré de photos aériennes représentant des traces décoratives que les paysans ou sylviculteurs ont laissées dans le paysage. (BEL)
348, 349 Couverture et l'une des feuilles d'un calendrier grand format publié par une maison d'édition de livres d'art, afin d'introduire une nouvelle méthode de reliure pour calendriers. Série de photos de jeunes filles à peine vêtues qui s'engagent dans diverses disciplines sportives réservées aux hommes. (GER)

**Calendars / Kalender
Calendriers**

348

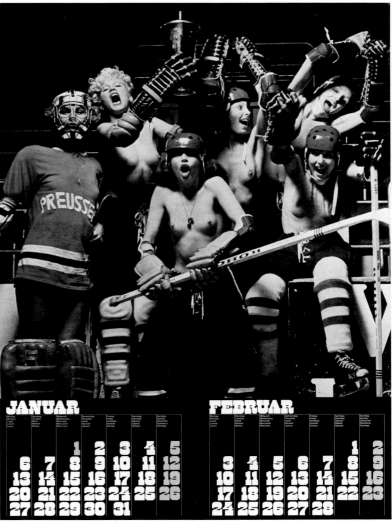

349

4

Editorial Photography

Magazine Covers

Book Jackets

Annual Reports

Redaktionelle Photographie

Zeitschriften-Umschläge

Buchumschläge

Jahresberichte

Photographie rédactionnelle

Couvertures de périodiques

Chemises des livres

Rapports annuels

352

353

354

355

PHOTOGRAPHER / PHOTOGRAPH:

350, 351 Bud Lee
352 Co Rentmeester
353, 354 Kennith Hope
355, 356 Farrell Grehan
357 Oscar van Alphen
358 Sacha

DESIGNER / GESTALTER / MAQUETTISTE:

350 Richard Weigand
352–358 Hans van Blommestein

ART DIRECTOR / DIRECTEUR ARTISTIQUE:

350, 351 Richard Weigand
352–358 Dick de Moei

PUBLISHER / VERLEGER / EDITEUR:

350, 351 Esquire, Inc.
352 Elsevier N.V.
353–358 De Geillustreerde Pers B.V.

350

Stanley Marsh Plays with His Money
by Gordon Chaplin

*These pictures are worth several thousand words.
The words follow . . .*

351

142

356

357

358

350 Opening spread of an article on Stanley Marsh in *Esquire* magazine. (USA)
351 Page in full colour from a series of disguises presented in *Esquire*—Mr. Peanut. (USA)
352 Double spread in full colour from an article on Indonesia in the magazine *Avenue*. (NLD)
353 Spread from an article in *Avenue* on fashion accessories. Pink glove on blue. (NLD)
354 From a fashion feature in *Avenue*. Double spread in full colour. (NLD)
355, 356 Two double spreads (both in full colour) from a feature in *Avenue* about the pollution of the Dutch fens. Fig. 356 with special reference to bird life. (NLD)
357 Spread from a feature about motor traffic in *Avenue* entitled "Dead-end Street". (NLD)
358 From a fashion feature in *Avenue*. Shades of golden brown. (NLD)

350 Page double initiale d'un article sur Stanley Marsh, publié dans le magazine *Esquire*. (USA)
351 Page en couleur d'une série consacrée à divers déguisements – ici M. Peanut. (USA)
352 Page double figurant dans un article du magazine *Avenue*, sur l'Indonésie. (NLD)
353 D'un article d'*Avenue* consacré aux accessoires de modes. Gant en rose sur bleu. (NLD)
354 D'un article de modes paru dans le magazine *Avenue*. Page double en couleur. (NLD)
355, 356 Deux pages doubles (en couleur) tirées d'un article du magazine *Avenue* sur la pollution des plaines marécageuses des Pays-Bas. Fig. 356 se réfère aux oiseaux. (NLD)
357 Page double d'un article intitulé «Cul-de-sac», qui est consacré à la circulation. (NLD)
358 D'un album de modes paru dans le magazine *Avenue*. Tons bruns doré. (NLD)

350 Doppelseite als Einleitung zu einem Artikel über einen Exzentriker, in *Esquire*. (USA)
351 Mehrfarbige Seite aus einer Folge über originelle Verkleidungen, in *Esquire*. (USA)
352 Mehrfarbige Doppelseite aus einem Artikel über Indonesien in der Zeitschrift *Avenue*. (NLD)
353 Doppelseite aus einem Artikel in *Avenue* über modische Accessoires. (NLD)
354 Aus einem Modebericht in *Avenue*. Mehrfarbige Doppelseite. (NLD)
355, 356 Zwei mehrfarbige Doppelseiten aus einem Bericht in *Avenue* über die Verschmutzung holländischer Marschlandschaften. Abb. 356 bezieht sich besonders auf die Vogelwelt. (NLD)
357 Doppelseite aus einem Aufsatz in *Avenue* über die mörderische Motorisierung. (NLD)
358 Aus einem Modebericht in *Avenue*. Goldbraune Farbtöne. (NLD)

Editorial Photography

359

360

361

Back when irons were really "irons" (heavy to lift and heated on the stove), ironing was a heavy, all-day job, traditionally done on Tuesdays. Somehow the hard-work stigma has stuck, even though today's irons are lightweight, well designed and equipped with extra features that make ironing and pressing jobs easier and faster.

Most of the recent improvements in irons are water related: steam, sprays, and the most recent—a self-cleaning action that flushes out water chambers and steam vents. The steam feature is so useful that Redbook considers it a basic requirement for all irons. Several brands have a device for releasing an additional amount of steam. You press a button and, depending on the iron, you get either a short blast of steam from all the holes in the soleplate or from just those in front or a continuous supply until you release the button. This feature is helpful for ironing badly wrinkled garments and for all pressing jobs, particularly during sewing. A spray is more effective than steam alone for badly wrinkled fabrics that aren't damp enough to iron. Press a button and a fine mist shoots from the front of the iron on a continuous spray while the button is depressed or a short shot at each press of the button. The latest iron development is a separate self-cleaning action that is supposed to clean minerals and other residue from the water chambers and steam vents. Regular tap water can be used in these irons instead of the distilled or demineralized water usually recommended. (Continued on page 208.)

114

PHOTOGRAPH BY HERMAN HIDOIHORA

IRONS & IRONING

362

CHARLESTON, CHRISTMAS

As dawn breaks over Charleston's East Battery a few days before Christmas, the scene is almost exactly as it was in the 1850s. Invisible across the Cooper River is Fort Sumter. (The rice and seafood in the foreground are mainstays of the Charlestonian diet and often are served on Christmas Eve. A recipe for Shrimp Pilau will be found on page 104.)

88

PHOTOGRAPH BY JACK WARD

363

364

365

366

359, 360 Detail of the photography and complete double spread from an article in *Redbook* magazine on how to make a perfect soufflé. (USA)
361 Black-and-white page opening a feature in *Redbook* magazine on ironing and the useful features incorporated in new models of irons. (USA)
362 Double spread in full colour from a feature in *Redbook* on Christmas and Christmas foods at Charleston, South Carolina. (USA)
363 Spread in full colour from an article in *Redbook* on homemade ice cream. (USA)
364 Spread from a feature in *McCall's* magazine on eye make-up. (USA)
365 "There's always a shrewd head under it." Double spread in full colour on motorcyclists from *Zeit Magazin*. (GER)
366 Spread opening a feature in *Stern* on Scotland "between whisky and melancholia". (GER)

359, 360 Ausschnitt der Farbaufnahme und ganze Doppelseite aus einem Artikel über die Zubereitung eines perfekten Auflaufs, erschienen in der Zeitschrift *Redbook*. (USA)
361 Schwarzweisse Seite, die einen Artikel in *Redbook* über technische Neuerungen bei Bügeleisen einleitet. (USA)
362 Mehrfarbige Doppelseite zur Einleitung eines Artikels über typische Weihnachtsgerichte in Charleston, Südkarolina, erschienen in der Zeitschrift *Redbook*. (USA)
363 Mehrfarbige Doppelseite aus *Redbook* mit Rezepten für Eisspezialitäten. (USA)
364 Doppelseite aus *McCall's* mit einem Artikel über Augenkosmetik. (USA)
365 Farbige Doppelseite aus dem *Zeit-Magazin* zu einem Artikel über Motorradfahrer. (GER)
366 Mehrfarbige Doppelseite aus der Zeitschrift *Stern* als Einleitung zu einem Reisebericht über Landschaft und Menschen in Schottland. (GER)

359, 360 Détail de la photo et page double qu'elle illustre. D'un article du magazine *Redbook* consacré à la préparation de soufflés. (USA)
361 Page en noir et blanc en tête d'un article du magazine *Redbook* consacré au repassage et aux avantages que les nouveaux fers à repasser peuvent offrir. (USA)
362 Page double (en couleur) figurant dans un article de *Redbook* sur les coutûmes et les spécialités de Noël à Charleston, Caroline du Sud. (USA)
363 Page double d'un article de *Redbook* consacré aux glaces faites à la maison. (USA)
364 Page double du magazine *McCall's*. Article consacré au maquillage des yeux. (USA)
365 «Là-dessous, il y a toujours un esprit perspicace.» Page double en couleur figurant dans un article du *Zeit Magazin* sur le motocyclisme. (GER)
366 Page en tête d'un article de *Stern* sur l'Ecosse, un pays «entre le whisky et la mélancolie». (GER)

PHOTOGRAPHER / PHOTOGRAPH / PHOTOGRAPHE:

359, 360 Phil Marco
361 Norman Nishimura
362 Jack Ward
363 Mort Mace
364 Irwin Horowitz
365 Ben Oyne
366 Will McBride

DESIGNER / GESTALTER / MAQUETTISTE:

359, 360, 362 363 Edward Sobel
361 Verdun P. Cook
364 Alvin Grossman
365 Ben Oyne/Markus Osterwalder

ART DIRECTOR / DIRECTEUR ARTISTIQUE:

359–363 William F. Cadge
364 Alvin Grossman
365 Markus Osterwalder
366 Rolf Gillhausen

AGENCY / AGENTUR / AGENCE – STUDIO:

365 Ben Oyne Studio
366 Gerd Plessl

PUBLISHER / VERLEGER / EDITEUR:

359–363 Reedbook Magazine
364 McCall Publishing Co.
365 Gerd Bucerius
366 Gruner & Jahr GmbH & Co.

Editorial Photography

367 ''Cardinal point of the winter: Richelieu style.'' Double spread in black and white on shoes and pantyhose fashions, from *Vogue*. (FRA)
368 From a fashion feature on jumpsuits in *Vogue*. Double spread in black and white. (FRA)
369 Double spread from *Vogue* on Japanese eye make-up. (FRA)
370, 371 Complete double spread (in full colour) and detail of the photography. From a feature in *Pardon* on love life in Germany. (GER)

367 «Kardinalpunkt ist diesen Winter der Richelieu-Stil». Schwarzweisse Doppelseite über Schuhmodelle und Strumpfhosen aus *Vogue*. (FRA)
368 Aus einem Modebericht über Jumpsuits in *Vogue*. Schwarzweisse Doppelseite. (FRA)
369 Doppelseite aus *Vogue* über Augenkosmetik im Stil der Japanerinnen. (FRA)
370, 371 Ganze Doppelseite (mehrfarbig) und Ausschnitt der Photographie zu einem Artikel in *Pardon* über das Liebesleben in Deutschland. (GER)

367 Page double en noir et blanc figurant dans un article sur les chaussures lacées style Richelieu et diverses marques de collants assortis. De la revue féminine *Vogue*. (FRA)
368 D'un article de *Vogue* présentant la nouvelle collection de jumpsuits. Noir et blanc. (FRA)
369 Page double de la revue *Vogue* consacrée au maquillage des yeux à la japonaise. (FRA)
370, 371 Page double complète (en couleur) et détail de la photo qui l'illustre. D'un article paru dans le magazine *Pardon* sur la vie amoureuse en Allemagne. (GER)

370

PHOTOGRAPHER / PHOTOGRAPH:

367 Alexis Stroukoff
368 Hans Feurer
369 Guy Bourdin
370, 371 Mike Berkofsky

DESIGNER / GESTALTER / MAQUETTISTE:

367–369 Paul Wagner
370, 371 Jürgen Horst Frickel

ART DIRECTOR / DIRECTEUR ARTISTIQUE:

367–369 Jocelyn Kargere
370, 371 Gerhard Kromschröder

AGENCY / AGENTUR / AGENCE – STUDIO:

367–369 Vogue

PUBLISHER / VERLEGER / EDITEUR:

367–369 Les Editions Condé Nast
370, 371 Pardon-Verlags GmbH

Point cardinal
de l'hiver :
le style richelieu

367

Près du corps, allongeant la silhouette, donc dans la ligne de la mode de cet hiver, rien de plus féminin que costume d'origine masculin. Le jumpsuit se porte dans des bottes, sur un pull, sous un manteau, une canadienne, un imperméable ou une fourrure. (De g. à dr.), Hama, en jumpsuit de velours côtelé. Kenzo pour Jap. Eeva, en jumpsuit de velours côtelé sous un gilet-canadienne, Kenzo pour Jap. Ceinture L'Aiglon. Bottes en serpent. Ah!. Écharpe Tunmer. Anne, en jumpsuit de flanelle beige. Jil Sander. Bottes Surplus Yankee. Écharpe Afghan House. Gunel, en jumpsuit de popeline kaki. Christian Aujard. Botte Ah!. Écharpe Afghan House. Pull Memmi. Michel, en jumpsuit de popeline beige de Saint Laurent-Rive Gauche. Écharpe frangée Afghan House. Coiffures Bruce de Jean-Marc Maniatis. Maquillages Daniel Demanjean pour Max Factor.

102   103
                                                                                                        368

371

Beauté
l'art
du
japon

renouvelle entièrement
le maquillage des yeux :
sur peau claire, œil
ocre doré. Au Japon, tout est dans le pinceau. On maquille comme on écrit. Ceux qui ont inventé les pinceaux en soies animales ou "Mohitsu", nous ont complètement ébahis et confondus, ici, à Paris. Ils sont venus toute une équipe, droit du Japon, envoyés par le "Kanebo Cosmetics", très grande marque de produits de beauté du Japon, ne comptant pas moins de dix crèmes pour la nuit, déjà extraordinairement répandues. Il faudrait pouvoir vous montrer, non seulement le résultat ci-contre, page de dr., d'une séance de maquillage, mais les étapes des préparatifs que nous avons vus devant nos yeux écarquillés. D'abord massage spécial de la nuque et des points d'acupuncture de la tête : cela détend les traits, relaxe le visage, active la circulation et surtout rend la peau plus vivante. Ensuite sous-maquillage différent selon le degré hydrométrique de l'air : lotion hydratante à base d'huile d'olive si l'atmosphère est sèche; lotion à la vitamine B6 si elle est humide, pour "poudrer" à l'avance. Enfin, extraordinaire virtuosité dans l'utilisation des pinceaux, changés pour chaque couleur, mouillés pour poudrer le tour de l'œil, gonflés pour "matifier" le menton par en-dessous, effilés pour dessiner le contour des lèvres.

Tout aux pinceaux

Sur un fond de teint très clair, sont calligraphiés au pinceau :
l'anti-cernes rose-violet, le rose à joues de trois couleurs
dégradées, puis le tour des yeux de trois couleurs aussi,
marron, beige et ocre. Sourcils brossés vers le haut.
Lip Gloss au pinceau, lui aussi : maquillage Kanebo "Josei".

GUY BOURDIN

369

147

PHOTOGRAPHER / PHOTOGRAPH:

372, 373 Jerry Sarapochiello
374, 375 Jean-Paul Mann
376 Albert Mackenzie Watson

DESIGNER / GESTALTER:

372, 373 Bill Reedy
374, 375 Helmut Mätzler

ART DIRECTOR:

372, 373 Bill Reedy
374, 375 Helmut Mätzler
376 Roger Schoening

AGENCY / AGENTUR / AGENCE:

374, 375 Sportive Werbe-
produktion GmbH + Co.

PUBLISHER / VERLEGER / EDITEUR:

372, 373 Eastman Kodak Co.
374, 375 Sportive Verlags-GmbH
376 Condé Nast Publications, Inc.

372

**Editorial
Photography**

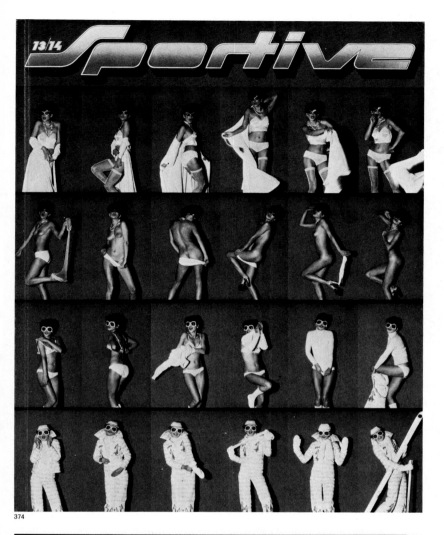

374

375

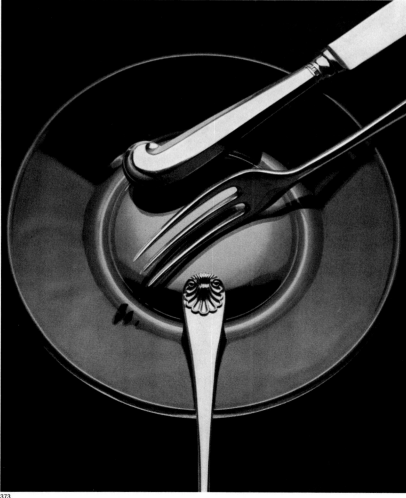

373

HEAD FOR SUMMER

YOU'VE GOT A GOOD MONTH TO GET READY

376

372 Photograph reproduced in *Applied Photography* (actual size). (USA)
373 Full-page illustration from an article on light as the essence of photography published in *Applied Photography*. Predominantly blue shades. (USA)
374 Cover of the magazine of advertising *Sportive* with a two-way striptease presented on a purple ground. (GER)
375 Opening illustration from the advertising magazine *Sportive*. Full colour. (GER)
376 Colour spread from *Mademoiselle* magazine: summer beauty care and fashions. (USA)

372 Originalgrosse Aufnahme aus der Zeitschrift *Applied Photography*. (USA)
373 Ganzseitige Illustration zu einem Artikel über das Licht als Grundlage der Photographie, erschienen in *Applied Photography*. Blautöne. (USA)
374 Umschlag der Zeitschrift *Sportive* für Sportmode und Sportartikel, mit einem originellen Striptease. Grund in Violett. (GER)
375 Ganzseitige, mehrfarbige Aufnahme aus der Zeitschrift *Sportive*. (GER)
376 Farbige Doppelseite aus *Mademoiselle*: Hautpflege im Sommer. (USA)

372 Photo (en grandeur nature) reproduite dans le magazine *Applied Photography*. (USA)
373 Illustration pleine page d'un article sur la lumière en tant qu'élément essentiel de la photographie. Du magazine *Applied Photography*. Prédominance de tons bleus. (USA)
374 Couverture du magazine publicitaire *Sportive* présentant un strip-tease en deux sens. Illustration en couleur sur fond lilas. (GER)
375 Illustration initiale du magazine publicitaire *Sportive*. Polychromie. (GER)
376 Page du magazine *Mademoiselle*: produits cosmétiques et modes d'été. (USA)

377

377 Double spread on shakes and sodas from the *Los Angeles Times Home Magazine*. Full colour. (USA)
378 Black-and-white photograph for an article on beauty care, as yet unpublished. (GER)
379 From a fashion reportage (first published in *Nova*), reproduced in an article on the photographer Hans Feurer in *Photo* magazine. Actual size. (FRA)

377 Mehrfarbige Doppelseite mit Rezepten für sommerliche Getränke, aus dem *Los Angeles Times Home Magazine*. (USA)
378 Schwarzweisse Photo aus einem unveröffentlichten Artikel über die Hautpflege im Sommer. (GER)
379 Aus einer Mode-Reportage, die in einem Artikel über den Photographen Hans Feurer in der Zeitschrift *Photo* verwendet wurde. Originalgrosse Aufnahme. (FRA)

377 Page double du *Los Angeles Times Home Magazine*, consacré aux cocktails et sodas. Polychrome. (USA)
378 Photo en noir et blanc illustrant un article sur les soins de beauté. Photo inédite. (GER)
379 D'un album de modes (paru pour la première fois dans *Nova*) figurant dans l'article «La mode survit» du magazine *Photo*, article consacré au photographe Hans Feurer. Grandeur nature. (FRA)

PHOTOGRAPHER / PHOTOGRAPH / PHOTOGRAPHE:

377 Hans Albers
378 Wolfgang Neeb
379 Hans Feurer

DESIGNER / GESTALTER / MAQUETTISTE:

377 Hans Albers
378 Wolfgang Neeb

ART DIRECTOR / DIRECTEUR ARTISTIQUE:

377 Hans Albers

AGENCY / AGENTUR / AGENCE – STUDIO:

378 Wolfgang Neeb

PUBLISHER / VERLEGER / EDITEUR:

377 Los Angeles Times
379 Publication Filipacchi

Editorial Photography

378

381

PHOTOGRAPHER / PHOTOGRAPH / PHOTOGRAPHE:

380 Hiro
381 Art Kane
382 Earl Gustie

DESIGNER / GESTALTER / MAQUETTISTE:

380 Patrick Lefrançois
381 Carl Barile

ART DIRECTOR / DIRECTEUR ARTISTIQUE:

380 Eric Colmet Daage
381 Carl Barile
382 Kaliopee Malagaris/Jim Nichols

PUBLISHER / VERLEGER / EDITEUR:

380 Publication Filipacchi
381 Viva International Ltd.
382 Chicago Tribune Magazine

380 From an article on the colour photography of Hiro in *Photo* magazine. Actual size. (FRA)
381 Colour photograph illustrating a feature entitled ''Woman as Erotic Fantasy'' published in the magazine *Viva*. (USA)
382 Double spread opening an article on tomatoes, published in *Chicago Tribune Magazine*. (USA)

380 Originalgrosse Aufnahme aus einem Artikel über Farbphotographien von Hiro, erschienen in der Zeitschrift *Photo*. (FRA)
381 Farbaufnahme aus dem Artikel «Frauen als erotische Phantasie» in der Zeitschrift *Viva*. (USA)
382 Doppelseite als Auftakt zu einem Artikel über Tomaten im *Chicago Tribune Magazine*. (USA)

380 Photographie pleine page (grandeur nature) de l'article «L'âge de la couleur». Cet article, consacré au photographe Hiro, a paru dans le magazine *Photo*. (FRA)
381 Photo couleur illustrant un article intitulé «La femme en tant que fantaisie érotique» qui a paru dans le magazine *Viva*. (USA)
382 Page double en tête d'un article du *Chicago Tribune Magazine* consacré aux tomates. (USA)

382

Editorial Photography

383

384

383 Double spread in colour opening an article on Rick Wakeman, a successful young musician, in the magazine *Rolling Stone*. (USA)
384 Double spread opening a feature in *Rolling Stone* magazine on a Friday night performance of the Rolling Stones in Los Angeles. Colour pictures. (USA)
385 Colour spread from a feature on lipsticks and nail varnishes in *Viva*. (USA)
386 Colour spread on jewellery from the German edition of *Playboy*. (GER)
387 Photographic studies of legs from a feature on the subject in *Playboy* magazine. (USA)
388 Colour spread from a feature on mechanical aids to getting fit, from *Playboy*. (USA)
389 Opening double spread (in colour) from an article on the actress and model Donyale Luna, from *Playboy* magazine. (USA)
390 Closing colour spread from an article on "Hindsight" in *Playboy* magazine. (USA)
391 From an article in the German *Playboy* on the last white hunters in Africa. Colour spread. (GER)

386

ART DIRECTOR / DIRECTEUR ARTISTIQUE:

383 Tony Lane
384 Tony Lane/Suzy Rice
385 Rowen Johnson
386, 391 Rainer Wörtmann
387–390 Arthur Paul

AGENCY / AGENTUR / AGENCE—STUDIO:

383, 384 Tony Lane Studios

PUBLISHER / VERLEGER / EDITEUR:

383, 384 Straight Arrow. Inc.
385 Viva International Ltd.
386, 391 Heinrich Bauer Verlag
387–390 Playboy Enterprises, Inc.

ARTHUR PAUL

Up against the wall, or how to liven up a decadent but dull soiree. Our satin doll and her Mr. Right (at least for the evening) find that "sitting this one out" can use up as much energy as the boogie. As choreographed by photographers Bob Keeling and Francois Robert, it's a *Last Tango*ish routine you won't learn at Arthur Murray's. Above and right: PLAYBOY Art Director Arthur Paul turned cameraman for these studies, which carry realism to a point beyond reality—first, as a female leg, viewed from above, acquires an abstractly sculptural quality; second, as a foot —with the aid of a stiletto heel, some black nail polish and a mysteriously missing shoe—takes on the potent role of fetish.

387

Editorial Photography

385

PHOTOGRAPHER / PHOTOGRAPH:

383 Neal Preston
384 Annie Leibovitz
385 Klaus Lucka
386 Charlotte March
387, 390 Arthur Paul
388 Paul Gremmler
389 Luigi Cazzaniga
391 Emil Perauer

DESIGNER / GESTALTER / MAQUETTISTE:

383 Tony Lane
384 Tony Lane/Suzy Rice
386, 391 George Guther/Angelika Bronder
Rudi Gill/Christl Schmidt
387, 388, 390 Tom Staebler
389 Chet Suski

383 Mehrfarbige Doppelseite aus der Zeitschrift *Rolling Stone* als Einleitung zu einem Artikel über den erfolgreichen jungen Musiker Rick Wakeman. (USA)
384 Doppelseitige Farbaufnahme mit einem Bericht über ein Konzert der Rolling Stones in Los Angeles, erschienen in der Zeitschrift *Rolling Stone*. (USA)
385 Farbige Doppelseite aus einem Artikel über Lippenstifte und Nagellack in *Viva*. (USA)
386 Farbige Doppelseite über Brillantschmuck aus der deutschen Ausgabe von *Playboy*. (GER)
387 Photographische Studien zu einem Artikel über Beine in *Playboy*. (USA)
388 Mehrfarbige Doppelseite zu einem Bericht über Fitness-Geräte in *Playboy*. (USA)
389 Farbige Doppelseite als Einleitung zu einem Artikel über Donyale Luna, eine schwarze Schauspielerin und Photomodell, erschienen in *Playboy*. (USA)
390 Doppelseite als Schluss eines Artikels in *Playboy*. (USA)
391 Farbige Doppelseite aus *Playboy* über die letzten weissen Jäger in Afrika. (GER)

383 Page double en couleur en tête d'un article sur Rick Wakeman, un jeune musicien de renom. Article publié dans le magazine *Rolling Stone*. (USA)
384 Page double initiale d'un article de *Rolling Stone* consacré à une présentation de fin de semaine des Rolling Stones à Los Angeles. Photos couleurs. (USA)
385 Page double d'un article du magazine *Viva* sur les rouges à lèvres et vernis à ongles. (USA)
386 Page double consacrée à la joaillerie. Article de l'édition allemande de *Playboy*. (GER)
387 Etudes photographiques de jambes illustrant un article de *Playboy* consacré à ce sujet. (USA)
388 Page double en couleur d'un article sur les agrès automatiques servant à se maintenir en forme. Article du magazine *Playboy*. (USA)
389 Page double initiale d'un article de *Playboy* consacré à l'actrice Donyale Luna. (USA)
390 Dernière page double d'un article de *Playboy*. (USA)
391 D'un article du *Playboy* allemand, sur les derniers chasseurs blancs en Afrique. (GER)

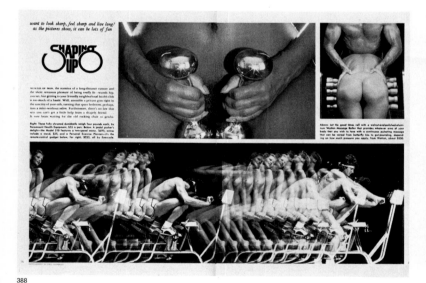

388

389

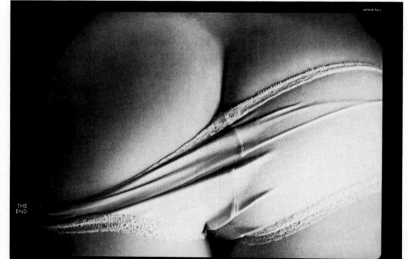

390

391

392, 393 Detail of the photography and complete page from a fashion feature on boots published in *The New York Times Magazine*. (USA)
394, 395 Complete double spread and detail of the photography from an article in *The Sunday Times Magazine* on parachuting and a record in "star building". (GBR)
396 Double spread in black and white from an article on "military" fashions in *The New York Times Magazine*. (USA)

392, 393 Photoausschnitt und ganze Seite eines Modeberichts über Stiefel, erschienen im *New York Times Magazine*. (USA)
394, 395 Ganze Doppelseite und Ausschnitt der Aufnahme zu einem Artikel über Fallschirmspringen im *Sunday Times Magazine*. (GBR)
396 Schwarzweisse Doppelseite aus einem Artikel über sportliche Damenmode mit militärischem Akzent im *New York Times Magazine*. (USA)

392, 393 Détail de la photo et page où elle figure. D'un article de mode de bottes «qui se plient agréablement aux chevilles», publié dans le *New York Times Magazine*. (USA)
394, 395 Page double et détail de la photographie qui l'illustre, figurant dans un article du *Sunday Times Magazine* consacré au parachutage. (GBR)
396 Page double en noir et blanc tirée d'un article sur la mode style militaire paru dans le *New York Times Magazine*. (USA)

PHOTOGRAPHER / PHOTOGRAPH / PHOTOGRAPHE:

392, 393 Elliott Erwitt
394, 395 Andy Keech
396 Bill King

DESIGNER / GESTALTER / MAQUETTISTE:

392, 393, 396 Ruth Ansel

393

394

392

395

By Patricia Peterson

The draft is on for
fatigues and Army issue.
Seventh Avenue
has commandeered
military designs, but the
adventurous can find
the authentic stuff,
new or used, in
Army surplus
stores.

AT EASE

This page, from left: Shirt with a cartridge-pleat pocket and walking shorts in khaki cotton. New or used. New, $3.95; used $1.99 to $2.99. Weiss & Mahoney, 142 Fifth Avenue. Undershirt in khaki-colored cotton. Used, 99 cents. Khaki cotton shorts, new or used. $4. Both from Kaufman Surplus.

man Surplus, 623 Broadway and 319 West 42d Street. Sam Browne belt (supply limited), $6.95. Weiss & Mahoney. Undershirt in khaki-colored cotton. Used, 99 cents. Khaki cotton shorts, new or used. $4. Both from Kaufman Surplus. Brief dress is a khaki-colored wool and cotton undershirt. New, $6. Kauf-

Girl in inset picture, left, wears a one-piece used Air Force coverall with zip front and pockets. Styles vary. Available in brown or olive drab, wool or cotton. $14.95-$19.95. Gyro, 654 Broadway. Wool jeep cap, $3. Kaufman Surplus. Right (and in blowup):

Olive-drab cotton fatigue shirt and jungle fatigue pants with roomy pockets. Shirt, new, $8.95; used, $2.95 to $4.95. Pants, new, $9.95; used, $4.95 to $7.95. Olive-drab cotton cap, $2.95. Shirt, pants and cap are all from Weiss & Mahoney.

The New York Times Magazine/March 16, 1975   73

72

396

ART DIRECTOR / DIRECTEUR ARTISTIQUE:

392, 393, 396 Ruth Ansel

PUBLISHER / VERLEGER / EDITEUR:

392, 393, 396 The New York Times Publishing Co.
394, 395 The Sunday Times Magazine

Editorial Photography

397

398

ON COMA

When you talk about the comatose or the unresponsive patient, definitions are hard to come by unless you break them down into various categories. From a clinical point of view, the comatose patient may be defined as one who is unresponsive to external stimuli. Obviously, this is a relative thing, because some patients may respond to severe tactile *continued*

Excerpts from a talk at the Emergency Medical Systems National Symposium at Walt Disney World, Fla., by Melvin Greer, M.D., professor and chief of neurology at the University of Florida.

399

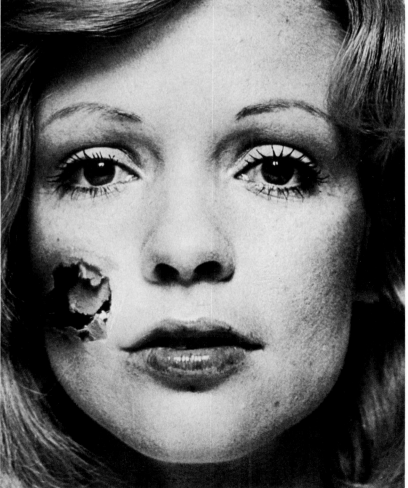

400

397, 398 From an article on the photography of Helmut Newton published in the magazine *Progresso Fotografico* (fig. 397 was taken in 1974, fig. 398 in 1973). (ITA)
399 Double spread in colour from an article on coma in *Emergency Medicine*. (USA)
400 Full-page colour illustration accompanying an article on the treatment of facial injuries, from *Emergency Medicine*. (USA)

397, 398 Aufnahmen aus einem Bericht über das Werk des Photographen Helmut Newton in der Fachzeitschrift *Progresso Fotografico* (Abb. 397: 1974; Abb. 398: 1973). (ITA)
399 Farbige Doppelseite aus einem Artikel über Patienten im Koma in einer medizinischen Fachzeitschrift. (USA)
400 Ganzseitige Farbphoto zur Illustrierung eines Artikels über Gesichtsverletzungen in einer medizinischen Fachzeitschrift. (USA)

397, 398 D'un article consacré à l'œuvre photographique de Helmut Newton. Elément du magazine *Progresso Fotografico* (la fig. 397 a été prise en 1974, la fig. 398 en 1973). (ITA)
399 Page double en couleur figurant dans un article d'*Emergency Medicine* sur le coma. (USA)
400 Illustration pleine page figurant dans un article d'*Emergency Medicine* sur le traitement de blessures faciales. (USA)

PHOTOGRAPHER / PHOTOGRAPH / PHOTOGRAPHE:

397, 398 Helmut Newton
399 Laszlo Hege
400 Shig Ikeda

DESIGNER / GESTALTER / MAQUETTISTE:

397, 398 Alberto Piovani
399, 400 Tom Lennon

ART DIRECTOR / DIRECTEUR ARTISTIQUE:

397, 398 Alberto Piovani
399, 400 Ira Silberlicht

PUBLISHER / VERLEGER / EDITEUR:

397, 398 Progresso Fotografico
399, 400 Emergency Medicine

Editorial Photography

401

405

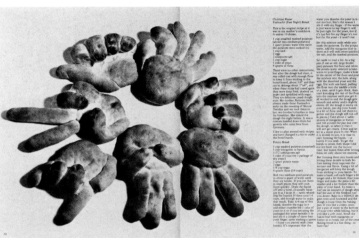

402

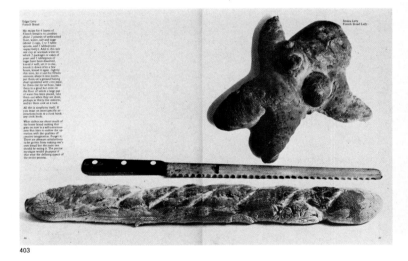

403

404

401–403 Double spreads from a yearbook by students of the Parsons School of Design on the subject of bread. The illustrations (in brown shades on yellowish stock) show Cuban, Carnival and French breads. (USA)
404 Photograph reproduced in the photographic magazine *Nikon World*. (JPN)
405 Colour fashion spread from the women's magazine *Elle*. (SWI)
406 "When summer girls go swimming ..." Black-and-white fashion page from the women's magazine *Elle*. (SWI)
407 Full-page black-and-white illustration opening a review of a book about the world of animals published in the magazine *Elle*. (FRA)

401–403 Doppelseiten aus dem Jahrbuch der *Parsons School of Design*, das dem Thema «Brot» gewidmet war. Die Aufnahmen (braun auf gelblichem Papier) zeigen Brot aus Kuba und Frankreich sowie (Abb. 402) Fastnachtsgebäck. (USA)
404 Schwarzweissaufnahme aus der Photozeitschrift *Nikon World*. (JPN)
405 Farbige Doppelseite aus der Frauenzeitschrift *Elle*. (SWI)
406 Schwarzweisse Photographie aus der Frauenzeitschrift *Elle*, mit neuen Modellen von Badekleidern. (SWI)
407 Schwarzweisse, ganzseitige Aufnahme als Einleitung zur Besprechung eines Buches über die Welt der Tiere, erschienen in der Zeitschrift *Elle*. (FRA)

401–403 Pages doubles figurant dans un répertoire annuel des étudiants de la *Parsons School of Design*. Les illustrations se réfèrent au pain: pains cubains, pains de carnaval, pains français. Tons bruns sur papier jaunâtre. (USA)
404 Photo reproduite dans le magazine photographique *Nikon World*. (JPN)
405 Page double d'un article de modes paru dans la revue féminine *Elle*. (SWI)
406 «Quand les jeunes filles 'estivales' vont se baigner.» Pleine page en noir et blanc d'un article de mode de plage, du magazine *Elle*. (SWI)
407 Illustration pleine page en noir et blanc en tête du compte rendu d'un livre consacré au règne animal. Article paru dans la revue féminine *Elle*. (FRA)

406

407

PHOTOGRAPHER / PHOTOGRAPH:

401–403 Parsons School of Design,
         Students of Publication Design,
         Class 73/74
404 Alan Kaplan
405 Ernst Wirz
407 Roman Cieslewicz

DESIGNER / GESTALTER:

401–403 Parsons School of Design,
         Students of Publication Design,
         Class 73/74
404 Ernest Scarfone
405 Roland Scotoni
407 Roman Cieslewicz

ART DIRECTOR:

401–403 Cipe Pineles Burtin
404 Ernest Scarfone
405 Roland Scotoni
406 Gianfranco Verna
407 Peter Knapp

PUBLISHER / VERLEGER / EDITEUR:

401–403 Parsons School of Design
404 Nikon World
405 Elle S.A.
406 Annabelle Verlag
407 Elle/France Editions
     et Publications

408

"Eve," Laura Ziegler, 1958

The Hirshhorn's smooth circular facade is broken only by a long balcony from which patrons can view an indelibly American image—the U.S. capitol. Most critics grant Washington's new museum an excellent chance to become another famed landmark, as it matures from a grand private collection into a great public institution.

A CAPITOL OF STATE—AND A CAPITAL OF ART

60

"Two Discs," Alexander Calder, 1965

409

411

412

408 Colour page from an article on the preparation of fish from a special issue of the magazine *Meine Familie und ich* devoted to cooking for children. (GER)

409, 410 Page and double spread with colour illustrations (the large sculptures are by Calder and Bourdelle) from an article on the new Hirshhorn Museum in New York published in the magazine *Horizon*. (USA)

411, 412 Double spreads from a feature on Martha Graham's women characters published in *Dance* magazine. Fig. 411 shows the three dancers who took the role of Clytemnestra in New York's 1974/75 season. (USA)

413 Double spread from a feature on structural steel in *Horizon*. It shows the Superdome in New Orleans against a blue sky. (USA)

408 Farbseite aus einem Artikel über Fischgerichte in der Zeitschrift *Meine Familie und ich*, die ein Sonderheft dem Kochen für Kinder widmete. (GER)

409, 410 Seite und Doppelseite mit Farbaufnahmen (die grossen Skulpturen stammen von Calder und Bourdelle) aus einem Artikel über das neue Hirshhorn-Museum in New York, erschienen in der Zeitschrift *Horizon*. (USA)

411, 412 Doppelseite aus einem Aufsatz über Charakterrollen in Ausdruckstänzen der Gruppe Martha Graham, erschienen in der Zeitschrift *Dance*. Abb. 411 zeigt drei Tänzerinnen, die 1974/75 in New York die Klytämnestra spielten. (USA)

413 Doppelseite aus einem Bericht über Stahlkonstruktionen in der Zeitschrift *Horizon*. Die Aufnahme zeigt die Riesenkuppel eines Sportzentrums in New Orleans. (USA)

SCULPTURAL MASTERWORKS ON DISPLAY—A GARDEN WHERE LOVE OF ART CAN GROW

"Juggler," Marino Marini, 1954 (top); "Needle Tower," Kenneth Snelson, 1968

Spotted throughout the large plaza underneath and surrounding the museum's doughnut-shaped concrete mass, and prominently featured in an adjacent multileveled garden, are massive bronzes and stones including many of the world's greatest works of sculpture. Indeed, the collection's sculpture has won widespread acclaim.

From the figurative masterpieces of the French sculptor Auguste Rodin (see "the Burghers of Calais," top) to abstract modern works such as the mobiles and stabiles of Alexander Calder or the powerful metallic creations of another American, David Smith, the Hirshhorn brilliantly shows the richness and variety of contemporary sculpture.

The arrangement of the sculpture exhibits is both striking and people-oriented. The plaza's centerpiece is a high-spraying fountain; and in the garden, strollers view a tasteful blend of sculpture and shrubbery around a peaceful pool.

"The Great Warrior of Montauban," Émile-Antoine Bourdelle, 1898

58

59

410

STEEL
The great strength of steel is being utilized in new design concepts that enable a steel building to bear greater loads as a whole than the strength of its individual parts would permit. In effect, through design, one steel part picks up strength from another. Standard steel bears as much as 248 megapascals; special steels are now proving to be three times as strong.

The steel skeleton of the Superdome, a mammoth sports and activities center being built in downtown New Orleans, Louisiana, has a span of 204 meters and will support a roof nearly four hectares in area.

413

PHOTOGRAPHER / PHOTOGRAPH / PHOTOGRAPHE:

408 Maria Harder
411, 412 Martha Swope/Frederika Davis
413 Robert Phillips

DESIGNER / GESTALTER / MAQUETTISTE:

408 Winfried Lang
411, 412 Herbert Migdoll/Augustus Ginnochio
413 James Keaton

ART DIRECTOR / DIRECTEUR ARTISTIQUE:

408 Noëlle Thieux
411, 412 Herbert Migdoll
413 Joseph Morgan/Lee E. Battaglia

PUBLISHER / VERLEGER / EDITEUR:

408 Co-Publica Verlagsgesellschaft mbH & Co.
411, 412 Dance Magazine
413 USIA

408 Page en couleur figurant dans un article sur la préparation de poissons. Numéro spécial du magazine *Meine Familie und ich,* consacré aux enfants qui «font la popote». (GER)
409, 410 Page et page double avec illustrations en couleur (les grandes sculptures ont été créées par Calder et Bourdelle) d'un article du magazine *Horizon,* consacré au nouveau bâtiment du Musée Hirshhorn à New York. (USA)
411, 412 Pages doubles tirées d'un article consacré aux caractères de Martha Graham. La fig. 411 représente trois danseuses qui ont joué le rôle de Clytemnestre pendant la saison 74/75 à New York. Article paru dans le magazine *Dance.* (USA)
413 Page double d'un article paru dans le magazine *Horizon* sur l'acier de construction. La photo présente le «Superdome» à la Nouvelle-Orléans. (USA)

Editorial Photography

414

PHOTOGRAPHER / PHOTOGRAPH:

414 Gene Butera
415, 416 Laszlo Hege
417 Ed Lettau
418 Victor Skrebneski
419 Seymour & Sol Mednick Studio, Inc.

DESIGNER / GESTALTER / MAQUETTISTE:

414 Gene Butera
415–417 Tom Lennon

415

416

417

ART DIRECTOR / DIRECTEUR ARTISTIQUE:

414 Gene Butera
415–417 Ira Silberlicht
418 Jack Lund/Dan Jursa
419 Frank Metz

AGENCY / AGENTUR / AGENCE – STUDIO:

419 Seymour & Sol Mednick Studio, Inc.

PUBLISHER / VERLEGER / EDITEUR:

414 Car and Driver
415–417 Emergency Medicine
418 The Chicago Tribune
419 Simon & Schuster, Inc.

Editorial Photography

418

419

420

420 Part of a double-spread illustration for an article on "Energy and the City" published in an issue of *The Lamp*, the *Exxon* house magazine. (USA)
421 Double spread in full colour on children's fashions from *The New York Times Magazine*. Attention is also drawn to the big wall painting in the background. (USA)
422 Fashion spread from *Chicago Tribune Magazine* on the subject of new satin evening gowns on the border of the peignoir and pyjama. Shades of beige and pink. (USA)

420 Ausschnitt aus einer doppelseitigen Illustration als Einleitung zu einem Artikel über den Energiehaushalt einer Stadt, erschienen in *The Lamp*, der Hauszeitschrift der *Exxon*. (USA)
421 Mehrfarbige Doppelseite über Kindermode aus dem *New York Times Magazine*, mit Hinweis auf die grosse Wandmalerei im Hintergrund. (USA)
422 Doppelseite mit neuen Abendkleidern im Stil von Pyjamas und Negligés aus *Chicago Tribune Magazine*. Die Modelle sind in zarten Rosa- und Beigetönen gehalten. (USA)

420 Partie d'une illustration sur page double, figurant dans un article sur «L'Energie et la ville». Article publié dans un numéro de *The Lamp*, journal d'entreprise d'*Exxon*. (USA)
421 Page double en couleur du *New York Times Magazine*, numéro consacré à la mode pour enfants. L'attention du lecteur est attirée aussi sur la grande peinture murale au fond. (USA)
422 Page double d'un album de modes du *Chicago Tribune Magazine* consacré aux robes de soir en satin, dont les modèles s'approchent du peignoir et du pyjama. Beiges et rose. (USA)

421

PHOTOGRAPHER / PHOTOGRAPH / PHOTOGRAPHE:

421 Bill Binzen
422 Victor Skrebneski

DESIGNER / GESTALTER / MAQUETTISTE:

420 Harry O. Diamond/Illustration: Fred Otnes
422 Jack Lund

422

ART DIRECTOR / DIRECTEUR ARTISTIQUE:

420 Harry O. Diamond
421 Ruth Ansel
422 Jack Lund

PUBLISHER / VERLEGER / EDITEUR:

420 Exxon Corporation
421 The New York Times Magazine
422 The Chicago Tribune

Editorial Photography

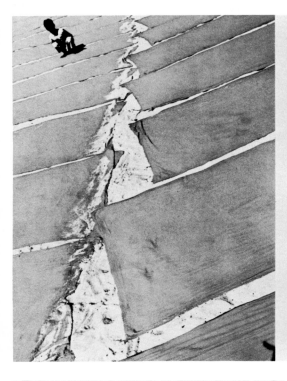

Ashvin Gatha looks for and finds both beauty and happiness among the poorest of his fellows. At left, dyed fabric glows in bright sunlight. Above, the sunrise lights three fishermen as they go after the day's catch. Below, temple lamplight contrasts with blueness of pre-sunrise.

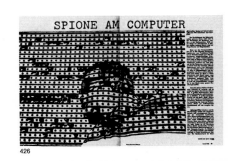

BY KENNETH POLI

". . . they all live happily in spite of all the misery. That's what I'm trying to show."

ASHVIN GATHA

he sound track twanged with the eccentric-sounding rhythms of a sitar, replaced eventually by the voice of a woman singing in high, keening tones as images flashed and changed on the multiple screens of the slide show being previewed at the offices of the India National Tourist Board in New York City.

The images were soaked in rich color, brimming with a sense of life, and had been created by the use of a full vocabulary of photographic expression from fisheye to telephoto.

The show was a recent production of Ashvin Gatha, a 31-year-old Indian fashion and commercial photographer from Bombay. Readers of POPULAR PHOTOGRAPHY have seen some of his previous work in the September, 1970, issue.

continued on page 167

Above. Gatha photographed five fisherwoman bringing salt water from the sea to preserve the fish caught by their husbands. An assignment for a Bombay fashion feature in Asian magazine resulted in this picture (r.). It was made in Bombay hotel room.

Combating the Medicare Squeeze

If physicians want to preserve their freedom, the author says, they must actively combat government edict and fiscal fiat.

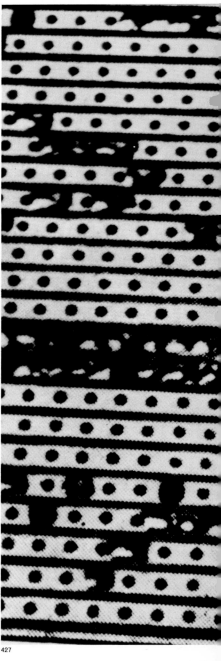

Editorial Photography

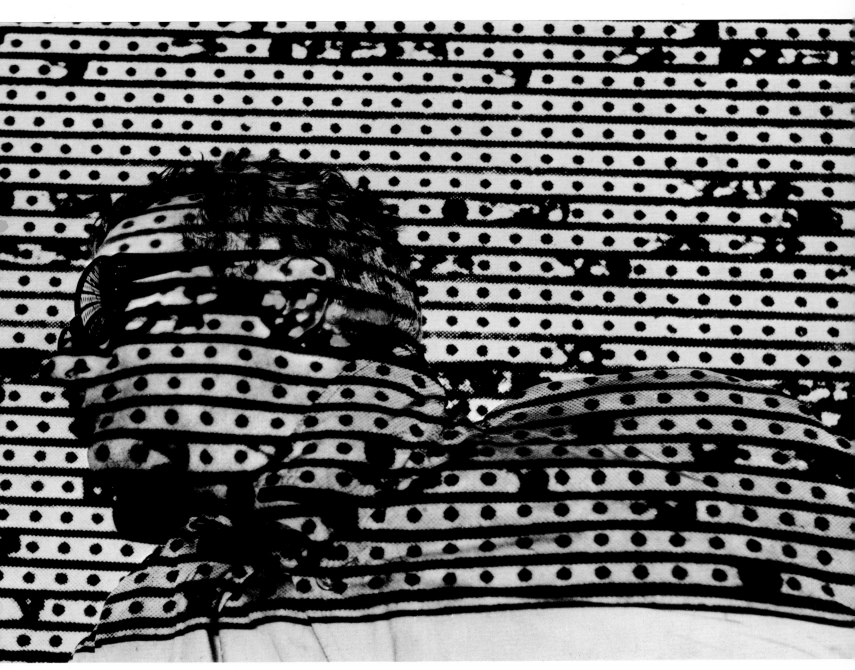

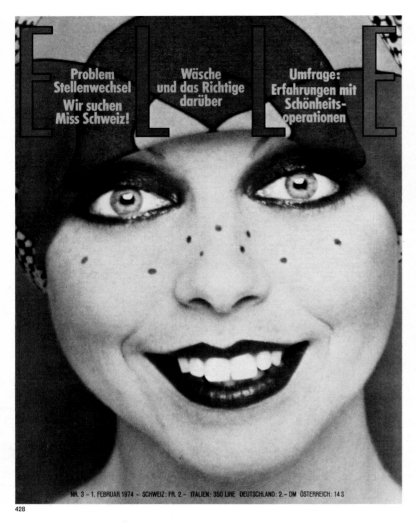

428

NR. 3 – 1. FEBRUAR 1974 – SCHWEIZ: FR. 2.– ITALIEN: 350 LIRE DEUTSCHLAND: 2.– DM ÖSTERREICH: 14 S

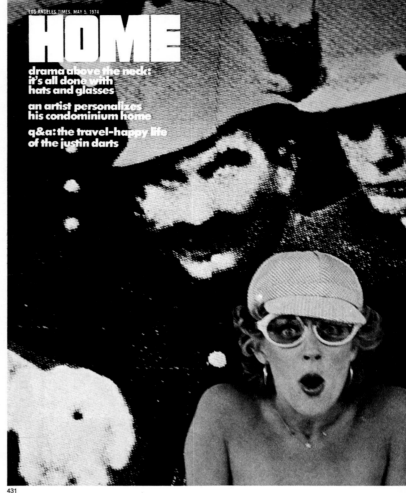

LOS ANGELES TIMES, MAY 5, 1974

HOME

drama above the neck:
it's all done with
hats and glasses

an artist personalizes
his condominium home

q&a: the travel-happy life
of the justin darts

431

PHOTOGRAPHER / PHOTOGRAPH / PHOTOGRAPHE:

428 Elisabeth Ely
429, 430 Ben Oyne
431–433 Antonin Kratochvil
434 Robert Freson

DESIGNER / GESTALTER / MAQUETTISTE:

429, 430 Rolf Gillhausen
431–433 Hans Albers
434 Urs Husmann

ART DIRECTOR / DIRECTEUR ARTISTIQUE:

428 Monika Frei-Herrmann
429, 430 Rolf Gillhausen
431–433 Hans Albers
434 Paul Kaelin

AGENCY / AGENTUR / AGENCE – STUDIO:

429, 430 Ben Oyne Studio

PUBLISHER / VERLEGER / EDITEUR:

428 Elle S.A.
429, 430 Gruner & Jahr GmbH & Co.
431–433 Los Angeles Times
434 Tages-Anzeiger für
Stadt und Kanton Zürich

429

430

170

LOS ANGELES TIMES, JUNE 8, 1975

HOME

EASING INTO SUMMER
with action clothes,
cool refreshments
& a neat city garden

home q&a:
the eddie alberts

432

TAGES ANZEIGER MAGAZIN
NR. 32, 13. AUGUST 1972

434

LOS ANGELES TIMES, APRIL 13, 1975

HOME

FOR THE YOUNG & SPIRITED
portable soups
sounds to please every ear
one-room lifestyles
home q&a: the robert goulets

433

428 Cover of the women's magazine *Elle*. Yellow, flesh and red shades, green eyes. (SWI)
429, 430 Cover of *Stern* magazine with an allusion to the emancipation of women, and detail of the photography. (GER)
431 Cover of *Home*, a magazine of the *Los Angeles Times*. The picture, with pink cap and sun glasses, refers to a feature on "drama above the neck". (USA)
432 Cover of an issue of *Home* magazine with an article on summer refreshments. (USA)
433 Cover of an issue of *Home* magazine containing an article on "portable soups". (USA)
434 Cover of *Tages-Anzeiger-Magazin* with an article on orange soufflés. The photograph appeared originally in the French women's magazine *Marie Claire*. (SWI)

428 Umschlag der Frauenzeitschrift *Elle*. Rot- und Gelbtöne, Augen grün. (SWI)
429, 430 Umschlag der Zeitschrift *Stern* und Ausschnitt der Photographie. Die Illustration bezieht sich auf das im Innern behandelte Thema der Frauenemanzipation. (GER)
431 Umschlag der Zeitschrift *Home*, ein Wochenmagazin der *Los Angeles Times*. Die Aufnahme (rosa Mütze und Brille) nimmt Bezug auf einen Artikel über Mode. (USA)
432 Umschlag einer Ausgabe der Zeitschrift *Home* mit einem Beitrag über sommerliche Erfrischungsgetränke. (USA)
433 Umschlag zu *Home* mit einem Artikel über Suppengerichte für unterwegs. (USA)
434 Umschlag des *Tages-Anzeiger-Magazins*, das einen Artikel über Orangenaufläufe enthält. Die Aufnahme erschien ursprünglich in einem Artikel in *Marie Claire*. (SWI)

428 Couverture de la revue féminine *Elle*. Tons jaunes, roses et rouges, yeux verts. (SWI)
429, 430 Couverture du magazine *Stern* avec une allusion à l'émancipation de la femme, et détail de la photographie. (GER)
431 Couverture de *Home*, supplément hebdomadaire du *Los Angeles Times*. La photo (chapeau et lunettes roses) se réfère à un article sur «le drame au-dessus du cou». (USA)
432 Couverture d'un numéro de *Home*, contenant un article sur les boissons rafraîchissantes en été. (USA)
433 Couverture d'un numéro du magazine *Home* avec un article concernant les soupes qui se prêtent à la préparation « en route ». (USA)
434 Couverture du *Tages-Anzeiger-Magazin*, supplément de fin de semaine du *Tages-Anzeiger*. L'illustration se réfère aux soufflés à l'orange. La photo a été publiée pour la première fois dans un article de *Marie Claire*. (SWI)

Magazine Covers
Zeitschriftenumschläge
Couvertures de périodiques

435

PHOTOGRAPHER / PHOTOGRAPH / PHOTOGRAPHE:

435, 436 Frank Aleksandrowicz
437, 438 Thomas Zamiar
439 Charles Compère
440—442 Heinz Kroehl/Peter Offenberg

DESIGNER / GESTALTER / MAQUETTISTE:

435, 436 Sue Connors
437, 438 Carl Hofman
439 Hanswerner Klein
440—442 Heinz Kroehl/Peter Offenberg

ART DIRECTOR / DIRECTEUR ARTISTIQUE:

435, 436 Joe Giacalone
437, 438 Carl Hofman
440—442 Heinz Kroehl/Peter Offenberg

AGENCY / AGENTUR / AGENCE – STUDIO:

440—442 Kroehl Design Gruppe

PUBLISHER / VERLEGER / EDITEUR:

435, 436 American Medical Association
437, 438 Realtors National Marketing Institute
439 Verlag form GmbH
440—442 B. Schott's Söhne

436

435, 436 Complete cover of *Prism,* a magazine published by the American Medical Association, and detail of the photography. The issue contains an article on Imhotep, the Egyptian architect and physician. (USA)
437, 438 Two covers of the magazine *Real Estate Today.* (USA)
439 Cover of the design magazine *Form.* Colour photograph in blue, red and yellow. (GER)
440–442 Title pages for pieces of music (here for oboe, recorder and horn) issued by a music publisher. (GER)

435, 436 Ganzer Umschlag der Ärztezeitschrift *Prism* und Ausschnitt der Aufnahme. Die Nummer enthält einen Artikel über Imhotep, einen ägyptischen Architekten und Arzt. (USA)
437, 438 Umschläge einer Zeitschrift für den Liegenschaftenhandel. (USA)
439 Umschlag der Zeitschrift für Gestaltung *Form.* Farbaufnahme in Blau, Rot und Gelb. (GER)
440–442 Notenheft-Umschläge des Musikverlages B. Schott's Söhne, Mainz. (GER)

435, 436 Couverture complète du magazine *Prism* (magazine de l'Association médicale américaine) et détail de la photo qui l'illustre. Ce numéro contient un article consacré à Imhotep, le grand architecte et médecin de l'Egypte. (USA)
437, 438 Couvertures du magazine *Real Estate Today.* (USA)
439 Couverture du magazine de création esthétique *Form.* Photo couleur en bleu, rouge et jaune. (GER)
440–442 Couvertures de cahiers de musique (pièces pour hautbois, flûte à bec et cor), publiés à Mayence. (GER)

437

438

439

440

441

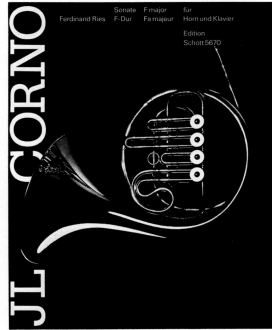

442

Magazine Covers
Zeitschriftenumschläge
Couvertures de périodiques

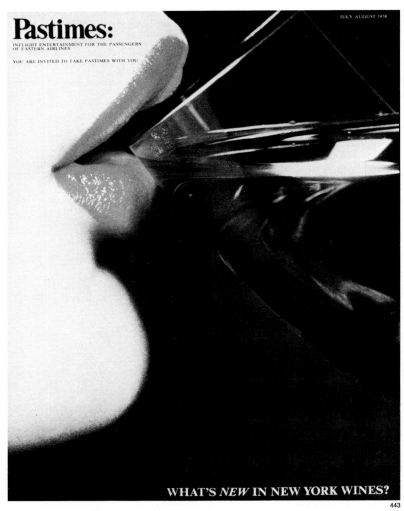

Pastimes:
INFLIGHT ENTERTAINMENT FOR THE PASSENGERS OF EASTERN AIRLINES

YOU ARE INVITED TO TAKE PASTIMES WITH YOU

JULY AUGUST 1974

WHAT'S *NEW* IN NEW YORK WINES?

443

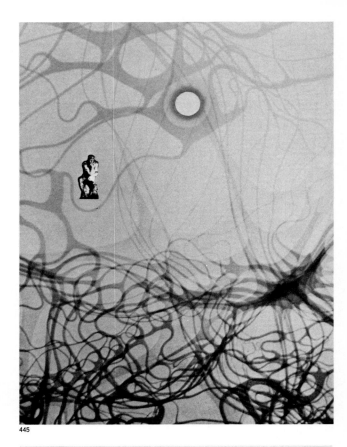

445

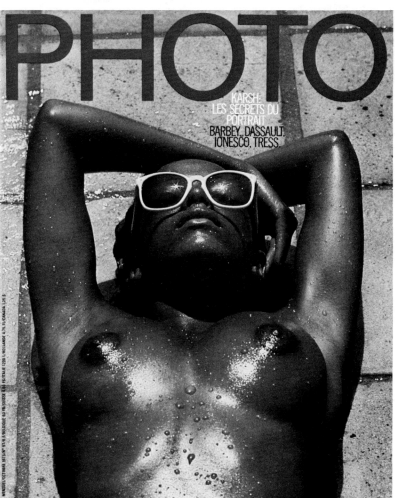

PHOTO

KARSH: LES SECRETS DU PORTRAIT
BARBEY, DASSAULT, IONESCO, TRESS.

444

progresso
FOTOGRAFICO

APRILE 1975
L. 1.000
4

448

443 Cover of *Pastimes*, the passenger magazine of *Eastern Airlines*. The issue contains a feature on wine. (USA)
444 Cover of the magazine *Photo*. Full colour. (USA)
445 Back cover of the magazine *Psychologie*. Turquoise, blue and purple network, black-and-white figure, yellow sun. (FRA)
446 Cover of an issue of the magazine *Psychologie* containing an article on sexual deficiencies. Title in green. (FRA)
447 Cover of AIA *Journal* (a publication of the American Institute of Architects) showing reflections in glass tiles. (USA)
448 Cover of *Progresso Fotografico*. Red kimono, blue title. (ITA)
449 Cover of *Spot*, a review of photography. Black and white. (YUG)
450 Cover of *Domus*, a review of architecture and art. (ITA)

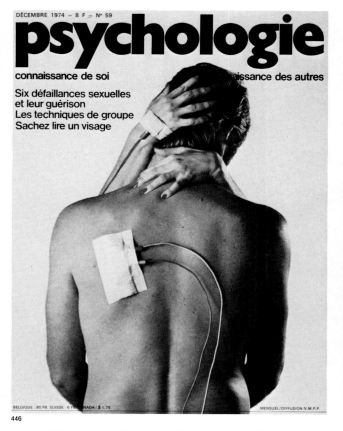

psychologie

connaissance de soi ...naissance des autres

Six défaillances sexuelles
et leur guérison
Les techniques de groupe
Sachez lire un visage

DÉCEMBRE 1974 – 8 F – N° 59

BELGIQUE : 80 FB. SUISSE : 6 F... ...NADA : $ 1.75   MENSUEL/DIFFUSION N.M.P.P.

446

447

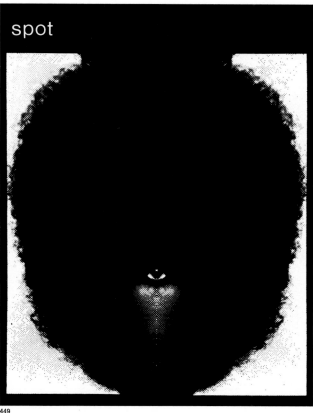

spot

449

450

PHOTOGRAPHER / PHOTOGRAPH:

443 Pat Field
444 James Baes
445 Thierry Vincens
446 Michel Tiziou
447 Sam Hall
448 Alberto Rizzo
449 Roman Cieslewicz

DESIGNER / GESTALTER:

443 B. Martin Pedersen
444 Patrick Lefrangois
445 Evelyne Doucet
448 Alberto Piovani
449 Roman Cieslewicz
450 Domus, Redaktion

ART DIRECTOR:

443 B. Martin Pedersen
444 Eric Colmet Daage
445, 446 Daniel Sinay
447 Don Canty/Suzy Thomas
448 Alberto Piovani

AGENCY / AGENTUR / AGENCE:

443 Pedersen Design
445, 446 Hollenstein Créations
447 Sam Hall & Associates
449 Roman Cieslewicz

PUBLISHER / VERLEGER:

443 Pastimes
444 Publication Filipacchi
445 C.E.P.L. (Centre d'étude et
     de promotion de la lecture)
446 C.A.L. Revue Psychologie
447 American Inst. of Architects
448 Progresso Fotografico
449 Musée d'Art Moderne
450 Editoriale Domus S.p.A.

443 Umschlag der Zeitschrift *Pastimes*, die von den *Eastern Airlines* an ihre Passagiere abgegeben wird. Das Heft enthält einen Artikel über Wein. (USA)
444 Mehrfarbiger Umschlag der Fachzeitschrift *Photo*. (USA)
445 Umschlagrückseite der Zeitschrift *Psychologie*. Nervensystem in Türkis, Blau und Violett, Figur schwarzweiss, Sonne gelb. (FRA)
446 Umschlag der Zeitschrift *Psychologie* mit einem Artikel über sexuelle Störungen. Titelschrift grün. (FRA)
447 Umschlag der Zeitschrift des amerikanischen Instituts für Architektur. Die Photo zeigt Spiegelungen in Glasziegeln. (USA)
448 Umschlag der Zeitschrift *Progresso Fotografico*. Roter Kimono. (ITA)
449 Schwarzweisser Umschlag von *Spot*, einer Photo-Zeitschrift. (YUG)
450 Umschlag der Zeitschrift für Architektur und Kunst *Domus*. (ITA)

443 Couverture de *Pastimes*, le magazine pour les passagers de la compagnie aérienne *Eastern Airlines*. Ce numéro présente un article sur les vins. (USA)
444 Couverture du magazine *Photo*. Polychromie. (USA)
445 Quatrième page de couverture du magazine *Psychologie*. Réseau en turquoise, bleu et violet, figure en noir et blanc, soleil jaune. (FRA)
446 Couverture d'un numéro du magazine *Psychologie*, contenant un article sur les défaillances sexuelles. Titre imprimé en vert. (FRA)
447 Couverture de l'AIA *Journal* (une publication de l'Institut américain d'architecture). Réflexions d'un bâtiment dans des carreaux en verre. (USA)
448 Couverture de *Progresso Fotografico*. Kimono rouge, titre bleu. (ITA)
449 Couverture de *Spot*, une revue photographique. Noir et blanc. (YUG)
450 Couverture de *Domus*, une revue d'art et d'architecture. (ITA)

Magazine Covers

451

452

PUBLISHER / VERLEGER:

451 IBM, Data Processing Div.
452 Litton Publications
453 Creative Communicator
454 The Cooper Union
455 First Federal Savings Bank
456 VNU Panorama
457 Emergency Medicine

453

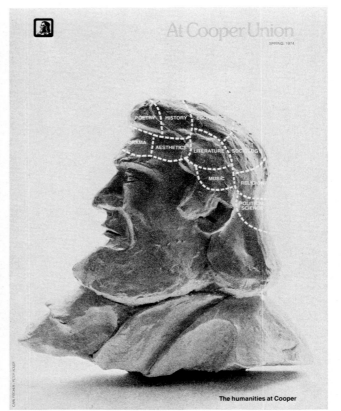

454

PHOTOGRAPHER / PHOTOGRAPH / PHOTOGRAPHE:

451 Beatrice Stocklin
452 Jerry Sarapochiello
453 Jean Moss
454 Carl Fischer
455 Jan Mar
456 Wim Baggelaar
457 Ed Lettau

DESIGNER / GESTALTER / MAQUETTISTE:

451 Fred Troller
452 Joann Cassela
453 Jim Lienhart
454 Peter Adler
455 Barry Lau
456 Panorama, Art Group
457 Mike Shenon

ART DIRECTOR / DIRECTEUR ARTISTIQUE:

452 Joann Cassela
453 Jim Lienhart
454 Peter Adler
455 Barry Lau
456 Jan Lips/Wim van Gogh
457 Mike Shenon

AGENCY / AGENTUR / AGENCE – STUDIO:

451 Fred Troller Associates
453 Murrie – White & Associates
454 Adler, Schwartz & Connes, Inc.
455 American Graphics Corp.
456 Fotostudio Baggelaar

455

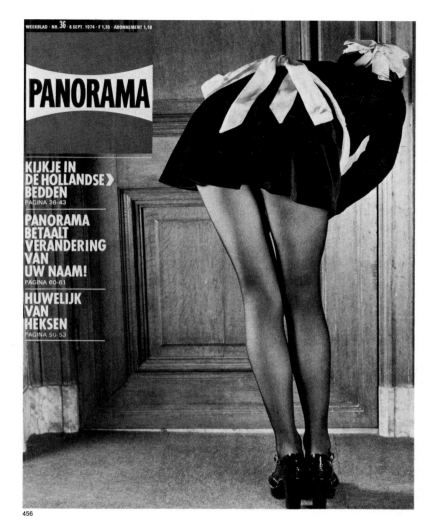

456

457

451 Cover of the IBM magazine *Data Processor*. Bright colours on beige. (USA)
452 Cover of RN *Magazine*, a publication for registered nurses. Full colour. (USA)
453 Cover of an issue of *Creative Communicator* announcing an exhibition in Chicago. (USA)
454 Cover of the alumni quarterly *At Cooper Union*, artifact with an allusion to phrenology in pale grey-brown, blue title. (USA)
455 Cover of *Saver* (autumn issue), published by First Federal Savings Bank, Chicago. (USA)
456 Cover of an issue of the weekly *Panorama* containing an article on a "peep into Dutch beds". Full colour. (NLD)
457 Cover of an issue of *Emergency Medicine* containing a feature on the detection of syphilis. Reddish figure, blue title. (USA)

451 Umschlag der IBM-Zeitschrift *Data Processor*. Leuchtende Farben auf beigem Grund. (USA)
452 Mehrfarbiger Umschlag einer Zeitschrift für diplomierte Krankenschwestern. (USA)
453 Umschlag eines Heftes von *Creative Communicator* mit der Ankündigung einer Ausstellung in Chicago. (USA)
454 Umschlag der vierteljährlich erscheinenden Zeitschrift der Altherren, *At Cooper Union*. Die Schädelfelder nennen die an dieser Kunstschule dozierten Fächer. (USA)
455 Umschlag für die Herbstnummer der Kundenzeitung einer Sparkasse. (USA)
456 Mehrfarbiger Umschlag der Wochenzeitschrift *Panorama*, die einen Artikel über «Holländische Betten durchs Schlüsselloch gesehen» enthält. (NLD)
457 Umschlag einer medizinischen Fachzeitschrift mit einem Artikel über Syphilis. «Sie wirkt sauber, aber ...» Figur in Rottönen, Titelschrift blau. (USA)

451 Couverture du magazine *Data Processor*, une publication de l'IBM. Couleurs vives sur fond beige. (USA)
452 Couverture du RN *Magazine*, une publication s'adressant aux infirmières diplômées. (USA)
453 Couverture d'un numéro du magazine *Creative Communicator* annonçant une exposition qui sera présentée à Chicago. (USA)
454 Couverture de la publication trimestrielle *At Cooper Union*, destiné aux anciens étudiants. Artefact avec allusion à la phrénologie, en gris brun pâle, titre bleu. (USA)
455 Couverture de *Saver* (numéro d'automne), périodique publié par une banque à Chicago. (USA)
456 Couverture d'un numéro de l'hebdomadaire *Panorama*, contenant un article sur «un coup d'œil dans le lit néerlandais». Polychromie. (NLD)
457 Couverture d'un numéro d'*Emergency Medicine*, avec un article sur la découverte de la syphilis. En couleur. (USA)

Magazine Covers
Zeitschriftenumschläge
Couvertures de périodiques

Magazine Covers
Zeitschriftenumschläge
Couvertures de périodiques

458 Cover of *Stethoscope,* house organ of the pharmaceutical company Sankyo Co. Ltd. Flesh shades with blue and pink shadows. (JPN)
459 Cover of *Stethoscope.* Purple ground, red and white carnation. (JPN)
460 Cover of an issue of the design magazine *Print* containing a critical article on the satirical monthly *National Lampoon.* Red blood. (USA)
461 Cover of *Tripping,* a bi-annual students' travel magazine. Black and white with yellow title. (USA)
462 Pipes for the Alaska pipeline on the cover of *The Lamp.* (USA)

458 Umschlag der Hauszeitschrift eines pharmazeutischen Unternehmens. Fleischfarbig mit Schattierungen in Blau und Rosa. (JPN)
459 Umschlag der Hauszeitschrift eines Arzneimittel-Konzerns. (JPN)
460 Umschlag der Zeitschrift *Print,* die einen kritischen Artikel über die satirische Zeitschrift *National Lampoon* enthält. Blutspritzer in Rot. (USA)
461 Umschlag einer Halbjahresschrift für Studentenreisen. (USA)
462 Röhren der Alaska-Pipeline auf dem Umschlag der Hauszeitschrift der Erdölgesellschaft *Exxon.* (USA)

458 Couverture de *Stethoscope,* journal d'entreprise d'une compagnie de produits pharmaceutiques. Tons roses avec des ombres en bleu et rouge. (JPN)
459 Couverture de *Stethoscope.* Fond lilas, œillet en tons rouges. (JPN)
460 Couverture de *Print* (magazine d'art graphique), avec un article critique sur la publication satirique *National Lampoon.* Sang rouge. (USA)
461 Couverture de *Tripping,* un magazine bi-annuel de voyages d'étudiants. Noir et blanc avec titre en jaune. (USA)
462 Tuyaux pour l'oléoduc de l'Alaska. Couverture de *The Lamp.* (USA)

458

460
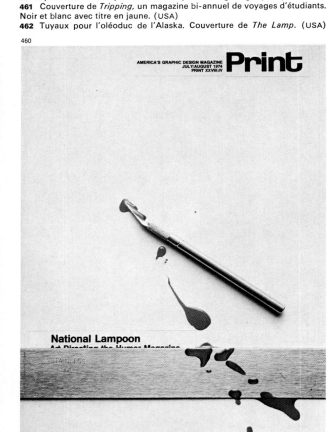

459

461

PHOTOGRAPHER / PHOTOGRAPH:

458, 459 Akio Suyama
460 Dick Frank
461 Randy LaMorte
462 Harald Sund

DESIGNER / GESTALTER / MAQUETTISTE:

458, 459 Kenji Itoh
460 Michael Gross
461 Walter Sparks/David Gauger
462 Harry O. Diamond

ART DIRECTOR / DIRECTEUR ARTISTIQUE:

458, 459 Kenji Itoh
460 Andrew Kner
461 David Gauger/Walter Sparks
462 Harry O. Diamond

AGENCY / AGENTUR / AGENCE – STUDIO:

461 Gauger Sparks Silva

PUBLISHER / VERLEGER / EDITEUR:

458, 459 Sankyo Co. Ltd.
460 RC Publications, Inc.
461 Student Services West, Inc.
462 Exxon Corporation

The Lamp
WINTER 1974

465

PHOTOGRAPHER / PHOTOGRAPH:

463 Henry Wolf
464–466 Dan Wynn
467, 468 Henry Wolf

DESIGNER / GESTALTER / MAQUETTISTE:

463 Walter Bernard/Milton Glaser
464 Milton Glaser
465, 466 Milton Glaser/Tom Bentkowski
467, 468 Walter Bernard

ART DIRECTOR / DIRECTEUR ARTISTIQUE:

463–466 Walter Bernard/Milton Glaser
467, 468 Walter Bernard

AGENCY / AGENTUR / AGENCE – STUDIO:

467, 468 Henry Wolf Productions, Inc.

PUBLISHER / VERLEGER / EDITEUR:

463–468 New York Magazine

463

464

463 Cover of *New York* magazine with a portrait of black dancer Judith Jamison. Red feathers and dress. (USA)
464 Cover of *New York* magazine featuring a "new kind of Hollywood star". Lettering red and green. (USA)
465, 466 Detail of the photography (bringing up to date Manet's famous painting) and complete cover of an issue of *New York* dealing with summer pleasures. (USA)
467, 468 Complete cover of an issue of *New York* magazine alluding to the revival of Art Déco, and detail of the colour photography. (USA)

463 Umschlag der Zeitschrift *New York* mit der Photographie einer Tänzerin. Federn und Kleid in Rot. (USA)
464 Umschlag der Zeitschrift *New York* mit einem Bericht über einen neuen Hollywoodstar. (USA)
465, 466 Ausschnitt der Aufnahme (die Manets berühmtes Gemälde in die Gegenwart transponiert) und ganzer Umschlag einer Nummer von *New York*, die den Sommerfreuden gewidmet ist. (USA)
467, 468 Ganzer Umschlag und Ausschnitt der Photographie für ein Heft von *New York* mit einem Artikel über die Wiederentdeckung von Art Déco. (USA)

463 Couverture du magazine *New York* avec un portrait de Judith Jamison. Plumes et robe rouges. (USA)
464 Couverture du magazine *New York* qui présente «le nouveau star de Hollywood». Texte en rouge et vert. (USA)
465, 466 Détail de la photo (mise à jour d'une célèbre peinture de Manet) et couverture complète où elle figure. D'un numéro du magazine *New York*, consacré aux plaisirs d'été. (USA)
467, 468 Couverture complète d'un numéro du magazine *New York* et détail de la photo qui l'illustre. Allusion à la renaissance de l'Art Déco. (USA)

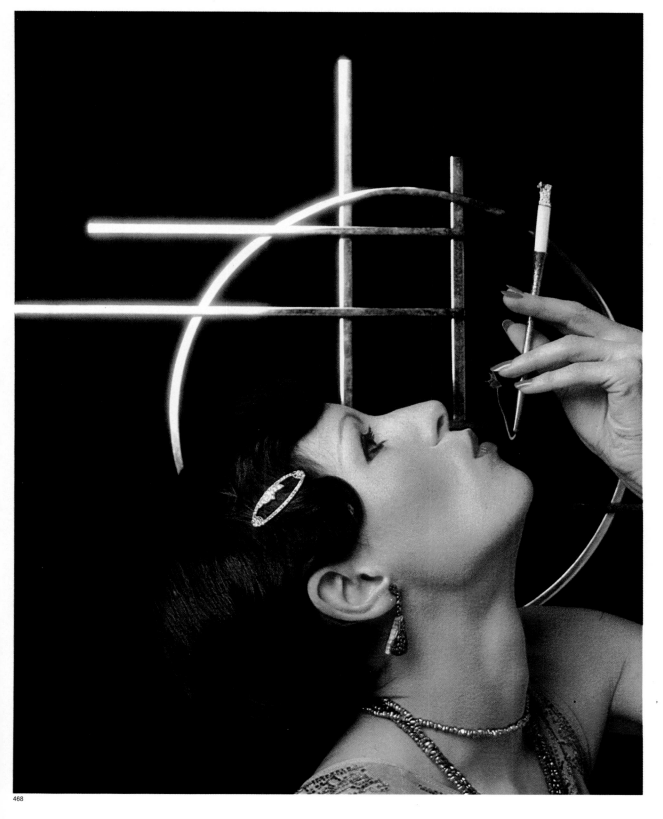

Magazine Covers

181

Magazine Covers
Zeitschriftenumschläge
Couvertures de périodiques

PHOTOGRAPHER / PHOTOGRAPH / PHOTOGRAPHE:

469, 470 Rolf Giger
471 James Moore
472 Richard L. Shaefer

DESIGNER / GESTALTER / MAQUETTISTE:

471, 472 Rowan G. Johnson

ART DIRECTOR / DIRECTEUR ARTISTIQUE:

471, 472 Rowan G. Johnson

PUBLISHER / VERLEGER / EDITEUR:

469, 470 Schweizer. Verkehrszentrale
471, 472 Viva International Ltd.

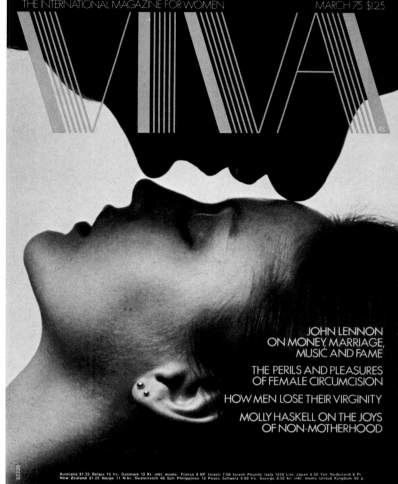

471

469, 470 Detail of the photography (roughly in the size of actual use) and complete cover of an issue of *Switzerland*, magazine of the Swiss National Tourist Office. (SWI)
471 Cover of the women's magazine *Viva*. Title in pale vermilion. (USA)
472 Cover of *Viva* contrasting white and sunburnt skins, black title. (USA)

469, 470 Annähernd originalgrosse Photographie und ganzer Umschlag der Zeitschrift *Schweiz* der Schweizerischen Verkehrszentrale. (SWI)
471 Umschlag der Frauenzeitschrift *Viva*. Titelschrift in hellem Zinnober. (USA)
472 Umschlag von *Viva* mit einem hellen Frauen- und einem sonnverbrannten Männerkörper. Titelschrift schwarz. (USA)

469, 470 Détail de la photo (approx. en grandeur nature) et couverture complète où elle figure. Numéro de la revue *Suisse*, publiée par l'Office National Suisse du Tourisme. (SWI)
471 Couverture du magazine féminin *Viva*. Titre en vermillon pâle. (USA)
472 Couverture de *Viva* avec une illustration qui met en contraste la peau pâle et la peau teintée. Titre en noir. (USA)

470

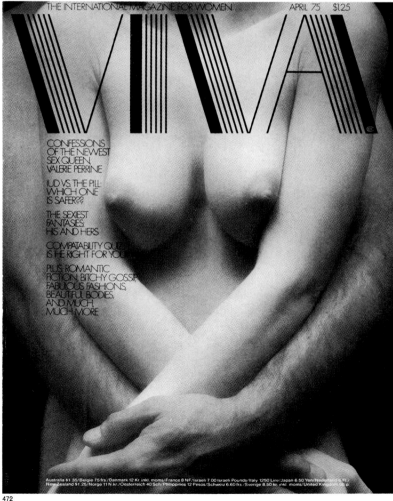

472

473

474

475

476

Magazine Covers
Zeitschriftenumschläge
Couvertures de périodiques

473 "Don't be alarmed, we're only looking for the nearest petrol station." Cover of *Zeit Magazin*. Brown ground. (GER)
474 "Our oil." Cover of the magazine *Nin*. Pale blue globe. (YUG)
475 Cover of the local *Hudson Valley* magazine. (USA)
476 Cover of a fiftieth anniversary issue of the *Philadelphia Daily News*. (USA)
477 Cover of *The New York Times Magazine* with two pictures of the same young lady. Full colour. (USA)
478 Black-and-white cover of *The New York Times Magazine* (blue title) showing a composite photograph as used by a rape squad. (USA)
479, 480 Two covers of *The New York Times Magazine* in full colour, alluding to a good-conscience Thanksgiving menu and to American football on television. (USA)

The New York Times Magazine

AUGUST 11, 1974   SECTION 6

Two
faces of
the
same Eve:
Ms.
versus
Cosmo

CONTENTS: PAGE 4

Also in this issue:

KIDS'
CLOTHES

PAGES 38-71

477

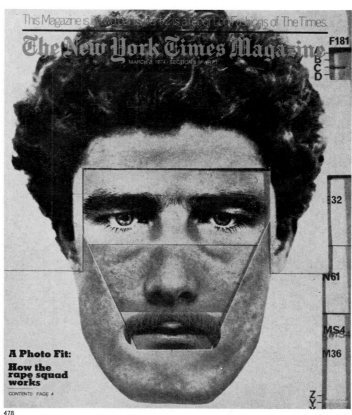

This Magazine is in two parts. Part 2 is a report on Fashions of The Times.

The New York Times Magazine

MARCH 3, 1974 / SECTION 6 PART 1

F181
B C
C D
D E

E32

N61

MS4

M36

A Photo Fit:
How the
rape squad
works

CONTENTS: PAGE 4

478

The New York Times Magazine

NOVEMBER 24, 1974 / SECTION 6

Thanksgiving,
with a
conscience

CONTENTS: PAGE 10

Thanksgiving
Menu 1974

Chilled Artichoke
Sunflower Seeds Vinaigrette

Clear Borscht
Sesame Seed Wafers

Vegetarian Coulibiac
Sour Cream Sauce
Broccoli Purée

Corn Relish

Bean Sprout & Citrus Salad
on Watercress

Pumpkin Flan

Fresh Apple Cider

479

The New York Times Magazine

SEPTEMBER 22, 1974   SECTION 6

Instant
Pre-Play:
TV football
for the
novice

CONTENTS PAGE: 10

480

473 Umschlag des *Zeit Magazins*. Vorwiegend in Brauntönen. (GER)
474 «Unser Öl.» Umschlag der Zeitschrift *Nin*. Erdkugel in hellem Blau. (YUG)
475 Umschlag einer lokalen Zeitschrift. (USA)
476 Umschlag der Jubiläumsnummer der *Philadelphia Daily News*, die anlässlich des 50jährigen Bestehens herausgegeben wurde. (USA)
477 Mehrfarbiger Umschlag des *New York Times Magazine* mit zwei Aufnahmen des gleichen Photomodells. (USA)
478 Schwarzweisser Umschlag des *New York Times Magazine*. Unter der blauen Titelschrift eine Photomontage, wie sie von der Kriminalpolizei erstellt wird. (USA)
479, 480 Mehrfarbige Umschläge des *New York Times Magazine*. Sie beziehen sich auf Menüvorschläge zum Erntedanktag sowie auf Sportsendungen im Fernsehen. (USA)

473 «Ne soyez pas alarmés, nous sommes en quête du prochain poste d'essence.» Couverture du supplément hebdomadaire *Zeit Magazin*. Fond brun. (GER)
474 «Notre pétrole.» Couverture du magazine *Nin*. Globe terrestre en bleu pâle. (YUG)
475 Couverture de *Hudson Valley*, un magazine régional. (USA)
476 Couverture d'un numéro célébrant les 50 ans du *Philadelphia Daily News*. (USA)
477 Couverture du *New York Times Magazine* présentant deux photos de la même jeune dame. Polychromie. (USA)
478 Couverture du *New York Times Magazine* (titre bleu) avec une photo combinée du type utilisé par la police. Noir et blanc. (USA)
479, 480 Deux couvertures du *New York Times Magazine* avec allusion à un menu de la fête de Thanksgiving et aux programmes de sport à la TV. (USA)

PHOTOGRAPHER / PHOTOGRAPH / PHOTOGRAPHE:

481 G. Routhier
482, 483 Eddi Brofferio

DESIGNER / GESTALTER / MAQUETTISTE:

481 Walter Rospert
482, 483 José Alvarez

ART DIRECTOR / DIRECTEUR ARTISTIQUE:

481 Peter Knapp
482, 483 José Alvarez

PUBLISHER / VERLEGER / EDITEUR:

481 Editions André Sauret
482, 483 Guide du livre et Clairfontaine/
Ehem. Kurt Desch Verlag

481 Dust jacket of a large book on the French sculptor César by Pierre Restany. Shades of blue, grey and black. (FRA)
482, 483 Complete dust jacket and detail of the photography for a large volume by and about Léonor Fini. The book contains photographs of the artist as well as reproductions of her works and extracts from her writings. (SWI)

481 Schutzumschlag zu einem grossformatigen Buch von Pierre Restany über den französischen Bildhauer César. Blau, grau und schwarz. (FRA)
482, 483 Ganzer Schutzumschlag und Photoausschnitt zu einem grossformatigen Buch von und über Léonor Fini. Es enthält Aufnahmen der Künstlerin, Abbildungen ihrer Werke und Auszüge aus ihren Schriften. (SWI)

481 Jaquette d'un livre grand format (édité par Pierre Restany) qui est consacré à César, un sculpteur français. Tons bleu, gris et noirs. (FRA)
482, 483 Jaquette complète et détail de la photo qui l'illustre. Cette publication est consacrée à Léonor Fini et comprend des photos de l'artiste ainsi que des reproductions de son œuvre et des extraits de ses essays. (SWI)

482

Book covers
Buchumschläge
Couvertures de livres

481

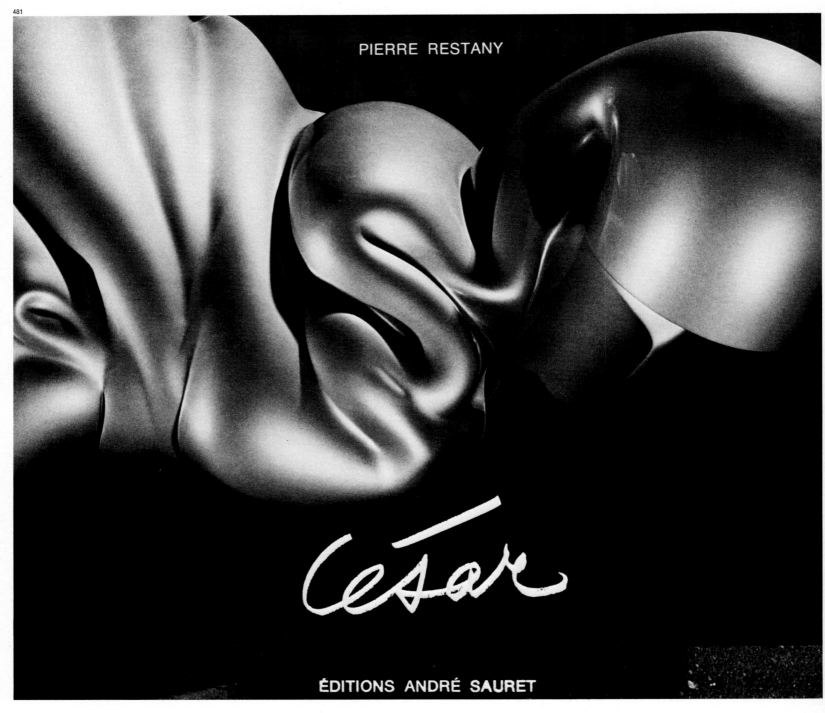

PIERRE RESTANY

César

ÉDITIONS ANDRÉ SAURET

484

PHOTOGRAPHER / PHOTOGRAPH / PHOTOGRAPHE:

484, 484a Beth Toming
485–487 Ralph Cowan/Ray Komorski
488, 488a Carl Fischer

DESIGNER / GESTALTER / MAQUETTISTE:

484, 484a Beth Toming
488, 488a Carl Fischer

ART DIRECTOR / DIRECTEUR ARTISTIQUE:

484, 484a Hans Jørgen Toming
485–487 Norman Perman
488, 488a Les Pockell

Book covers
Buchumschläge
Couvertures de livres

484a

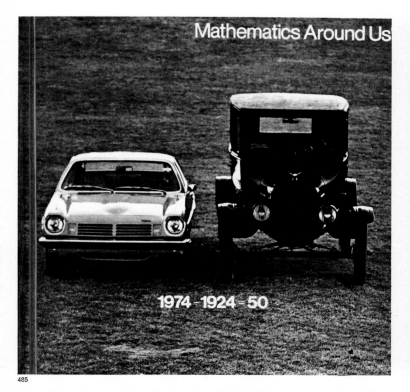

Mathematics Around Us

1974−1924=50

485

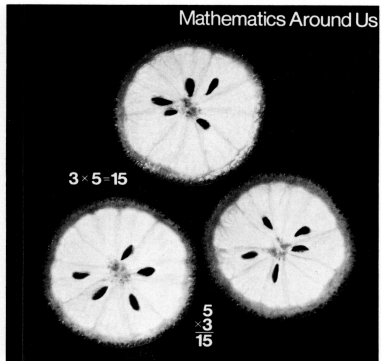

Mathematics Around Us

3×5=15

$\frac{\begin{array}{r}5\\\times3\end{array}}{15}$

486

Mathematics Around Us

.68m 1.10m 1.28m 1.06m 1.17m .65m

487

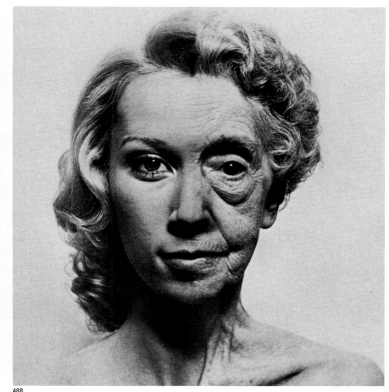

488

484, 484a Detail of the photography in actual size and complete cover for a book from a poetry series, with lyrics by Nils Ferlin, a Swedish worker poet. (NOR)
485−487 Covers of educational books from a series dealing with practical applications of mathematics, published by Scott, Foresman & Co. (USA)
488, 488a Detail and complete dust jacket for a book on beauty care, published by St. Martin's Press. Colour photograph on light blue ground. (USA)

484, 484a Aufnahme in Originalgrösse und vollständiger Umschlag zu einem Band Gedichte von Nils Ferlin, einem schwedischen Arbeiterdichter. (NOR)
485−487 Umschläge aus einer Serie von Lehrbüchern über die praktische Anwendung der Mathematik, herausgegeben von Scott, Foresman & Co. (USA)
488, 488a Ausschnitt und vollständiger Schutzumschlag für ein Buch über Schönheitspflege. Farbaufnahme auf hellblauem Grund. (USA)

484, 484a Photo en grandeur nature et couverture complète d'une publication qui fait partie d'une série d'anthologies. Ce volume-ci est consacré aux poèmes de Nils Ferlin, un poète-ouvrier suédois. (NOR)
485−487 Couvertures d'une série de manuels sur l'emploi pratique de la mathématique. Publication de Scott, Foresman & Cie. (USA)
488, 488a Détail et jaquette complète pour un livre consacré aux soins de beauté. Photographie en couleur sur fond bleu pâle. (USA)

The Art of Being Beautiful at Any Age

Bedford Shelmire, Jr. M.D.
An essential guide to beauty care with the revolutionary Personal Skin Index by the best-selling author of The Art of Looking Younger

488a

AGENCY / AGENTUR / AGENCE − STUDIO:
484, 484a Beth & Hans Jørgen Toming

PUBLISHER / VERLEGER / EDITEUR:
484, 484a Den norske Bokklubben
485−487 Scott, Foresman & Co.
488, 488a St. Martin's Press

ORGANIZATION
WILFRED BROWN

PELICAN LIBRARY OF BUSINESS AND MANAGEMENT

489

AN INSIGHT
INTO MANAGEMENT
ACCOUNTING
JOHN SIZER

PELICAN LIBRARY OF BUSINESS AND MANAGEMENT

490

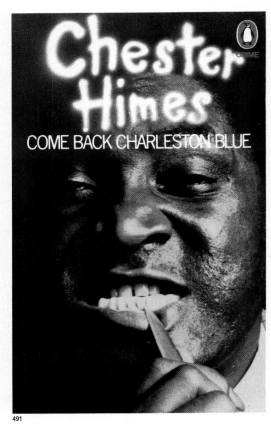

Chester
Himes
COME BACK CHARLESTON BLUE

491

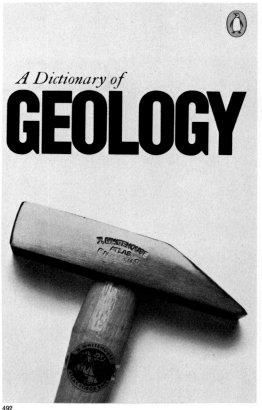

A Dictionary of
GEOLOGY

492

VICTORIAN
ENGINEERING

L.T.C. ROLT

493

Income Distribution
Jan Pen

494

489, 490 Covers of two *Pelican* paperbacks from a series on business and management. In colour on dark blue. (GBR)
491 Cover of a paperback from a *Penguin* crime series. (GBR)
492 Cover of a *Penguin* geological dictionary. Hammer in full colour on white. (GBR)
493 Cover of a *Pelican* paperback. Green, red and black, white lettering. (GBR)
494 Cover of a *Pelican* paperback. The colour photograph comments on the title. (GBR)
495 Black-and-white cover of a large work on the modern artist Lucio Fontana. (BEL)

489, 490 Umschläge zweier Taschenbücher aus einer Serie über Geschäftsführung. Mehrfarbig auf dunkelblauem Grund. (GBR)
491 Taschenbuchumschlag für einen Kriminalroman. (GBR)
492 Umschlag zu einem geologischen Wörterbuch. Mehrfarbiger Hammer auf weissem Grund. (GBR)
493 Umschlag zu einem Taschenbuch über die Technik im Zeitalter der Königin Victoria. Mehrfarbig. (GBR)
494 Mehrfarbiger Umschlag eines Taschenbuches über Einkommensverteilung. (GBR)
495 Schwarzweisser Umschlag zu einem grossformatigen Band über das Werk des Künstlers Lucio Fontana. (BEL)

489, 490 Couvertures de deux livres de poche figurant dans une série sur la gestion et le management. Fond bleu foncé. (GBR)
491 Couverture d'un roman policier. (GBR)
492 Couverture d'un dictionnaire géologique, d'une collection de poche. Marteau en couleur sur fond blanc. (GBR)
493 Couverture d'un livre de poche *Pelican*. Vert, rouge et noir, titre en blanc. (GBR)
494 Couverture d'un livre de poche *Pelican*. La photo couleur se réfère au titre de cette publication. (GBR)
495 Couverture d'un ouvrage grand format consacré à l'œuvre de l'artiste Lucio Fontana. Noir et blanc. (BEL)

495

PHOTOGRAPHER / PHOTOGRAPH:

489, 490 Pentagram Design
491 John Claridge
493 Humphrey Sutton
495 Ugo Moulas

DESIGNER / GESTALTER:

489, 490 Mervyn Kurlansky
491 Paul May
492 Omnific Design
494 Delaney & Ireland
495 Sylvia Goldschmidt

ART DIRECTOR

489–491, 493, 494 David Pelham
492 Derek Birdsall

AGENCY / AGENTUR / AGENCE:

489, 490 Pentagram Design
492 Omnific Design

PUBLISHER / VERLEGER / EDITEUR:

489–494 Penguin Books Ltd.
495 La Connaissance

Book covers
Buchumschläge
Couvertures de livres

Materials

For Colt Industries' materials business, 1974 was a year of record sales and earnings performance. The year was characterized by a high level of demand for Crucible specialty steels, high efficiency and productivity at near-capacity operation, a lower level of import competition, the ability to recover increased costs following decontrol of prices, and improved profit margins.

The materials business is conducted by three divisions: the Crucible Alloy Division and Crucible Stainless Steel Division, both at Midland, Pennsylvania; and the Crucible Specialty Metals Division at Syracuse, New York. Together, they comprise one of the nation's foremost producers of specialty steels.

A Unique Niche

Specialty steels occupy a unique niche in the steel industry. They differ from the carbon, or tonnage, steels in their use of costly alloying elements, the extreme precision required in their alloying and subsequent heat treatment or other processing, and the extent to which they are custom-formulated in scores of different grades to meet specific requirements. As a result, they are priced and sold by the pound rather than by the ton.

Specialty steels typically require substantial quantities of chromium, nickel, vanadium, molybdenum, tungsten or other relatively costly materials. Combinations of these alloying elements impart such valued properties as resistance to corrosion, abrasion, and extremes of temperature; machinability and formability; hardness and high tensile strength; and high strength-to-weight ratios. These are the properties, singly or in combination, that enable specialty steels to perform reliably in extremely demanding work environments.

Their applications range, therefore, from highly polished kitchenware, surgical instruments, and automobile trim to heavy construction equipment, refinery catalytic cracking towers, and metalworking tools.

Meeting Industry Needs

As American industry becomes more advanced technologically, its requirements for advanced materials with specific properties grow ever greater and more rigorous. Thus, the demand for specialty steels has increased steadily over the years, and in 1974 reached new highs as many basic industries moved to increase their production capacities. While demand slackened during the year in such areas as automobile and major appliance

496

Industrial and Power Equipment

Demand was high for the company's broad range of industrial products and power equipment in 1974, with the exception of electric transformers. Industrial and power equipment encompasses six major product areas: Trent and Crucible fabricated metal products, Pratt & Whitney and Elox production equipment, Fairbanks scales, Quincy compressors, Fairbanks Morse diesel engines, and Central Moloney electric distribution transformers.

Trent Paces Growth

The company's 1974 sales of Trent welded stainless steel pipe and tubing and Crucible industrial springs and permanent magnets were well above 1973 levels. The demand for Trent products was particularly strong and resulted in a sharp increase in orders from the energy, chemical, and food processing industries.

Illustrative of this demand were 1974 orders totaling more than $10 million for pipe for use in facilities for the loading of liquefied natural gas aboard ship in Algiers and unloading it at the Columbia Gas System's offshore terminal at Cove Point, Maryland. Demand for Trent products was also so substantial from such other energy-related industries as petroleum refining and electric power generation.

The Trent Tube Division supplied all of the nuclear quality welded stainless steel piping for the Duke Power Company's Maguire Station, Units One and Two, at Cowans Ford, North Carolina; and has received the order for the nuclear piping to be used at Duke Power's Catawba Station at Newport, South Carolina.

Substantial Orders

Among other substantial orders during the year were those from public utilities in Alabama, Arkansas, Florida, Louisiana, and Michigan and from the Atomic Energy Commission for its fast-flux uranium test facility in Hanford, Washington. The division will also supply all of the welded power piping for the Almaraz and Lemoniz nuclear stations in Spain and the feed-water heater tubing for the Colmenles station on the Costa del Sol.

Demand is also increasing for welded stainless steel piping for use in breweries and wineries.

To meet growing demand, the division is significantly increasing production capacity. The Carrollton, Georgia, plant was expanded and new equipment added to increase by some 50 percent its large-diameter pipe pro-

497

 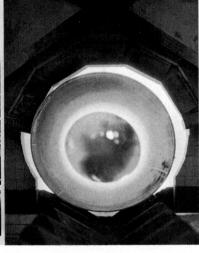

Die Unternehmen: Partner einer bewegten Welt

Keine Frage, für viele Unternehmen war das Jahr 1971 nicht ohne gravierende Probleme. Das äußerte sich zunächst darin, daß die Investitionen zurückgingen. Denn wenn beispielsweise der Export in wirtschaftlich unsicheren Zeiten besonders aktuell ist.

[Text body in German]

Tront zur Partnerschaft

Es leuchtet ein, daß gerade in unsicheren Zeiten der Wunsch zum Zusammengehen besonders aktuell ist.

499

PHOTOGRAPHER / PHOTOGRAPH / PHOTOGRAPHE:

496–498 Burk Uzzle
499 C. J. Winter
500 Burt Glinn

DESIGNER / GESTALTER / MAQUETTISTE:

496–498 Arnold Saks/Tomas Nittner
499 Wolfgang Quak
500 Arnold Saks/Ingo Scharrenbroich

ART DIRECTOR / DIRECTEUR ARTISTIQUE:

496–498, 500 Arnold Saks
499 Moritz S. Jaggi

AGENCY / AGENTUR / AGENCE – STUDIO:

496–498, 500 Arnold Saks, Inc.
499 Barlogis & Jaggi

496–498 Spreads from the 1974 annual report of Colt Industries, with detail of one page. The illustrations relate to the production of iron in a blast furnace and to the manufacture of springs and pipes. The detail shows a pipe in the annealing furnace. (USA)
499 Black-and-white double spread from the annual report of Girokasse, a Stuttgart bank, here relating to the financing of private enterprise. (GER)
500 Full-colour cover of the 1974 annual report of Pfizer Inc., a company involved in pharmaceuticals, chemicals, agricultural and consumer products and materials science. (USA)

496–498 Doppelseiten und Umschlag in Originalgrösse des Jahresberichts 1974 eines Unternehmens für Fabrikheizung und -lüftung. Die Illustrationen beziehen sich auf die Herstellung von Eisen in einem Hochofen sowie auf die Fabrikation von Federn und Röhren. Die Detailaufnahme zeigt ein Stahlrohr im Glühofen. (USA)
499 Schwarzweisse Doppelseite aus dem Jahresbericht der Girokasse Stuttgart, einer öffentlichen Bank. Die Illustration bezieht sich auf die Finanzierung von Privatunternehmen. (GER)
500 Mehrfarbiger Umschlag zum Jahresbericht 1974 des pharmazeutischen Unternehmens *Pfizer*. Die Aufnahme weist auf die vielfältigen Produkte der Firma hin, die in der Medizin, in der Landwirtschaft und in der Technik Verwendung finden. (USA)

496–498 Pages doubles figurant dans le rapport annuel 1974 de Colt Industries et détail d'une page. Les illustrations se rapportent à la production de fer dans un haut fourneau ainsi qu'à la fabrication de ressorts et de tuyaux. Le détail sous fig. 498 représente un tuyau dans un four à recuir. (USA)
499 Page double en noir et blanc tirée du rapport annuel d'une banque à Stuttgart. Les illustrations se réfèrent au financement d'entreprises privées. (GER)
500 Couverture (en couleur) du rapport annuel 1974 de Pfizer, Inc., une entreprise de production diversifiée (produits pharmaceutiques, chimiques et agricoles, biens de consommation). (USA)

500

501

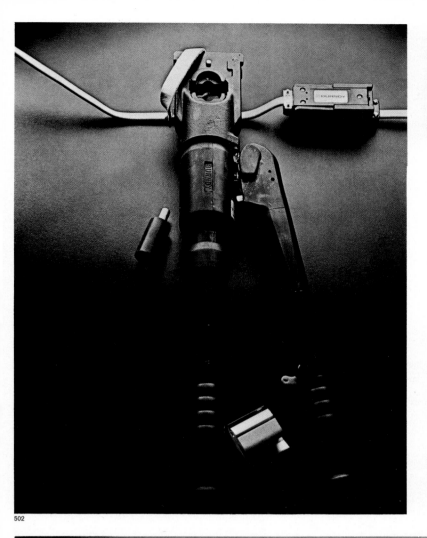

502

503

PHOTOGRAPHER / PHOTOGRAPH:

501 Bill Farrell
502–504 Phil Marco

DESIGNER / GESTALTER / MAQUETTISTE:

501 Barry Ostrie
502–504 Richard Rogers

ART DIRECTOR / DIRECTEUR ARTISTIQUE:

502–504 Richard Rogers

AGENCY / AGENTUR / AGENCE – STUDIO:

501 John Heiney & Associates
502–504 Richard Rogers, Inc.

501 Photographic illustration from an annual report of Automatic Data Processing, Inc. (USA)
502, 503 Detail of a colour page and complete corresponding spread from an annual report of Burndy Corporation. (USA)
504 Complete cover of the 1973 annual report of the Burndy Corporation, makers of electric and electronic equipment. Chiefly blue and yellow shades on a blue ground. (USA)

501 Aufnahme aus dem Jahresbericht der Automatic Data Processing, Inc. (USA)
502, 503 Farbaufnahme und dazugehörige Doppelseite aus dem Jahresbericht einer Fabrik für elektrische und elektronische Bestandteile. (USA)
504 Ganzer Umschlag zum Jahresbericht 1973 eines Herstellers von Bestandteilen für elektrische Apparate. Vorwiegend Blautöne mit Gelb auf blauem Grund. (USA)

501 Illustration photographique figurant dans le rapport annuel d'une entreprise qui fabrique des appareils électroniques. (USA)
502, 503 Détail d'une page (en couleur) et page double correspondante. Eléments tirés d'un rapport annuel de la Burndy Corporation. (USA)
504 Couverture du rapport annuel 1973 de la Burndy Corporation, fabricant d'équipements électriques et électroniques. Prédominance de tons bleus et jaunes sur fond bleu. (USA)

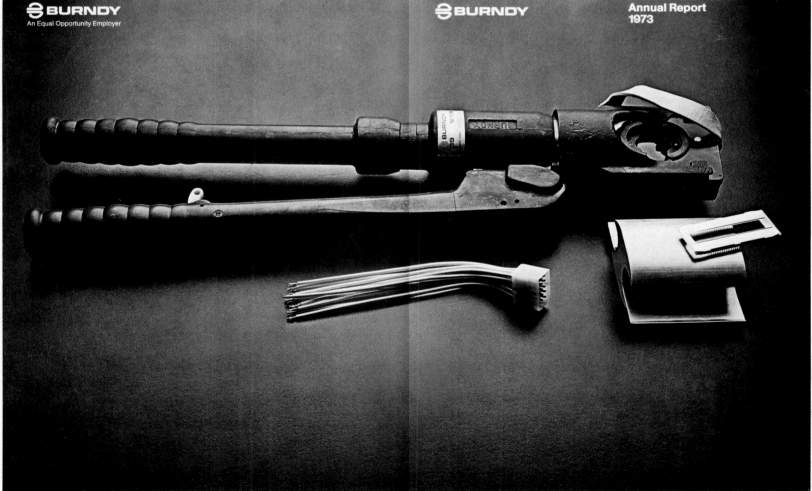

504

505, 506 Cover and double spread, both in full colour, from the 1974 annual report of Continental Can Company, Inc. Both refer to the company's forest product operations, involving the development of superior strains of pine trees and the manufacture of paperboard. (USA)
507 Cover of an annual report of the Brown Group, Inc., a diversified shoe company. Brown shades. (USA)
508 Cover of an annual report for Health Industries, Inc. (USA)
509 Cover of the 1973 annual report of the Torin Corp. (USA)
510 Illustration in colour from the 1973 annual report of the Otis Elevator Company. (USA)
511, 512 Two double spreads in full colour from the 1973 annual report of US Industries, Inc., a diversified company, here referring to bicycles and clothing. (USA)

505, 506 Umschlag und Doppelseite, beide mehrfarbig, aus dem Jahresbericht 1974 einer Papier- und Dosenfabrik. Die Aufnahme auf dem Umschlag bezieht sich auf die Entwicklung einer besseren Föhrenart, die Innenaufnahme auf die Herstellung von Karton. (USA)
507 Umschlag zum Jahresbericht einer Schuhfabrik. (USA)
508 Umschlag eines Jahresberichts der *Health Industries*. (USA)
509 Jahresbericht-Umschlag der Torin Corporation. (USA)
510 Mehrfarbiger Umschlag des Jahresberichts 1973 einer Aufzügefabrik. (USA)
511, 512 Zwei mehrfarbige Doppelseiten aus dem Jahresbericht eines amerikanischen Unternehmens, das Fahrräder, Kleider, Spielzeug und andere Verbrauchsgüter für den allgemeinen Bedarf anbietet. (USA)

505, 506 Couverture et page double (en couleur) du rapport annuel 1974 d'une entreprise industrielle. Les illustrations se réfèrent aux recherches forestières – au développement d'un genre de pin supérieur et à la fabrication de carton. (USA)
507 Couverture du rapport annuel du Brown Group, Inc., société diversifiée spécialisée dans la chaussure. Prédominance de tons bruns. (USA)
508 Couverture du rapport annuel de *Health Industries*. (USA)
509 Couverture du rapport annuel 1973 de la Torin Corp. (USA)
510 Illustration en couleur figurant dans le rapport annuel 1973 d'une entreprise industrielle. (USA)
511, 512 Deux pages doubles en couleur, tirées du rapport annuel 1973 de US Industries, entreprise diversifiée. Les photos se réfèrent aux bicyclettes et aux vêtements. (USA)

505

With 1.5 million acres of U.S. timberlands, Forest Products Operations has grown to 4 paper mills, 9 sawmills and 42 converting plants. Sales were $614 million; earnings reached $85 million before taxes and interest.

506

507

508

509

Annual Reports
Jahresberichte
Rapports annuels

PHOTOGRAPHER / PHOTOGRAPH / PHOTOGRAPHE:

505, 506 Burk Uzzle
507 Tom Freece
508 Roger Marshutz
509 Ivan Chermeyeff
510 Joseph Brignolo
511, 512 Bill Farrell

511

512

510

DESIGNER / GESTALTER / MAQUETTISTE:

505, 506 Arnold Saks/Ingo Scharrenbroich
507 Morton Goldsholl
509 Ivan Chermayeff/Steven Haines
510 Irving D. Miller
511, 512 Alicia Landon

ART DIRECTOR / DIRECTEUR ARTISTIQUE:

505, 506 Arnold Saks
507 Morton Goldsholl
508 Carl Seltzer
509 Ivan Chermayeff
510 Robert McElrath
511, 512 Alicia Landon

AGENCY / AGENTUR / AGENCE – STUDIO:

505, 506 Arnold Saks, Inc.
507 Goldsholl Associates, Inc.
508 Harry Boller
509 Chermayeff & Geismar Assoc.
510 Irving D. Miller, Inc.
511, 512 Corporate Annual Reports, Inc.

Annual Reports / Jahresberichte / Rapports annuels

ART DIRECTOR / DIRECTEUR ARTISTIQUE:

513, 514 Bob Salpeter
515 Tets Yamashita
517, 518 Don Weller

AGENCY / AGENTUR / AGENCE – STUDIO:

513, 514 Lopez Salpeter, Inc.
515 Harte Yamashita & Harte
516 Orell Füssli Graphische Betriebe AG
517, 518 Weller Institute

PHOTOGRAPHER / PHOTOGRAPH:

513, 514 Bob Colton
515 Tets Yamashita/Bill Miller
516 Annemarie + Peter Schudel
517, 518 Roger Marshutz

DESIGNER / GESTALTER / MAQUETTISTE:

513, 514 Bob Salpeter
515 Tets Yamashita
516 Walter Wieser
517, 518 Don Weller/Chikako Matsubayashi

517

513

514

515

513, 514 Double spreads with colour illustrations from the 1974 annual report of the Polychrome Corporation, whose products were used in the printing of the tickets for the Aztec Stadium in Mexico City and the cheques used by Lloyds Bank in London. (USA)
515 Double spread from the 1973 annual report of Early California Industries, Inc. The photomontage relates to the operation of rice mills. (USA)
516 A colour shot of the Mauvoisin Dam from an *Elektro-Watt* annual report. (SWI)
517, 518 Double spread and page in actual size from the 1974 annual report of Standard Brands Paint Company. The shot shows an angler's hand-painted fly. (USA)

513, 514 Doppelseiten mit Farbaufnahmen aus dem Jahresbericht 1974 einer Druckfarbenfabrik, deren Produkte beim Druck von Eintrittskarten und von Bankschecks Verwendung finden. (USA)
515 Doppelseite aus dem Jahresbericht 1973 einer kalifornischen Industriegesellschaft. Die Photomontage bezieht sich auf den Betrieb von Reismühlen. (USA)
516 Aufnahme der Staumauer der Kraftwerke Mauvoisin als Illustration des Jahresberichts von *Elektro-Watt*, Zürich. (SWI)
517, 518 Doppelseite und originalgrosse Aufnahme aus dem Jahresbericht 1974 einer Farbenfabrik. Die Photographie zeigt eine vom Angler handbemalte künstliche Fliege. (USA)

513, 514 Pages doubles avec illustrations en couleur. Eléments du rapport annuel 1974 de la Polychrome Corporation, dont les encres ont été utilisées pour l'impression des billets du Stade Aztec à Mexico City et des chèques bancaires de Lloyds Bank à Londres. (USA)
515 Page double du rapport annuel 1973 de Early California Industries. La photo se réfère au fonctionnement d'une rizerie. (USA)
516 Photo couleur du barrage de Mauvoisin. Elément du rapport annuel de l'*Elektro-Watt*. (SWI)
517, 518 Page double et pleine page (grandeur nature) figurant dans le rapport annuel 1974 de la Standard Brands Paint Co. La photo représente une mouche peinte à la main. (USA)

516

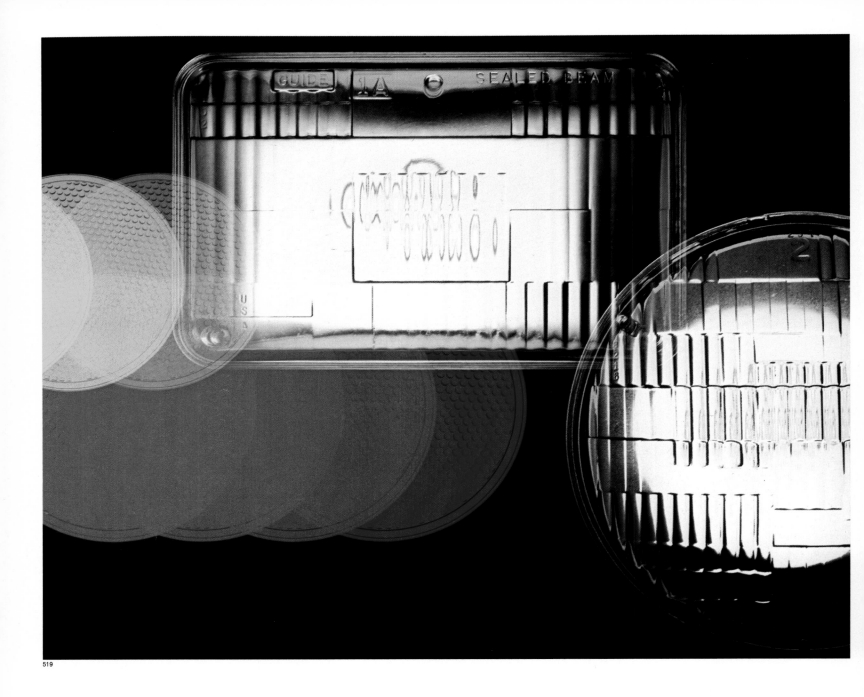

519

519–523 Detail in colour and four photographic spreads from the 1974 annual report of Corning Glass Works. The spreads relate to glass and ceramic parts for emission control, heat exchangers and sealed beams (Figs. 519 and 520), refractory blocks and high-temperature components (Fig. 521), bulb blanks and lamp tubing (Fig. 522) and ophthalmic glassware (Fig. 523). (USA)

519–523 Ausschnitt der Farbaufnahme und vier Doppelseiten aus dem Jahresbericht 1974 der *Corning* Glaswerke. Die Farbseiten zeigen Gläser für verschiedene technische Zwecke, unter anderem für Glühbirnen, Brillen usw. (USA)

519–523 Détail (en couleur) et quatre pages doubles avec illustrations photographiques figurant dans le rapport annuel 1974 d'une verrerie. Les pages doubles se réfèrent à diverses pièces en verre ou en céramique qu'on utilise pour les systèmes de contrôle des gaz d'échappement, les échangeurs de chaleur et les scellements de phares (figs. 519 et 520), à des blocs réfractaires et des parties résistant aux températures élevées (fig. 521), à des ampoules et tubes à décharge (fig. 522) et à des verres ophtalmiques (fig. 523). (USA)

520

Annual Reports / Jahresberichte / Rapports annuels

PHOTOGRAPHER / PHOTOGRAPH / PHOTOGRAPHE:
519–523 Jerry Sarapocchiello

DESIGNER / GESTALTER / MAQUETTISTE:
519–523 Fred Vapenik

ART DIRECTOR / DIRECTEUR ARTISTIQUE:
519–523 Fred Vapenik

AGENCY / AGENTUR / AGENCE – STUDIO:
519–523 Corning Glass Works, Design Dept.

521

522

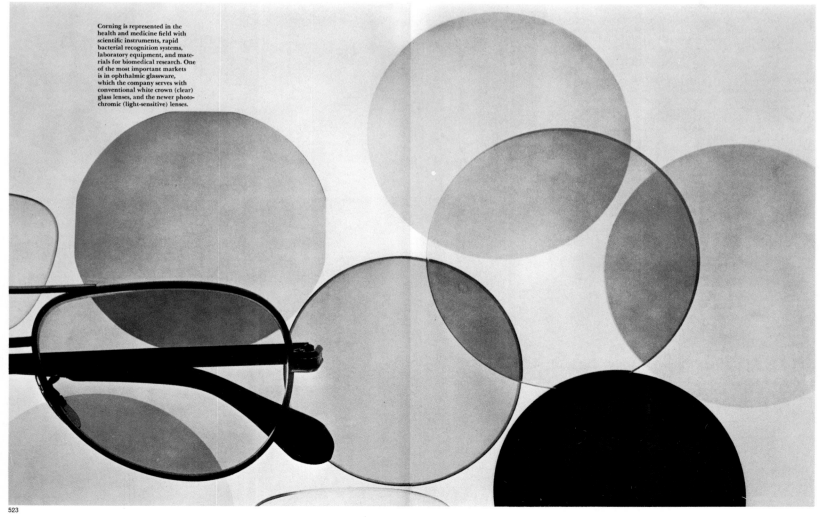

Corning is represented in the
health and medicine field with
scientific instruments, rapid
bacterial recognition systems,
laboratory equipment, and materials for biomedical research. One
of the most important markets
is in ophthalmic glassware,
which the company serves with
conventional white crown (clear)
glass lenses, and the newer photo-
chromic (light-sensitive) lenses.

523

Revlon.
Through cosmetics and pharmaceuticals, we're working to improve the appearance and health of people everywhere. Our 1973 annual report.

524

525

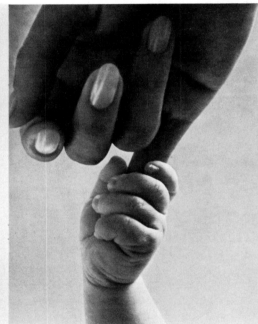

526

524–526 Cover and two colour spreads with interleaved texts from the *Revlon* 1973 annual report. The references are to cosmetics and pharmaceuticals. (USA)
527 Complete cover of the 1974 annual report of the Sea Pines Company, builders of sea and lake resorts. (USA)
528–530 Complete colour cover of the folder, view of the three-part 1973 annual report of The Hongkong and Shanghai Banking Corporation contained in it, and double spread from the report showing the resort of Macau. The report is devoted to tourism and all three covers show suitcases. (HGK)

524–526 Umschlag und mehrfarbige Doppelseiten mit halbseitigen Textblättern aus dem Jahresbericht 1973 von *Revlon*, Fabrik für kosmetische und pharmazeutische Produkte. (USA)
527 Ganzer Umschlag des Jahresberichts 1974 einer Firma, die sich auf die Erstellung von Kurorten an Seen und am Meer spezialisiert hat. (USA)
528–530 Ganzer, mehrfarbiger Umschlag der Mappe, die den dreiteiligen Jahresbericht 1973 der Hongkong und Shanghai Banking Corporation enthält, sowie Doppelseite mit Ansicht des Kurortes Macau. Der Jahresbericht gilt besonders dem Thema Tourismus. (HGK)

524–526 Couverture et deux pages doubles (en couleur), avec textes intercalés, du rapport annuel 1973 de *Revlon*. Les photos se réfèrent aux produits cosmétiques et pharmaceutiques. (USA)
527 Couverture du rapport annuel 1974 d'une entreprise qui s'est spécialisée dans la conception de stations balnéaires. (USA)
528–530 Couverture d'un portefeuille (en couleur), rapport annuel tripartite de la Hongkong and Shanghai Banking Corp. et page double qui y figure et qui présente une station de vacances. Le rapport est entièrement consacré au tourisme. Les trois couvertures représentent des valises. (HGK)

PHOTOGRAPHER / PHOTOGRAPH / PHOTOGRAPHE:

524   Richard Avedon/Jay Maisel
525   R. Avedon/J. Maisel/A. Vogel
526   Jay Maisel/Allen Vogel
527   Bill Cornelius
528, 529   Derek Dutton
530   Keith Macgregor

DESIGNER / GESTALTER / MAQUETTISTE:

524–526   Arnold Saks/Robert Jakob/Ingo Scharrenbroich
527   Leslie A. Segal
528–530   Henry Steiner

ART DIRECTOR / DIRECTEUR ARTISTIQUE:

524–526   Arnold Saks
527   Leslie A. Segal

AGENCY / AGENTUR / AGENCE – STUDIO:

524–526   Arnold Saks, Inc.
527   Corporate Annual Reports, Inc.
528–530   Graphic Communications Ltd./Gainsborough Studio

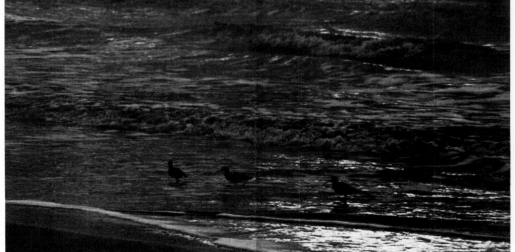

Sea Pines Company Annual Report Year Ended February 28, 1974

527

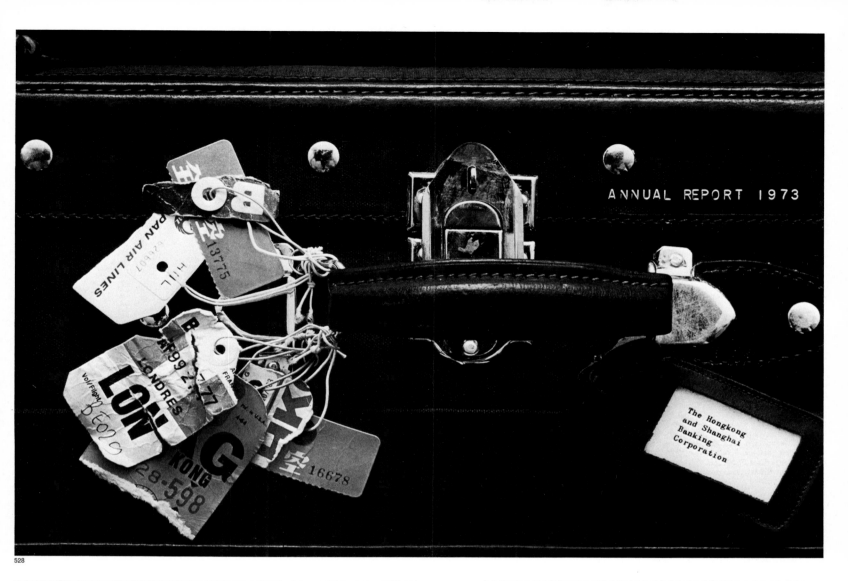

528

529

530

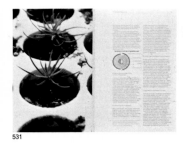

531

PHOTOGRAPHER / PHOTOGRAPH:

531, 532 Ty Hyon
533 Bill Farrell
534 Ken Whitmore
536–539 John Zoiner

DESIGNER / GESTALTER / MAQUETTISTE:

531–533 Richard Hess
534 Ronald Jefferies
535 Alicia Landon
536–539 Robert S. Nemser

532

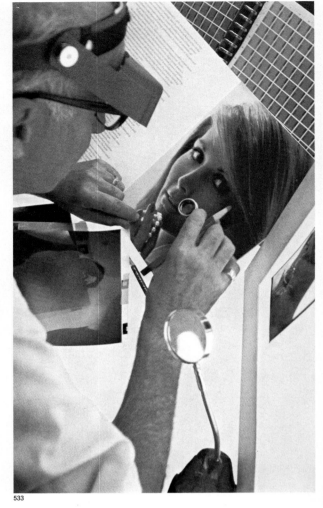

533

536

ART DIRECTOR / DIRECTEUR ARTISTIQUE:

531–533 Richard Hess
534 Robert Miles Runyan
535 Alicia Landon
536–539 Robert S. Nemser

AGENCY / AGENTUR / AGENCE:

531–533 Richard Hess, Inc.
534 Robert Miles Runyan & Associates
535 Corporate Annual Reports, Inc./
    S. D. E. Conseils en Information
536–539 Nemser & Howard, Inc.

537

538

534

535

539

531–533 Double spread and detail of two of the full-page colour illustrations from the 1974 annual report of Champion International Corp. The pictures relate to tree breeding and to reproduction quality obtained on the papers made by the corporation. (USA)
534 Cover of the 1974 annual report of the VSI Corporation, makers of metal products. (USA)
535 Colour illustration of ampoules from the 1974 annual report of L'Air Liquide S.A. (FRA)
536–539 Double spread, two pages and cover of the 1973 annual report of Monica Simone Cosmetics, Inc. Eyes and lips in full colour on a very pale ground. (USA)

531–533 Doppelseite und Ausschnitte aus den ganzseitigen, mehrfarbigen Illustrationen zum Jahresbericht 1974 einer Papierfabrik. Die Aufnahmen zeigen die fabrikeigene Baumschule und die Wiedergabequalität auf Kunstdruckpapier. (USA)
534 Umschlag zum Jahresbericht 1974 eines Unternehmens der Metallverarbeitung. (USA)
535 Farbaufnahme mit Ampullen aus dem Jahresbericht 1973 von L'Air Liquide S.A. (FRA)
536–539 Doppelseite, Seite und Umschlag des Jahresberichts 1973 einer Kosmetikfirma. Augen und Lippen mehrfarbig auf ganz hellem Grund. (USA)

531–533 Page double et détail de deux illustrations pleines pages. Elément figurant dans le rapport annuel 1974 de la papeterie Champion International Corp. Les photos se rapportent à la culture des arbres et à la qualité des reproductions obtenue grâce aux papiers couchés fabriqués par cette compagnie. (USA)
534 Couverture du rapport annuel d'une entreprise de produits en métal. (USA)
535 Ampoules illustrant le rapport annuel 1974 de L'Air Liquide SA. En couleur. (FRA)
536–539 Page double, pleines pages et couverture du rapport annuel 1973 d'une fabrique de produits cosmétiques. Les yeux et les lèvres sont en couleur sur fond pâle. (USA)

Annual Reports
Jahresberichte
Rapports annuels

540

PHOTOGRAPHER / PHOTOGRAPH / PHOTOGRAPHE:

540 Werner Bischof
541 George Meinzinger
542 Jan Erik Friis
543–545 Jay Maisel

DESIGNER / GESTALTER / MAQUETTISTE:

541 James Cross
543–545 Leslie A. Segal

ART DIRECTOR / DIRECTEUR ARTISTIQUE:

541 James Cross
542 Jon Kvaestad/Odd Bolstad
543–545 Leslie A. Segal

AGENCY / AGENTUR / AGENCE – STUDIO:

541 James Cross Design Office, Inc.
542 Ingar Jensen a/s
543–545 Corporate Annual Reports, Inc.

Annual Reports
Jahresberichte
Rapports annuels

541

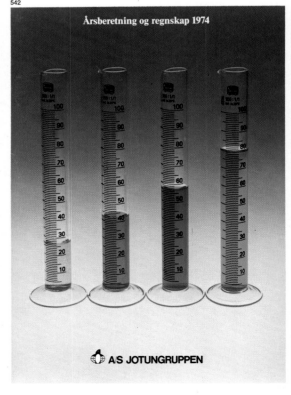

542

543

544

545

540 Complete black-and-white cover of the 1973 annual report of The Henry Luce Foundation, Inc., which furthers higher education in the USA and the Far East. (USA)
541 Cover of an annual report of ICN Pharmaceuticals, Inc. (USA)
542 Cover of the 1973 annual report of A/S Jotungruppen, a company manufacturing paints and chemicals. (NOR)·
543, 544 Two pages (in full colour) from the 1973 annual report of Chesebrough-Pond's Inc., a diversified company making foods, cosmetics, etc. (USA)
545 Full-colour cover of the 1974 annual report of Chesebrough-Pond's Inc. (USA)

540 Ganzer, schwarzweisser Umschlag zum Jahresbericht 1973 der Henry-Luce-Stiftung zur Förderung der höheren Ausbildung in den USA und im Fernen Osten. (USA)
541 Umschlag zum Jahresbericht 1973 eines pharmazeutischen Unternehmens. (USA)
542 Umschlag des Jahresberichts 1973 einer Fabrik für Farben und Chemikalien. (NOR)
543, 544 Mehrfarbige Seiten aus dem Jahresbericht 1973 einer Firma für Nahrungsmittel, Kosmetik und weitere Produkte. (USA)
545 Mehrfarbiger Umschlag des Jahresberichts 1974 einer Firma für Nahrungsmittel, Kosmetik usw. Siehe auch Abb. 543, 544. (USA)

540 Couverture en noir et blanc du rapport annuel 1973 de la Henry Luce Foundation, Inc. Cette fondation se propose de faire avancer l'éducation et d'augmenter le niveau d'instruction aux Etats-Unis et à l'Extrême-Orient. (USA)
541 Couverture du rapport annuel d'une entreprise de produits pharmaceutiques. (USA)
542 Couverture du rapport annuel 1973 de la A/S Jotungruppen, compagnie spécialisée dans le domaine des colorants et des produits chimiques. (NOR)
543, 544 Deux pages (en couleur) figurant dans le rapport annuel 1973 d'une entreprise de production diversifiée – produits alimentaires, produits cosmétiques, etc. (USA)
545 Couverture (en couleur) du rapport annuel 1974 d'une entreprise de production diversifiée (voir aussi les figs. 543 et 544). (USA)

546

547

548

546 Page in full colour from the 1973 annual report of the MD Group, manufacturers of paper and board. This and three other colour pages in the report show paper reliefs and sculptures which incorporate the initials MD and are printed in each case on the backs of gatefolds. (GER)
547–550 Page, two double spreads, and detail of the photography from one of them, from the 1974 annual report of Distillers Corporation-Seagrams Limited. The illustrations, all in full colour, show champagnes and wines of various provenances. (CAN)

546 Mehrfarbige Seite aus dem Jahresbericht 1973 der MD Verwaltungsgesellschaft Nicolaus & Co., München, einer Gruppe von Papierfabriken. Die ganzseitigen Farb-illustrationen mit Abwandlungen des Firmensignets wurden auf auslegbare Seiten ge-druckt. (GER)
547–550 Seite, zwei Doppelseiten und originalgrosse Aufnahme aus dem Jahresbericht 1974 der Distillers Corporation-Seagrams Ltd., einer Getränkefirma. Die mehrfarbigen Aufnahmen zeigen Champagner und Weine verschiedener Provenienzen. Die Doppel-seite in Abb. 548 eröffnet den Finanzbericht. (CAN)

546 Illustration pleine page (en couleur) figurant dans le rapport annuel 1973 d'une fabrique de papiers. (GER)
547–550 Pleine page, pages doubles et détail de la photo qui figure sur l'une d'elles. Eléments du rapport annuel 1974 de la Distillers Corporation-Seagrams Ltd. Les illus-trations – entièrement en couleur – présentent des bouteilles de champagne et de vin provenant de différentes régions du monde. Fig. 548: page double initiale du rapport financier qui est imprimé sur papier teinté. (CAN)

PHOTOGRAPHER / PHOTOGRAPH / PHOTOGRAPHE:

546 Studio Springmann
547–550 Phil Marco

DESIGNER / GESTALTER / MAQUETTISTE:

546 Bärbel Skarabela
547–550 Phil Marco/Arnold Saks

ART DIRECTOR / DIRECTEUR ARTISTIQUE:

546 Hein Popp
547–550 Arnold Saks

AGENCY / AGENTUR / AGENCE – STUDIO:

546 MD Papierfabriken Heinrich Nicolaus GmbH,
     Werbeabteilung
547–550 Arnold Saks, Inc.

Annual Reports

549

551

Annual Reports
Jahresberichte
Rapports annuels

PHOTOGRAPHER / PHOTOGRAPH / PHOTOGRAPHE:

551 Michel Tcherevkoff
552 Jay Maisel
554 Leonard Soned
555 Paul Fusco

DESIGNER / GESTALTER / MAQUETTISTE:

551 Alicia Landon
552 Leslie A. Segal
553 Arnold Saks
554 David Kaestle/Bob Pellegrini
555 Michael Reid

ART DIRECTOR / DIRECTEUR ARTISTIQUE:

551 Alicia Landon
552 Leslie A. Segal
553 Arnold Saks
554 David Kaestle/Bob Pellegrini
555 Michael Reid

AGENCY / AGENTUR / AGENCE – STUDIO:

551, 552 Corporate Annual Reports, Inc.
553 Arnold Saks, Inc.
554 Pellegrini, Kaestle + Gross
555 Michael Reid Design, Inc.

552

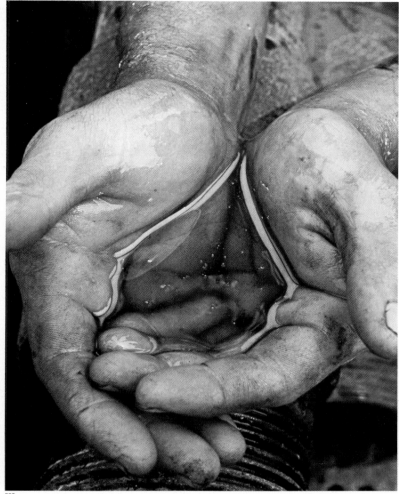

553

554

555

551 Ganzseitige Illustration aus einem Jahresbericht der Coca-Cola Company. (USA)
552 Umschlag des Jahresberichts 1975 einer Kette von Restaurants. Mehrfarbig, Gitarre in sattem Rot. (USA)
553 Ganzseitige Farbaufnahme aus dem Jahresbericht 1975 der Seagram Company, die auch am Erdölgeschäft beteiligt ist. (CAN)
554 Vorwiegend in Blau und Rot gehaltener Umschlag des Jahresberichts 1974 von *Texstar*. (USA)
555 Doppelseite aus dem Jahresbericht 1974 eines Unternehmens, das sich unter anderem auch mit Verpackungen befasst. Mehrfarbig. (USA)

551 Illustration pleine page figurant dans un rapport annuel de la Coca-Cola Company. (USA)
552 Couverture du rapport annuel 1975 publié par une chaîne de restaurants. Photographie en couleur, guitare rouge. (USA)
553 Illustration pleine page (en couleur) tirée du rapport annuel 1975 de la Seagram Company Ltd., compagnie qui s'est engagé aussi dans l'industrie pétrolière. (CAN)
554 Couverture du rapport annuel 1974 de *Texstar*. Prédominance de tons bleus et rouges. (USA)
555 Bemis Company, Inc. est une entreprise de fabrication diversifiée. La page double figurant dans le rapport annuel 1974 se rapporte à une branche de production: le conditionnement. (USA)

211

5

Packaging
Record Covers
Advertising Films
Television Commercials

Packungen
Schallplatten-Hüllen
Kino-Werbefilme
Fernseh-Werbefilme

Emballages
Pochettes de disques
Films publicitaires
Publicité télévisée

556

557

556 Folding box for a heavy-duty laundry detergent without phosphates. Flower with yellow petals, blue centre. (USA)
557 Folding box for a detergent for synthetics. Pink rose, white lettering, blue Y. (SWI)
558, 559 Cartons for mechanical toys by Systematic Learning Corp. designed to help children train their perceptive faculties, improve their spelling, etc. (USA)
560 Folding box for a water purifying apparatus made by Arnold Industries. (USA)
561 Folding box for a L'Oréal tinting shampoo. Hair in natural colour, white lettering. (FRA)
562 Folding box for a portable drinking-water purifier made by Better Living Laboratories. Photographic design. (USA)

556 Faltschachtel für ein Hochleistungswaschmittel ohne Phosphate. Gelbe Blume mit blauem Mittelpunkt. (USA)
557 Faltschachtel für Minyl, ein Waschmittel für Kunstfasern. Rosa Rose, weisse Schrift mit blauem Y. (SWI)
558, 559 Schachteln für didaktisches Spielzeug, mit dessen Hilfe Kinder ihre Beobachtungsgabe schärfen und die Rechtschreibung üben können. (USA)
560 Faltschachtel für ein Gerät zur Reinigung von Wasser. (USA)
561 Faltschachtel für ein Haarwaschmittel, das zugleich tönt. (FRA)
562 Faltschachtel für ein Trinkwasser-Reinigungsgerät. (USA)

556 Boîte pliante pour un détergent efficace sans phosphates. Fleur avec des pétales jaunes, centre bleu. (USA)
557 Boîte pliante pour un détergent qui se prête particulièrement au lavage de tissus synthétiques. Rose rouge, texte blanc, «Y» bleu. (SWI)
558, 559 Cartons contenant des jouets mécaniques, conçus par une institution engagée dans le domaine de l'enseignement. Les jouets sont conçus de façon à encourager la perception et à perfectionner l'orthographe des enfants. (USA)
560 Boîte pliante contenant un appareil pour l'épuration de l'eau. (USA)
561 Boîte pliante pour le shampooing colorant Récital de L'Oréal. Cheveux en couleur naturelle, texte en blanc. (FRA)
562 Boîte pliante contenant un appareil portable servant à l'épuration de l'eau potable. Conception photographique. (USA)

560

Packaging / Packungen / Emballages

PHOTOGRAPHER / PHOTOGRAPH:	DESIGNER / GESTALTER / MAQUETTISTE:	ART DIRECTOR / DIRECTEUR ARTISTIQUE:	AGENCY / AGENTUR / AGENCE – STUDIO:
556 Phillip Harrington	556 Robert P. Gersin	556 Robert P. Gersin	556 Robert P. Gersin Associates
557 Achille B. Weider	557 Migros, Abteilung Packungen	557 Hans Uster	557 Migros, Abteilung Packungen
560 Mason Pawlak	558, 559 Tomoko Miho	558, 559 John Massey	558, 559 Center for Advanced Research in Design
561 Hans Mauli	560 Terry Lesniewicz	560 Terry Lesniewicz	560 Flournoy & Gibbs Inc.
562 Tom Kelley	561 Annegret Beier	561 Annegret Beier	561 Delpire Advico S. A.
	562 John Boatright/Ed Bailey/Jim Osborn	562 Ed Bailey	562 John Malmo Advertising

558

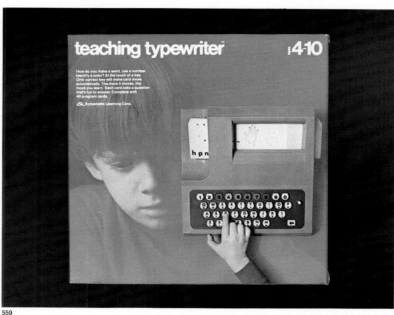

559

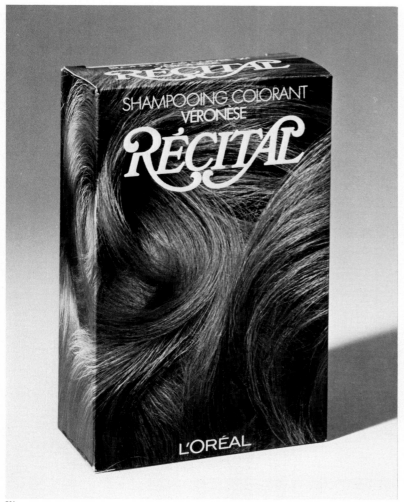

561

562

563

563, 564 Detail of *Orrefors* glass and carton (in dark green with white lettering and blue and yellow stripe) for four glasses with handles. The glasses are specially designed for hot or chilled drinks. (SWE)
565 Set-up box for *Lancôme* cosmetics. Shades of cream, pale orange, green and light brown. (SWI)
566 Folding box for pantyhose. Photograph in duotone, vignettes in full colour. (SPA)

564

565

563, 564 Aufnahme eines *Orrefors*-Henkelglases und einer Schachtel für vier Gläser (dunkelgrün mit weisser Schrift, blaue und gelbe Streifen). Die Gläser sind besonders für heisse oder kalte Getränke entworfen. (SWE)
565 Stulpschachtel für kosmetische Produkte von *Lancôme*. In Elfenbein, Hellorange, Grün und Hellbraun. (SWI)
566 Faltschachtel für Strumpfhosen. Photo in Zweifarbendruck mit mehrfarbigen Vignetten. (SPA)

563, 564 Détail présentant un verre *Orrefors* et carton (en vert foncé avec texte en blanc, rayures en bleu et jaune) pour quatre verres à anse. Ces verres ont été conçus spécialement pour des boissons chaudes ou glacées. (SWE)
565 Carton monté contenant des produits cosmétiques de *Lancôme*. Tons atténués, orange pâle, vert et brun pâle. (SWI)
566 Boîte pliante servant d'emballage pour des collants. Photo imprimée en deux couleurs, vignettes en couleur. (SPA)

PHOTOGRAPHER / PHOTOGRAPH / PHOTOGRAPHE:

563, 564 Svante Fischerström
566 Jeroni Vives

DESIGNER / GESTALTER / MAQUETTISTE:

563, 564 Karlerik Lindgren
566 Ramón Roda/Francisco Soro

ART DIRECTOR / DIRECTEUR ARTISTIQUE:

563, 564 Karlerik Lindgren
566 Ramón Roda

AGENCY / AGENTUR / AGENCE – STUDIO:

563, 564 Sivert Ahringer AB
566 Industrias Graficas PAUTA

566

567

568

571

PHOTOGRAPHER / PHOTOGRAPH / PHOTOGRAPHE:

567 David Hamilton
568 Joel Baldwin
569, 572 Manfred Vormstein
571 John Brown
573 Alain Marouani

DESIGNER / GESTALTER / MAQUETTISTE:

567 Claude Caudron
568 John H. Berg
570 Graham Hughes
571 Roslav Szaybo
573 Jean Paul Theodule

ART DIRECTOR / DIRECTEUR ARTISTIQUE:

567, 573 Alain Marouani
568 John H. Berg
569, 572 Manfred Vormstein
570 Graham Hughes
571 Roslav Szaybo

AGENCY / AGENTUR / AGENCE – STUDIO:

568, 571 CBS Records
569, 572 Ariola-Eurodisc, Atelier

PUBLISHER / VERLEGER / EDITEUR:

567, 573 Barclay Disques
568, 571 CBS, Inc.
569, 572 Ariola-Eurodisc GmbH
570 Track Records

**Record Covers / Schallplattenhüllen
Pochettes de disques**

567 Cover of a *Riviera* record with music by Raymond Lefèvre's dance orchestra. Yellow, pink and brown shades. (FRA)
568 Cover of a *Columbia* recording of popular hits. (USA)
569 Cover of a booklet accompanying a complete Russian recording of Prokofieff's ballet *Cinderella* issued by *Eurodisc*. Very pale colouring. (GER)
570 Die-cut cover for a recording of rock music by The Who (Track Records). (GBR)
571 Cover for a CBS record of songs by a group. (GBR)
572 For a *Eurodisc* recording of piano suites from Prokofieff's *Cinderella*. (GER)
573 Cover of a *Barclay* record of chansons by Lydia Verkine. Brown and green shades. (FRA)

569

570

572

573

567 Umschlag einer *Riviera*-Schallplatte mit dem Orchester Raymond Lefèvre. (FRA)
568 Umschlag einer *Columbia*-Schallplatte mit Erfolgsschlagern. (USA)
569 Umschlag eines Textheftes zu einer vollständigen Schallplattenaufnahme von Prokofieffs Ballett *Cinderella* (Aschenbrödel), aufgeführt vom Rundfunk-Sinfonieorchester der UdSSR, herausgegeben von *Eurodisc*. Hellgrau und hellrosa. (GER)
570 Gestanzte Hülle für eine Platte mit Rockmusik. (GBR)
571 Umschlag einer CBS-Schallplatte mit Liedern einer Gruppe. (GBR)
572 Für eine *Eurodisc*-Schallplatte mit Klaviersuiten von Prokofieff. (GER)
573 Umschlag einer *Barclay*-Schallplatte mit Liedern von Lydia Verkine. (FRA)

567 Pochette de disque pour l'enregistrement de musique de danse de l'orchestre Raymond Lefèvre. Tons jaunes, roses et bruns. (FRA)
568 Pochette pour un enregistrement de mélodies populaires. (USA)
569 Couverture d'un cahier accompagnant l'enregistrement du ballet *Cendrillon* de Prokofiev, présenté par l'orchestre symphonique de l'URSS. Couleurs atténuées. (GER)
570 Pochette de disque en découpe pour le groupe de rock The Who. (GBR)
571 Pochette pour un enregistrement de songs par un groupe. (GBR)
572 Pochette pour un enregistrement des suites pour piano de *Cendrillon* de Prokofiev. (GER)
573 Pochette pour un disque de chansons de Lydia Verkine. Tons bruns et verts. (FRA)

574 Complete cover for a *Warner Bros.* recording of popular hits. Coloured photomontage. (USA)
575 Cover of an ABC record by a black singer. Red lips, brown skin, pink neon. (USA)
576 Cover in brownish shades for an A&M record. (USA)
577 Complete cover of a double *Warner Bros.* record. Brightly coloured beads. (USA)
578 Cover of a *Salvation* record with music by a jazz quartet. Red apple. (USA)
579 "Art-head Indian." Cover of an MPS record of music by a group. Red, white and blue nails. (GER)
580 Cover of a *Blue Sky* record by Edgar Winter. Robe in dark red and gold. (USA)
581 Complete record cover. Green bottle and ground. (IRN)
582 Cover of a *Fantasy* record. Subdued colours. (USA)
583 Cover of a *Milestone* record of beat music. Pale blue-green ground. (USA)
584 Cover of a CTI record. Deep yellow signboard against a full-colour landscape. (USA)
585 Cover for a *Barclay* record of songs by Steve Davis. Bottle in red and blue shades. (FRA)
586 Cover for an A&M record. Red neon, purple stockings, green shoes on black. (USA)
587 Cover for 20th Century Records. (USA)

PHOTOGRAPHER / PHOTOGRAPH / PHOTOGRAPHE:
574 John Craig/Jim Ladwig
575 Brian Leatart
576 Stewart Grant
577 Albert Mackenzie Watson
578 Jerry Sarapocchiello
579 Frieder Grindler
580 Steinbecker-Houghton
581 Masod Masomi
582, 583 Tony Lane
584 Pete Turner
585 Dennis Wile
586 Geoff Halpin
587 Norman Seeff

575

574

578

579

574 Ganzer Umschlag zu einer *Warner-Bros.*-Schallplatte mit bekannten Schlagern. Kolorierte Photomontage. (USA)
575 Hülle einer Platte mit Liedern einer schwarzen Sängerin. Rote Lippen, braune Haut, rosa Neonröhren. (USA)
576 Umschlag einer Platte mit Cowboyliedern. (USA)
577 Ganzer Umschlag einer *Warner-Bros.*-Schallplatte. Mehrfarbig, bunte Perlstickerei. (USA)
578 Umschlag einer *Salvation*-Platte mit Jazzmusik. (USA)
579 Hülle einer MPS-Platte. Nägel rot-weiss-blau. (GER)
580 Umschlag einer *Blue Sky*-Schallplatte mit Edgar Winter. Dunkelrotes Samtkleid mit Goldverzierung. (USA)
581 Ganzer Schallplattenumschlag. Flasche und Hintergrund vorwiegend grün. (IRN)
582 Umschlag einer *Fantasy*-Schallplatte in verhaltenen Farbtönen. (USA)
583 Umschlag einer *Milestone*-Platte mit Schlagzeugmusik und Trommelsoli. (USA)
584 Umschlag einer CTI-Schallplatte. Gelbe Signaltafel vor mehrfarbiger Landschaftsaufnahme. (USA)
585 Umschlag einer *Barclay*-Platte mit Liedern von Steve Davis. Flasche in Rot und Blau. (FRA)
586 Umschlag einer A&M-Platte. Violette Strümpfe, grüne Schuhe und rote Neonschrift auf schwarzem Grund. (USA)
587 Umschlag einer Platte der 20th Century Records. (USA)

582

574 Recto et verso d'une pochette pour un enregistrement de mélodies populaires. Montage en couleur. (USA)
575 Pochette pour le disque d'une chanteuse noire. Lèvres rouges, peau brune, tubes néon roses. (USA)
576 Pochette en tons brunâtres pour un disque A&M. (USA)
577 Recto et verso d'une pochette contenant deux disques. Perles en couleurs vives. (USA)
578 Pochette pour le disque d'un quatuor, enregistré lors d'une tournée au Japon. Pomme rouge. (USA)
579 «L'Indien à la tête artificielle.» Pochette pour le disque d'un groupe. Clous rouges, blancs et bleus. (GER)
580 Pochette pour un enregistrement d'Edgar Winter. Robe en rouge foncé et or. (USA)
581 Recto et verso d'une pochette pour le disque d'un chanteur iranais. Bouteille verte sur fond vert. (IRN)
582 Pour un disque *Fantasy*. Couleurs atténuées. (USA)
583 Pochette pour un disque de Milt Jackson. Ecriteau en jaune foncé, photo couleur du paysage au fond. (USA)
584 Pochette pour un enregistrement de musique beat. Fond en tons bleu-vert pâle. (USA)
585 Pochette pour un enregistrement de chansons de Steve Davis. Bouteille en tons rouges et bleus. (FRA)
586 Pochette d'un disque A&M. Tubes néon en rouge, bas violets, chaussures vertes sur fond noir. (USA)
587 Pochette pour un enregistrement de chansons. (USA)

Record Covers / Schallplattenhüllen
Pochettes de disques

585

576

577

580

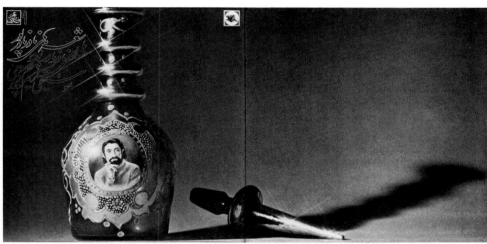

581

583

584

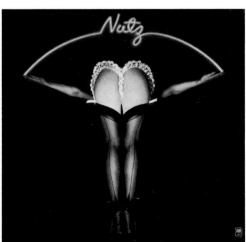

586

587

DESIGNER / GESTALTER / MAQUETTISTE:

574 Jim Ladwig
575 Peter Whorf/Brian Leatart
577 John Casado
578 Bob Ciano
579 Frieder Grindler
580 Teresa Alfieri
581 Farshid Mesgahali
582, 583 Tony Lane
586 Geoff Halpin
587 Philip Chiang

ART DIRECTOR / DIRECTEUR ARTISTIQUE:

574 Jim Ladwig
575 Peter Whorf
576 Fabio Nicoli
577 Ed Thrasher
578 Bob Ciano
579 Frieder Grindler
580 John H. Berg
581 Farshid Mesgahali
582, 583 Tony Lane
584 Bob Ciano
586 Michael Doud
587 Rod Dyer

AGENCY / AGENTUR / AGENCE – STUDIO:

574 Album Graphics, Inc.
575 ABC Records
577 John & Barbara Casado Design
579 Frieder Grindler
580 CBS Records
582, 583 Fantasy/Prestige/Milestone Records
587 Rod Dyer, Inc.

PUBLISHER / VERLEGER / EDITEUR:

574, 577 Warner Bros. Records, Inc.
575 Bluesway
576, 586 A & M Records, Inc.
578, 584 CTI Records
579 MPS Records GmbH
580 CBS, Inc.
582, 583 Fantasy/Prestige/ Milestone Records
585 Compagnie Phonographique Française
587 20th Century Records

588–591

593–596

597–600

601–604

605–608

588–592 Sequence from a commercial film for the *Faber* company, with detail of one of the frames. (ITA)
593–596 Sequence from a television commercial set in a library, for the soft drink *Dr. Pepper*. Winner of a silver award in The One Show, New York 1975. See also Figs. 601–604. (USA)
597–600 Sequence from a television commercial for ACRAF S.p.A., Rome, for the liqueur *Amargo*. (ITA)
601–604 Sequence from a television commercial set in a factory for the soft drink *Dr. Pepper*. See Figs. 593–596. (USA)
605–608 Sequence from a commercial film for a *Certina* watch showing the day of the week and the date. (SWI)

588–592 Sequenz aus einem Werbefilm für die Firma *Faber*, mit Einzelbild. (ITA)
593–596 Sequenz aus einer Fernsehwerbung für das Erfrischungsgetränk *Dr. Pepper*. Die Handlung spielt in einer Bibliothek. Silbermedaille der One Show, New York 1975. Siehe auch die Abbildungen 601–604. (USA)
597–600 Sequenz aus einer Fernsehwerbung für den Likör *Amargo* der ACRAF SpA, Rom. (ITA)
601–604 Sequenz aus einer Fernsehwerbung für *Dr. Pepper*. Ort der Handlung: eine Fabrik. Vergl. Abb. 593–596. (USA)
605–608 Sequenz aus einem Werbefilm für *Certina*-Uhren, die Datum und Wochentag angeben. (SWI)

588–592 Séquence d'un film publicitaire pour *Faber* et détail d'une image. (ITA)
593–596 Images d'un film publicitaire tourné dans une librairie. Publicité pour une eau minérale. Ce film a remporté une médaille d'argent du One Show 1975, New York. (USA)
597–600 Séquence d'un film publicitaire pour le liqueur *Amargo*, produit par ACRAF S.p.A., Rome. (ITA)
601–604 Séquence d'un film publicitaire pour une eau minérale (voir fig. 593–596). Lieu du tournage: une fabrique. (USA)
605–608 Images d'un film publicitaire pour les montres *Certina* avec indication de la date et du jour. (SWI)

PHOTOGRAPHER / PHOTOGRAPH / PHOTOGRAPHE:

588–592 David Hamilton
593–596 Bob Gaffney
597–600 Franco Boursier
601–604 Ray Long
605–608 Vorkapich & Hughes

ART DIRECTOR / DIRECTEUR ARTISTIQUE:

593–596, 601–604 Jim Swan
597–600 Aldo Lanfranco / Ciro Ciri

DIRECTOR / REGISSEUR:

588–592 Jed Falby
593–596 Dennis Powers
597–600 Ezio Perardi
601–604 Ed Bianchi
605–608 Contini Sjösted Impact

AGENCY / AGENTUR / AGENCE – STUDIO:

588–592 Young & Rubicam Italia S.p.A.
593–596, 601–604 Young Rubicam International, Inc.
597–600 Armando Testa
605–608 Contini Sjösted Impact

PRODUCER / PRODUZENT / PRODUCTION:

597–600 Arno Film

592